POLITICS AND ECONOMICS OF THE MIDDLE EAST

POLITICS AND ECONOMICS OF THE MIDDLE EAST

WILLIAM EVANS AND DANIEL J. HARRIS
EDITORS

Nova Science Publishers, Inc.
New York

For permission to use material from this book please contact us:
Telephone 631-231-7269; Fax 631-231-8175
Web Site: http://www.novapublishers.com

LIBRARY OF CONGRESS CATALOGING-IN-PUBLICATION DATA

Politics and Economics of the Middle East/William Evans and Daniel J. Harris,editors.

P. cm.

Includes bibliographical references and index.

ISBN 978-1-60456-719-9(hardcover)

1.Arab countries—Politics and government—1945-2.Arab countries—Econimic conditions. 3. Arab countries—Relations—United States—Relations—Arab countries.I. Evans,William,1970- II.Harris,Daniel J.

DS39.P634 2008

303.48'256073—dc22

2008016988

Published by Nova Science Publishers, Inc. ✢ New York

Contents

PREFACE

This new book includes the entire spectrum of contemporary politics and economics of the Middle East. The coverage is intended to deal with the Middle East, its political dynamics, economic policies, and institutions.

Chapter 1 - The U.S.-led war to overthrow Saddam Hussein virtually ended Iraq's ability to militarily threaten the region, but it has produced new and unanticipated security challenges for the Persian Gulf states (Saudi Arabia, Kuwait, Bahrain, Qatar, Oman, and the United Arab Emirates). The Gulf states, which are all led by Sunni Muslim regimes, fear that Shiite Iran is unchecked now that Iraq is strategically weak. The Gulf states strongly resent that pro-Iranian Shiite Muslim groups and their Kurdish allies (who are not Arabs) have obtained preponderant power within Iraq. This has led most of the Gulf states, particularly Saudi Arabia, to provide only halting support to the fledgling government in Baghdad and to revive the focus on U.S.-Gulf defense cooperation that characterized U.S.-Gulf relations during the 1990s.

The new power structure in Iraq has had political repercussions throughout the Gulf region, particularly as Sunni-Shiite violence in Iraq has come to overshadow direct insurgent violence against U.S. forces as the key threat to Iraqi stability. The Sunni-Shiite tensions in Iraq apparently are spilling over into the Gulf states. Shiite communities, particularly that in Bahrain, have been emboldened by events in Iraq to seek additional power, and Sunni-Shiite tension in the Gulf states is said by observers to be increasing.

Some Shiite communities, which view themselves as long repressed, are attempting to benefit politically from the Bush Administration's focus on promoting democracy and political reform in the region. Domestically, all of the Gulf states are undertaking substantial but gradual economic and political liberalization to deflect popular pressure and satisfy U.S. calls for reform.

However, the reforms undertaken or planned do not aim to fundamentally restructure power in any of these states. The Bush Administration advocates more rapid and sweeping political and economic liberalization as key to long-term Gulf stability and to reducing support in the Gulf states for terrorist groups such as Al Qaeda. The Administration is funding civil society programs in the Gulf states — funding that is not necessarily welcomed by the Gulf leaderships — but it is also promoting the bilateral free trade agreements that most of the Gulf leaders seek.

The Bush Administration also is working to maintain or improve post-September 11 cooperation with the Gulf states against Al Qaeda. Some Gulf states allegedly tolerated the presence of Al Qaeda activists and their funding mechanisms prior to the September 11 attacks. Fifteen of the nineteen September 11 hijackers were of Saudi origin, as is Al Qaeda founder Osama bin Laden.

See also CRS Report RL33533, *Saudi Arabia: Current Issues and U.S. Relations;* CRS Report RS21513, *Kuwait: Post-Saddam Issues and U.S. Policy*; CRS Report RS21852, *The United Arab Emirates: Issues for U.S. Policy*; CRS Report RL31718, *Qatar: Background and U.S. Relations*; CRS Report 95-1013 F, *Bahrain: Key Issues for U.S. Policy*; and CRS Report RS21534, *Oman: Reform, Security, and U.S. Policy.*

Chapter 2 - This report provides an overview of Egyptian politics and current issues in U.S.-Egyptian relations. It briefly provides a political history of modern Egypt, an overview of its political institutions, and a discussion of the prospects for democratization in Egypt. U.S.-Egyptian relations are complex and multi-faceted, and this chapter addresses the following current topics: the Arab-Israeli peace process, Iraq, terrorism, democratization and reform, human rights, trade, and military cooperation. For more information on Egypt, see CRS Report RS22274, *Egypt: 2005 Presidential and Parliamentary Elections*.

U.S. policy on Egypt is aimed at maintaining regional stability, improving bilateral relations, continuing military cooperation, and sustaining the March 1979 Egyptian-Israeli peace treaty. Successive Administrations have long viewed Egypt as a leader and moderating influence in the Middle East, though in recent years, there have been increasing calls for Egypt to democratize.

Congressional views of U.S.-Egyptian relations vary. Some lawmakers view Egypt as stabilizing the region and helping to extend U.S. influence in the most populous Arab country. Others would like the United States to pressure Egypt to implement political reforms, improve its human rights record, and take a more active role in reducing Arab-Israeli tensions.

Among the current issues in U.S.-Egyptian relations are a shared concern about international terrorism. Egypt can claim some experience with the subject, having defeated domestic Islamist terrorists intent on overthrowing the government. As the war on terror continues, the United States relies on Egypt for intelligence cooperation. Egypt provided valuable support during Operation Enduring Freedom in Afghanistan. On the issue of Iraqi reconstruction, Egypt is helping to train Iraqi security forces and has offered to increase its efforts. Egypt and the United States agree on the importance of the Egyptian-Israeli peace treaty and the need to continue current Arab-Israel peace talks. In support of this process, Egypt has been training Palestinian police and has sent 750 Egyptian soldiers to the Egypt-Gaza border in order to prevent weapons smuggling following Israel's recent withdrawal from Gaza.

The United States and Egypt disagree over the speed and depth of, but not the need for, some of Egypt's economic reforms. The two governments differ on Egypt's need to introduce democratic reforms, and many U.S. officials argue that Egypt is not moving quickly enough toward full democracy or in improving the human rights situation. Others caution that movement toward democracy carries a risk of establishment of an Islamist government.

The United States has provided Egypt with an annual average of over $2 billion in economic and military foreign assistance since 1979. The United States will reduce Economic Support Funds (ESF) to about $400 million per year by 2008 in keeping with a plan to reduce aid to both Israel and Egypt. The Administration requested $455 million in economic grants and $1.3 billion in military grants for FY2007 for Egypt.

Chapter 3 - U.S.-Egyptian relations are aimed at maintaining regional stability, improving bilateral relations, continuing military cooperation, and sustaining the March 1979 Egyptian-Israeli peace treaty. Experience gained from Egyptian-U.S. joint military exercises proved valuable in easing coordination during the February 1991 Desert Storm operation to reverse Iraqi aggression against Kuwait. Egypt is seen by U.S. policy makers as a leader and moderating influence among many Arab, African, Islamic, and Third World states.

Among the current issues in U.S.-Egyptian relations are a shared concern about international terrorism. Egypt can claim some experience with the subject, having defeated domestic Islamic terrorists intent on overthrowing the Egyptian government. The two countries disagree over the speed and depth, but not the need for some of Egypt's economic reforms. Egypt and the United States agree on the importance of the Egyptian-Israeli peace treaty, the need to continue current Arab-Israel peace talks, and the need for regional stability. The two nations agree on Egypt's need to introduce democratic reforms in Egypt, although critics argue that Egypt is not moving quickly enough toward full democracy or in improving the human rights situation. The United States has provided Egypt with an annual average of over $2 billion in economic and military foreign assistance since 1979.

The United States will reduce Economic Support Funds (ESF) to about $400 million per year by 2008 in keeping with a plan to reduce aid to Israel. The Administration requested $575 million in economic grants and $1.3 billion in military grants for FY2004 for Egypt.

Chapter 4 - In 1996, Congress authorized the creation of *Qualifying Industrial Zones* (QIZs), thereby entitling goods jointly produced by Israel and either Jordan or Egypt to enter the United States duty free. The QIZ creation vehicle was an amendment to the *United States-Israel Free Trade Area Implementation Act of 1985* (P.L. 99-47), and its purpose was to promote peace and development between Israel and her Arab neighbors. Although Israeli-Palestinian violence has continued, some observers have praised QIZs for helping to spark Jordan's economic growth. Others note that QIZs, while promoting U.S.-Jordanian trade, have had modest impact on promoting job growth in Jordan. In 2005, Egypt began participating in the QIZ program. This chapter provides an overview of QIZs in the context of promoting regional development and peace. For more information on Jordan, see CRS Issue Brief IB93085, *Jordan: U.S. Relations and Bilateral Issues*, by Alfred Prados. For more information on Egypt, see CRS Report RL33003, *Egypt: Background and U.S. Relations*, by Jeremy M. Sharp.

Chapter 5 - In aiming to fight terrorism with trade, the United States has negotiated and the President signed on January 19, 2006, the U.S.'s fifth bilateral free trade agreement (FTA) in the proposed 20-entity Middle East Free Trade Area (MEFTA). This proposed FTA is with Oman. Other U.S.-FTAs are with Israel, Jordan, Morocco, and Bahrain. A sixth is being negotiated with the United Arab Emirates. Oman is a small oil-exporting U.S. trade partner that has been supportive of U.S. policies in the Middle East and is strategically located at the mouth of the Persian Gulf. Because its oil reserves could be exhausted within 15-20 years, Oman is trying to liberalize and diversify its trade regime beyond oil and gas to provide economic opportunities for its fast growing workforce. Supporters of the agreement typically cite political and economic reasons. Opponents typically point to labor and human rights issues.

The proposed FTA with Oman is similar to other MEFTA FTAs and has three basic parts: new tariff schedules, broad commitments to open markets and provisions to support those commitments, and protections for labor and the environment. It would provide immediate duty-free access for almost all consumer and industrial goods, with special provisions for agriculture and textiles and apparel.

Among all U.S. trade partners, Oman ranks 88th for the United States, while the United States ranks third for Oman (after the United Arab Emirates and Japan). U.S.-Oman trade at about $1 billion for 2005 represents 0.04% (four-one hundredths of one percent) of total U.S. trade. In 2005, the most important U.S. imports from Oman were oil and natural gas (75%), and apparel (10%). The most important U.S. exports to Oman were transport equipment (56%), and machinery (24%). The U.S. International Trade Commission (USITC) predicts that the economic effect of the proposed U.S.-Oman FTA is likely to be minimal since trade levels are low; and any increase in U.S. imports of apparel would come at the expense of workers elsewhere in the world, not in the United States. Total U.S. foreign direct investment in Oman was $358 million in 2003, up from $193 million in 2002.

Supporters argue that a U.S.-Oman FTA would contribute to bilateral economic growth and trade, generate export opportunities for U.S. companies, farmers, and ranchers, and help create jobs in both countries. Critics argue that labor protections are inadequate for Omani workers, compared to those they receive under the Generalized System of Protections, and that the proposed FTA would not help level the playing field for Omani and U.S. workers. Critics also argue that a provision in Annex II of the FTA could obligate the United States to open up landside aspects of its port activities to operation by companies doing business in Oman — the very activities about which Congress expressed national security concerns during the Dubai Ports World debate. (See sections on "Current Labor Issues," and "Current Issues on Port Security.") After the President submits the agreement and the implementing legislation to Congress, relevant committees have 45 days to consider (or not consider) it, and either chamber has 15 more days to vote the legislation up or down without amendment to the agreement itself or the legislation. The Senate passed implementing legislation for the U.S.-Oman FTA on June 29, 2006; and the House passed it on July 20.

Chapter 6 - On May 9, 2003, the Bush Administration proposed the establishment of a U.S. Middle East Free Trade Area (MEFTA) within a decade (by about 2013). This proposal came a year and a half after the September 11, 2001 terrorist attacks on the U.S. World Trade Center and the Pentagon. The MEFTA was billed as part of a plan to fight terrorism — in this case, by supporting the growth of Middle East prosperity and democracy — through trade. On June 23, 2003 the Bush Administration described a six-step process for Middle East entities to become part of that MEFTA: (1) joining the World Trade Organization (WTO); (2) possibly participating in the Generalized System of Preferences; successively entering into (3) trade investment framework agreements (TIFAs), (4) bilateral investment treaties (BITs), and (5) free trade agreements (FTA) with the United States; and (6) participating in trade capacity building.

The MEFTA would cover 20 entities in what many refer to as the Middle East/North Africa — 16 in the Middle East: Bahrain, Cyprus, Egypt, the Gaza Strip/West Bank, Iran, Iraq, Israel, Jordan, Kuwait, Lebanon, Oman, Qatar, Saudi Arabia, Syria, the United Arab Emirates and Yemen; and four in North Africa: Algeria, Libya, Morocco, and Tunisia.

Although U.S.-Middle East trade is small (4-5% of total U.S. trade), oil and gas are key imports, accounting for roughly one-tenth of all oil and gas consumed in the United States each year. Textiles and apparel are the second most important imports from these entities. The most important U.S. exports to these entities are machinery and transportation equipment.

The Bush Administration's initiative aims to help diversify and improve the economies of the Middle East, provide jobs for the rapidly growing population, stimulate U.S. exports, and help Middle East countries make economic reforms — values echoed by *The 9-11 Commission Report* as part of a comprehensive strategy to countering terrorism.

Since the Bush Administration first announced its trade initiative, it has made substantial progress in working with MEFTA entities to support WTO membership, and to develop TIFAs, BITs, and FTAs and progress along the steps outlined above. Since the beginning of 2003: Saudi Arabia has joined the WTO, and Iraq, Iran, Lebanon, Yemen, and Algeria are negotiating accession. In addition, TIFAS have been completed with seven countries: Kuwait, Oman, Saudi Arabia, the United Arab Emirates, Yemen, Qatar, and Iraq, bringing the total to 12. Other TIFA partners are Bahrain, Egypt, Jordan, Algeria, Morocco, and Tunisia. BITs have been completed with one country, Jordan, bringing the total to five. Other BIT partners are Bahrain, Egypt, Morocco, and Tunisia. Finally, a bilateral free trade agreement has been implemented with Jordan, Israel, Morocco, and Bahrain; signed with Oman (January 19, 2006); and is under negotiation with the United Arab Emirates. This brings the number of MEFTA FTAs to four implemented, one awaiting congressional action, and one under negotiation. FTA negotiations underway with Egypt have been suspended over human rights issues.

Chapter 7 - Fair and transparent elections are seen by experts and policymakers as a necessary step in Palestinian democratization and for the peace process. In 2002, the Palestinian Authority (PA), under increasing internal and external pressure, announced a so-called "100-Day Reform Plan" for institutional reform and elections in order to rejuvenate PA leadership. The 2006 legislative elections were the final and perhaps most critical test for Palestinian democratic institutions. On the one hand, the Palestinian Legislative Council elections may improve the day-to-day lives of Palestinians, renew public confidence in the PA, and bolster the peace process. On the other hand, the clear-cut legislative victory of Hamas, which does not recognize the state of Israel and calls for an Islamized Palestinian state, may increase the possibility that Palestinians will find themselves isolated.

Palestinian political reform is an important element in the U.S. policy of promoting democracy, civil society, and good governance in the Middle East. Still, a PA that is dominated by a democratically elected Hamas is uncharted diplomatic territory for the United States government and international community. It remains unclear how U.S. policy toward the Palestinians will change now that a designated terrorist organization is set to head the government. Additionally, as Israel holds its own parliamentary election this spring, any new government will face decisions whether to curb economic and diplomatic relations with the Palestinians.

The Palestinian political landscape has changed dramatically since the death of Yasir Arafat in 2004. Violence between Palestinians and Israelis, ineffective PA government, and an elusive political solution to the Israeli-Palestinian conflict prompted Palestinians to opt for change. The shift from a secular Fatah government toward a militant, Islamist government, however, does not necessarily mean all Palestinians accept the ideology of Hamas. The public's support for Hamas is conditional and may erode if Hamas does not improve the lives of Palestinians in demonstrable ways.

President Bush expressed support for the conduct of the Palestinian elections, but he and other Administration officials contend that there should be no place in the political process for groups and individuals who refuse to denounce terror and violence, recognize Israel's right to exist, or disarm. Since 1993, Congress has authorized over $1.5 billion in assistance to the Palestinians, and U.S. assistance to the Palestinians has increased over the past few years. Some in Congress support restricting or ending economic assistance to the Palestinians so that U.S. aid does not benefit a foreign terrorist organization. Others are wary of initiatives that may weaken Palestinian President Abbas.

The report will be updated periodically as events warrant. For discussion of the Palestinian-Israeli conflict, see CRS Report RS21235, *Palestinian Factions*, by Aaron Pina and CRS Issue Brief IB91137, *The Middle East Peace Talks*, by Carol Migdalovitz, and CRS Report RS22370, *U.S. Foreign Aid to the Palestinians*, by Jeremy M. Sharp.

Chapter 8 - In recent years, the ruler of Qatar, Shaikh Hamad bin Khalifa Al-Thani, has embarked upon a limited course of political liberalization and aligned Qatar firmly with the United States. In 1992, Qatar and the United States concluded a Defense Cooperation Agreement that has been progressively expanded. In April 2003, the Bush Administration announced that the U.S.

Combat Air Operations Center for the Middle East will be moved from Prince Sultan Airbase in Saudi Arabia to Qatar's Al-Udeid airbase, which served as a logistics hub for U.S. operations in Afghanistan under Operation Enduring Freedom, as well as a key center for Operation Iraqi Freedom. Camp As-Sayliyah, the largest pre-positioning facility of U.S. equipment in the world, served as the forward command center for CENTCOM personnel during Operation Iraqi Freedom. Qatar also has assisted the United States in the war on terrorism by stepping up its efforts to prevent Al Qaeda from engaging in money laundering. With the third largest proven gas reserves in the world, U.S. companies, such as ExxonMobil, have worked to increase trade and economic ties with Qatar. Qatar has the highest per capita income of any country in the Middle East.

As part of Qatar's experiment with limited political liberalization, the Qatari monarchy started Al Jazeera, the Arab world's first all-news network. In a national referendum in April 2003, Qatari voters approved a new constitution that provides for a partially elected national assembly and grants women the right to vote and run for office. For further information, see CRS Report RL31889, *The Al-Jazeera News Network: Opportunity or Challenge for U.S. Foreign Policy in the Middle East*, and CRS Report RL31533, *The Persian Gulf: Issues for U.S. Policy, 2003.*

In: Politics and Economics of the Middle East
Editors: W. Evans & D.J. Harris
ISBN: 978-1-60456-719-9

Chapter 1

THE PERSIAN GULF STATES: ISSUES FOR U.S. POLICY, 2006*

Kenneth Katzman

ABSTRACT

The U.S.-led war to overthrow Saddam Hussein virtually ended Iraq's ability to militarily threaten the region, but it has produced new and unanticipated security challenges for the Persian Gulf states (Saudi Arabia, Kuwait, Bahrain, Qatar, Oman, and the United Arab Emirates). The Gulf states, which are all led by Sunni Muslim regimes, fear that Shiite Iran is unchecked now that Iraq is strategically weak. The Gulf states strongly resent that pro-Iranian Shiite Muslim groups and their Kurdish allies (who are not Arabs) have obtained preponderant power within Iraq. This has led most of the Gulf states, particularly Saudi Arabia, to provide only halting support to the fledgling government in Baghdad and to revive the focus on U.S.-Gulf defense cooperation that characterized U.S.-Gulf relations during the 1990s.

The new power structure in Iraq has had political repercussions throughout the Gulf region, particularly as Sunni-Shiite violence in Iraq has come to overshadow direct insurgent violence against U.S. forces as the key threat to Iraqi stability. The Sunni-Shiite tensions in Iraq apparently are spilling over into the Gulf states. Shiite communities, particularly that in Bahrain, have been emboldened by events in Iraq to seek additional power, and Sunni-Shiite tension in the Gulf states is said by observers to be increasing.

---

* Excerpted from CRS Report RL31533, dated August 21, 2006.

Some Shiite communities, which view themselves as long repressed, are attempting to benefit politically from the Bush Administration's focus on promoting democracy and political reform in the region. Domestically, all of the Gulf states are undertaking substantial but gradual economic and political liberalization to deflect popular pressure and satisfy U.S. calls for reform. However, the reforms undertaken or planned do not aim to fundamentally restructure power in any of these states. The Bush Administration advocates more rapid and sweeping political and economic liberalization as key to long-term Gulf stability and to reducing support in the Gulf states for terrorist groups such as Al Qaeda. The Administration is funding civil society programs in the Gulf states — funding that is not necessarily welcomed by the Gulf leaderships — but it is also promoting the bilateral free trade agreements that most of the Gulf leaders seek.

The Bush Administration also is working to maintain or improve post-September 11 cooperation with the Gulf states against Al Qaeda. Some Gulf states allegedly tolerated the presence of Al Qaeda activists and their funding mechanisms prior to the September 11 attacks. Fifteen of the nineteen September 11 hijackers were of Saudi origin, as is Al Qaeda founder Osama bin Laden.

See also CRS Report RL33533, *Saudi Arabia: Current Issues and U.S. Relations;* CRS Report RS21513, *Kuwait: Post-Saddam Issues and U.S. Policy*; CRS Report RS21852, *The United Arab Emirates: Issues for U.S. Policy*; CRS Report RL31718, *Qatar: Background and U.S. Relations*; CRS Report 95-1013 F, *Bahrain: Key Issues for U.S. Policy*; and CRS Report RS21534, *Oman: Reform, Security, and U.S. Policy.*

The Persian Gulf region is rich in oil and gas resources but has a history of armed conflict and of challenging U.S. national security. The Gulf states — Saudi Arabia, Kuwait, the UAE, Qatar, Bahrain, and Oman, bound together in a 1981 alliance called the Gulf Cooperation Council (GCC) — have experienced three major wars in the past twenty five years: the Iran-Iraq war (1980-1988), the Persian Gulf war (1991), and Operation Iraqi Freedom (2003-current). This report, which will be revised periodically, discusses U.S. and Gulf efforts to manage the new challenges posed by the September 11, 2001, attacks on the United States and the aftermath of the overthrow of Saddam Hussein. The report is derived from a wide range of sources, including press reports, unclassified U.S. government documents, U.N. documents, observations by the author during visits to the Gulf, and conversations with U.S., European, Iranian, and Gulf state officials, journalists, and academics.

THREAT PERCEPTIONS AND U.S.-GULF SECURITY COOPERATION

Prior to the 2003 war against Iraq, the United States was repeatedly drawn into conflicts in the Gulf to counter Iranian or Iraqi aggression and contain regional escalation. In the "Iran-Iraq War," Iran and Saddam Hussein's Iraq fought each other from Iraq's invasion on September 22, 1980, until August 20,1988, jeopardizing the security of the Gulf monarchy states, which collectively backed Iraq. Similarly, the United States tilted toward Iraq in that war to defeat the radical Islamist threat posed by Iran's Islamic revolutionary government, which came to power in February 1979 after ousting the U.S.-backed Shah. Iran and the United States fought minor naval skirmishes during 1987-1988, at the height of the Iran-Iraq war. During one such skirmish (*Operation Praying Mantis,* April 18, 1988) the United States fought a day long naval battle with Iran that destroyed almost half of Iran's largest naval vessels. On July 3, 1988, the United States mistakenly shot down an Iranian passenger aircraft flying over the Gulf (Iran Air flight 655), killing all 290 aboard.[1] After about 400,000 Iraqi and almost 1 million Iranian casualties, the Iran-Iraq war ceased in August 1988 after Iran's forces collapsed from a series of successful Iraqi offensives and Iran accepted U.N. Security Council Resolution 598, amounting to an Iraqi victory in the war.

The Iran-Iraq war victory emboldened Saddam Hussein to assert himself as the "strongman" of the Gulf. He invaded and occupied Kuwait on August 2, 1990, asserting that he did so because Kuwait (and UAE) were overproducing oil and thereby betraying Iraq (by lowering world oil prices). Others believe Saddam Hussein wanted to position Iraq to control, directly or indirectly, oil exports from the Gulf. To liberate Kuwait, the United States deployed over 500,000 U.S. troops, joined by about 200,000 troops from 33 other countries. That war (Operation Desert Storm, January 16- February 27, 1991) resulted in the death in action of 148 U.S. service personnel and 138 non-battle deaths, along with 458 wounded in action. The 1991 Gulf war reduced Iraq's conventional military capabilities roughly by half, but, prior to Operation Iraqi Freedom (March 2003), Iraq was still superior to Iran and the Gulf states in ground forces.

The Gulf is one of the few theaters where weapons of mass destruction (WMD) and ballistic missiles have been used in hostilities. Iraq's missile, chemical, nuclear, and biological programs, accelerated during the Iran-Iraq war, were among the most sophisticated in the Third World at the time of Iraq's invasion of Kuwait. Israel was sufficiently concerned about Iraq's nuclear program that it conducted an air-strike against Iraq's French-built Osirak nuclear reactor on June 7, 1981, temporarily setting back Iraq's nuclear effort. During the Iran-Iraq war, Iraq fired enhanced Scud missiles at Iranian cities,[2] and Iran fired its own Scud missiles at Iraqi cities as well in the so-called "war of the cities." On ten occasions during the Iran-Iraq war, Iraq used chemical weapons against Iranian troops and Kurdish guerrillas and civilians, killing over 26,000 Iranians and Kurds.[3] U.N. investigation missions found that Iran also used some chemical weapons against Iraq during the war, although Iran's capability was less advanced than that of Iraq during that period.[4] During the 1991 Gulf war, Iraq fired 39 enhanced Scud missiles at Israel, a U.S. ally, and 39 enhanced Scud missiles on targets in Saudi Arabia. One Iraqi missile, fired on coalition forces on February 25, 1991 (during Desert Storm) hit a U.S. barracks near Dhahran, Saudi Arabia, killing 28 military personnel and wounding 97. U.N. weapons inspectors dismantled much of Iraq's WMD infrastructure during 1991-1998, but they left in 1998 due to Iraqi obstructions and without clearing up major unresolved questions about Iraq's WMD. New U.N. inspections began, under threat of U.S. force, in November 2002, but were ended after the Bush Administration and its allies determined that Iraq's regime was not fully disarming and that it was necessary to overthrow the regime by force (Operation Iraqi Freedom, OIF).

The "Dual Containment" Approach of the 1990s

During 1993-1997, the Clinton Administration articulated a policy of "dual containment," an effort to keep both Iran and Iraq weak rather than alternately tilting toward one or the other to preserve a power balance between them. During this period, Saudi Arabia and Kuwait were primarily concerned about the conventional threat from Iraq and saw Iran as a counterweight to Iraqi power. The states of the lower Gulf were further from Iraq and tended to view Iran as a greater danger than Iraq. Bahrain, in 1981 and again in 1996 — the latter a period of substantial Shiite-inspired unrest — openly accused Iran of plotting to destabilize that country by supporting radical Shiite movements there. In 1992, the UAE became alarmed at Iranian intentions when Iran asserted complete control of the largely uninhabited Persian Gulf island of Abu Musa, which Iran and UAE shared under a 1971 bilateral agreement.

All the Gulf states improved relations with Iran significantly at the end of the decade, particularly after the May 1997 election of the relatively moderate president Mohammad Khatemi, who curtailed Iran's support for Shiite dissident movements in the Gulf states. Despite the rapprochement, which was matched by unsuccessful attempts by the Clinton Administration to open direct talks with Khatemi's government, the United States continued to try to constrain Iran's WMD programs, but with mixed success. Unlike Iraq, which was the target of U.N. sanctions after it invaded Kuwait, Iran faced no mandatory international restrictions on its imports of advanced conventional weapons or of "dual use" technology (civilian goods useful for WMD). Some of Iran's WMD programs made significant strides during the 1990s, reportedly with substantial help from Russia, China, North Korea, and other countries and entities, such as the network of Pakistani nuclear scientist A.Q. Khan.

The dual containment policy also had little success in curbing Iran's (or Iraq's) support for international terrorism. Iran has been on the U.S. list of terrorism state sponsors ("terrorism list") since 1984 (the list was created in 1979). Iraq was on the terrorism list during 1979-1982, and again from 1990 until the U.S.-led overthrow of Saddam Hussein. Over the past decade the State Department's annual report on terrorism has described Iran as "the most active state sponsor of terrorism. The Islamic regime in Iran had held American diplomats hostage during November 1979-January 1981, a seizure for which Iran has not apologized. The pro-Iranian Lebanese Shiite Muslim organization Hizballah held Americans hostage in Lebanon during 1984-1991, occasionally releasing some and then abducting others. Some U.S. law enforcement officials say Iranian operatives were involved in the June 1996 bombing in Saudi Arabia of the Khobar Towers housing complex for U.S. military officers, in which 19 U.S. airmen were killed, although some indications from the "September 11 Commission" final report (p.60) says Al Qaeda operatives might have had some role in that bombing. According to the recent annual State Department reports on international terrorism ("Country Reports on Terrorism: 2005," released April 2006) Iran provides material support to the following groups that oppose the U.S.-sponsored Arab-Israeli peace process: Hizballah and the Palestinian groups Hamas, Palestinian Islamic Jihad, the Al Aqsa Martyr's Brigade, and the Popular Front for the Liberation of Palestine-General Command.

Iraq's former regime was on the terrorism list and publicly supported Palestinian violence against Israel. According to the September 11 Commission report, neither Iran nor Saddam's Iraq was linked to the September 11 attacks and neither had an "operational" relationship with Al Qaeda. However, press accounts say that some Al Qaeda activists fleeing Afghanistan transited or took refuge in both countries, including Al Qaeda-Iraq leader Abu Musab al-Zarqawi,[5] and there apparently were some limited contacts between Al Qaeda and the Saddam Hussein regime. The new government in Iraq, which consists of political leaders who are generally well disposed toward the United States, was removed from the terrorism list on September 24, 2004. No observer is predicting that Iran will soon be removed from the U.S. list of state sponsors of terrorism ("terrorism list").

The Post-Saddam Gulf Threat Profile[6]

The Gulf threat profile has been altered — but not necessarily reduced — by the overthrow of Saddam Hussein's regime in Iraq. The fall of Saddam had initially generated a sense of relief among the Gulf states because the conventional and WMD threat posed by Iraq was essentially ended. However, no clear U.S. Gulf security architecture has emerged, and the Gulf states now sense new and different threats, although no major security crises have erupted in any of the GCC states since Saddam's fall. Others note that, in the past, crises have erupted on short notice, including Saddam Hussein's invasion of Kuwait and the internal unrest in Bahrain in the 1990s, neither of which were widely predicted.

Iran Strategically Strengthened

First and foremost, the Gulf states believe that the strategic weakness of post-Saddam Iraq has emboldened Iran to take a more active role in Gulf security and to seek to enlist the Gulf states in an Iran-led Gulf security structure. Iran has a long coastline and a well-honed sense of nationhood; it was not created by colonial powers and believes it is entitled to a major role in Gulf security. All of the Gulf state fears about Iran have been compounded by the Iranian presidency of hardliner Mahmoud Ahmadinejad. He has appointed to key positions longtime associates from his career in the Revolutionary Guard and Basij militia — both bastions of hardline sentiment and armed force and sponsors of radical activity in the Gulf in the past. However, to date, GCC leaders have leveled no specific allegations of renewed Iranian meddling in the GCC states, and the Gulf leaders have been receiving visiting Iranian leaders, including Ahmadinejad.

Yet, Gulf and U.S. concerns continue that further progress on Iran's WMD programs, particularly its nuclear program, could embolden Iran to try to intimidate the Gulf states. Qatar, for example, is wary that Iran might try to encroach on its giant natural gas North Field, which the two share. In response, in 2006, the Gulf states and the United States have renewed and expanded discussions on some of the joint defense initiatives that have been de-emphasized in the past five years.[7] Some of these steps are discussed in the section on defense issues below. Many U.S. experts believe that the GCC states would likely back U.S. action, including military action, to halt or set back Iran's nuclear program, despite fears of Iranian retaliation against them for any U.S. military move against Iran.

At the same time, Iran is not perceived as militarily able to move in force across the Gulf to invade any of the Gulf states, even if the United States were not present in the Gulf to block such a move. Senior U.S. military officials say Iran could use its coastal missiles, patrol boats, mines, aircraft, submarines, and other capabilities to try to block the Strait of Hormuz, the key oil shipment route, but U.S. officials express confidence that the U.S military presence in the Gulf could quickly overwhelm Iran's relatively older equipment and thwart any such Iranian action. Others argue that even a failed Iranian attempt to block the Strait could raise shipping insurance rates and drive up oil prices to unprecedented levels.

Shiite Communities Emboldened

Compounding the threat perception of the Gulf states is the rise of Shiite Islamist factions in post-Saddam Iraq —particularly revered clerical leader Grand Ayatollah Ali al-Sistani, the Supreme Council of the Islamic Revolution in Iraq (SCIRI), the Da'wa (Islamic Call) Party, and the faction of radical young cleric Moqtada Al Sadr. The Shiite Islamists have dominated Iraq's two elections for a parliament - in January and again in December 2005. The rise of Iraqi Shiite parties are reportedly prompting growing Shiite demands for power in the Gulf states themselves. As shown in the Appendix, several of the Gulf states have substantial Shiite populations; in Bahrain they are a majority (about 60%), but most Gulf Shiite communities consider themselves under-represented in government and lacking key opportunities in the economy. Bahraini Shiite groupings, including those that boycotted 2002 parliamentary elections, are planning to compete in the October 2006 parliamentary elections in the hopes of asserting Shiite rights against the Sunni-dominated government there. To prevent the emergence of Sunni-Shiite tensions that have erupted in Iraq, Bahraini leaders have begun reconciliation efforts, such as ending the distinction between Sunni and Shiite mosques and encouraging joint worship.

Kuwait's concerns are also high even though Shiites (about 25% of Kuwaitis) are well integrated into the political system. Radical factions of an Iraqi Shiite Islamic party, the Da'wa Party, attacked the U.S. and French embassies in Kuwait City in December 1983, and attacked the Amir's motorcade in May 1985, injuring him slightly. Although Kuwaiti fears of a resumption of such activity have faded, Kuwait remains wary of potential Shiite militance and has engaged Iraq's Shiite clerics and provided about $500 million in humanitarian aid to Iraq through a Kuwait based Humanitarian Operations Center. Kuwait has pledged to send an ambassador to Baghdad, although no ambassador has been named, to date. In Saudi Arabia, there is acute fear of potential Shiite unrest, in part because Shiites are concentrated in the eastern provinces where many of Saudi Arabia's oil fields are located and in which much of its oil export infrastructure is based. Resenting Shiite domination in Iraq,

Saudi Arabia has disbursed little of its $1 billion in aid pledges to Iraq, and it has not committed to appointing an ambassador to Iraq.

Spillover from Iraq Battlefield

Prior to the U.S. intervention in Iraq, the Gulf states had predicted that ousting Saddam would not necessarily produce stability in Iraq, and several were reluctant to support it. For the most part, Gulf leaders publicly indicated that they would only support a U.S. attack if such action were authorized by the United Nations and had broad international support. Two of the Gulf states, Kuwait and Qatar, were more openly supportive of the U.S. position, and both hosted substantial buildups of U.S. forces and equipment that were used in the offensive against Iraq. Kuwait, which strongly wanted to see the former invader, Saddam Hussein, overthrown, hosted the bulk of the personnel and equipment used in the ground assault. Saudi Arabia was the most vocally opposed to a U.S. offensive against Iraq, even though the prospect of the overthrow of Saddam Hussein held out the possibility that the 6,000 U.S. personnel that were based there in anti-Iraq containment operations would be able to depart. That redeployment happened after Saddam's fall.

Judging from the final statement of the 26th Gulf Cooperation Council summit in Abu Dhabi, UAE (December 2005), the Gulf leaders are expressing concern that spillover from the Iraq war could be worse than they had anticipated. Some Sunni Islamist insurgents have tried or succeeded in entering some of the Gulf states, particularly Kuwait, to commit acts of retribution against the Gulf governments or to try to attack U.S. forces staging for deployment into Iraq. The Sunni militants perceive the Gulf governments — even though they are Sunni-led — as traitors for having backed or acquiesced in the U.S. invasion of Iraq and ouster of Saddam Hussein. The Gulf states believe that parts of Iraq might become a safe haven for Sunni Islamic militants if the United States were to withdraw militarily from Iraq, an outcome that the Gulf states fear could result if U.S. casualties continue to mount. This issue is discussed in greater depth in the final section of this paper.

At the same time, efforts by the Gulf states to promote ethnic and sectarian balance in Iraq might be increasing the potential for spillover from Iraq. Saudi Arabia, and possibly other Gulf states, are said to have tacitly permitting some Saudis to enter Iraq to assist the Sunni insurgency there. Observers say there is an active debate in the Kingdom about whether to provide more active support to the Sunnis but that King Abdullah has decided against it out of concern that doing so would stimulate Iran to step up aid to Shiite groups in Iraq. U.S. military officers say that Saudi fighters accounted for about half of the foreign insurgents killed in Iraq in 2005.[8] In November 2004, 26 radical Saudi clerics issued a pronouncement calling on Iraqis to fight U.S.-led forces in Iraq, although the Saudi religious establishment subsequently contradicted that pronouncement. At the same time, Saudi Arabia has pursued diplomacy to increase the role of Sunni Arabs in Iraq's government. Press reports say the Saudis were influential in persuading hardline Iraqi Sunni clerics to attend a November 2005 Arab League-sponsored reconciliation meeting in Cairo.

Post-Saddam U.S.-Gulf Defense Cooperation

The post-Saddam Gulf is somewhat less stable than the United States initially expected, and the pillars of U.S.-Gulf defense cooperation that were put in place after the 1991 Gulf war are drawing renewed emphasis as Iran's power is perceived to be rising. The U.S.-GCC relationships enable the United States to continue to operate militarily in Iraq and have facilitated ongoing operations in Afghanistan as well. After the September 11, 2001, attacks, the Gulf states willingly and openly hosted U.S. forces performing combat missions in Afghanistan in Operation Enduring Freedom (OEF, the war against the Taliban and Al Qaeda). As discussed above, the Gulf states, perceiving potential fallout, were far less enthusiastic about the war to topple Saddam Hussein, although all the Gulf states did make facilities available for Operation Iraqi Freedom (OIF).

The cornerstones of U.S.-Gulf defense relations are broad bilateral defense pacts between the United States and each Gulf state except Saudi Arabia. The text of the agreements, most of which were adopted after the 1990-91 Gulf crisis, are classified. However, observers report that the pacts provide for:[9] facilities access for U.S. forces, but also for U.S. advice, training, and joint exercises; lethal and non-lethal U.S. equipment pre-positioning; and arms sales. The pacts do not include security guarantees that formally require the United States to come to the aid of any of the Gulf states if they are attacked, according to U.S. officials familiar with their contents. Nor, say officials, do the pacts give the United States automatic permission to conduct military operations from Gulf facilities; the United States must obtain permission on a case by case basis. None of the Gulf states has moved to suspend or end these formal pacts now that Saddam Hussein is gone from power.

The approximate number of U.S. military personnel in the Gulf theater of operations is listed in table 1 below, based on unclassified tables provided to CRS by the Department of Defense in late 2005.

Table 1. Gulf Hosting of U.S. Troops and Equipment (2005)

Country	U.S. Forces/Facilities Access
Saudi Arabia	• About 400 U.S. military personnel, mostly to train Saudi military and national guard
Kuwait	• About 90,000 mostly Army, supporting OIF • Ali al-Salem air base: hosts U.S. 386th Air Expeditionary Group supporting OIF • Camp Arifjan: main facility for US forces supporting OIF • Camp Buehring: firing range for U.S. training prior to OIF deployment • Camp Doha: was main facility for U.S., but was vacated in Dec. 05
UAE	• About 1,800 mostly Air Force supporting OIF and OEF • Al Dhafra air base: 380th Air Expeditionary Group, KC-10, KC-135 refueling aircraft and surveillance craft • Jebel Ali: port facilities for U.S. ships resupplying Al Dhafra
Qatar	• About 6,000 mostly Air Force supporting OEF and OIF • Al Udeid airbase, a hub of U.S. air operations in the Gulf: hosts U.S. F-16's, KC-10 and KC-135 refueling planes, surveillance aircraft, and CAOC • CENTCOM forward hq (since 2003) and hq for special operations component of CENTCOM (Socent) • As Saliyah: pre-positioned U.S. Army materiel • Millenium Village: built to house U.S. personnel
Oman	• About 25 mostly Air Force • equipment, U.S. Air Force access to Seeb, Thumrait, Masirah, Khasab air bases mostly for contingencies
Bahrain	• About 4,700, mostly Navy supporting OIF and OEF • Manama: large portside site for U.S. Fifth fleet headquarters and naval (Navcent) and Marine (Marcent) components of CENTCOM. These commands direct U.S. and allied anti-Al Qaeda, anti-drug, anti-proliferation naval operations and Iraq oil terminal defense • Mina al-Sulman port: docking for small U.S. warships, is being improved to handle carriers • Shaikh Isa air base: mainly for contingencies and pre- positioned U.S. equipment • Muharraq Airfield for U.S. Navy reconnaissance aircraft

Sources: Factsheets provided to CRS by the Department of Defense in 2005; Overseas Basing Commission (May 2005). U.S. force figures per country from November 2005.

During the U.S.-led containment operations against Iraq during the 1990s, there were about 20,000 U.S. military personnel stationed in the Gulf at most times, although about 60% of those were afloat on ships. Although there are fewer U.S. forces in most of the Gulf states than there were at the height of OEF and OIF, the aggregate is still higher than the 20,000 "baseline" during the 1990s — almost entirely due to the large numbers of U.S. personnel still in Kuwait supporting OIF. U.S. forces in Iraq number about 130,000. The following is an overview of U.S. defense cooperation with the GCC states:

- Saudi Arabia, concerned about internal opposition to a U.S. presence, did not sign a formal defense pact with the United States. However, it has entered into several limited defense procurement and training agreements (for both the regular military and the Saudi Arabia National Guard, SANG) with the United States.[10] During 1992-2003, U.S. combat aircraft based in Saudi Arabia flew patrols to enforce a "no fly zone" over southern Iraq (Operation Southern Watch, OSW), but Saudi Arabia did not permit preplanned strikes against Iraqi air defenses, only retaliatory strikes for tracking or firing by Iraq. OSW ended after the fall of Saddam Hussein and most of the 6,000 Saudi-based U.S. personnel, along with all Saudi-based U.S. combat aircraft, were withdrawn in September 2003. For OEF, Saudi Arabia did not offer to allow U.S. pilots to fly missions in Afghanistan from Saudi Arabia, but it reportedly did openly permit the United States to use the Combined Air Operations Center (CAOC) at Prince Sultan Air Base, south of Riyadh, to coordinate U.S. air operations over Afghanistan. Despite reservations about the war against Iraq, the Kingdom also quietly allowed use of the CAOC for OIF and permitted some U.S. special operations forces staging missions from there into Iraq.[11]
- Bahrain has hosted the headquarters for U.S. naval forces in the Gulf since 1948, long before the United States became the major Western power in the Gulf. (During the 1970s and 1980s, the U.S. presence was nominally based offshore.) Bahrain signed a separate defense cooperation agreement with the United States on October 28, 1991, and the pact remains in effect. In June 1995, the U.S. Navy reestablished its long dormant Fifth fleet, responsible for the Persian Gulf region, and headquartered in Bahrain. Bahrain allowed U.S. combat aircraft missions from Bahrain in both OEF and OIF, and it publicly deployed its U.S.-supplied frigate naval vessel in support of both operations, according to

the State Department. It was the only Gulf state to deploy its own forces to provide humanitarian aid inside Afghanistan.

- After Iran's 1979 revolution, Oman on April 21, 1980 signed a facilities access agreement providing the United States access to Omani airbases and allowing some prepositioning of U.S. Air Force equipment. The agreement was renewed in 1985, 1990, and 2000. In keeping with an agreement reached during the 2000 access agreement renewal negotiations, the United States provided the $120 million cost to upgrade the air base near al-Musnanah (Khasab).[12]
- On September 19, 1991, Kuwait, which saw itself as the most vulnerable to Iraqi aggression, signed a 10-year pact with the United States (renewed in 2001 for another 10 years) allowing the United States to preposition enough equipment to outfit two U.S. brigades. Joint U.S.-Kuwaiti exercises were held almost constantly, and about 4,000 U.S. military personnel were in Kuwait at virtually all times during the 1990s. The United States opened a Joint Task Force headquarters in Kuwait in December 1998 to better manage the U.S. forces in Kuwait, and the United States spent about $170 million in 1999-2001 to upgrade two Kuwaiti air bases (Ali al-Salem and Ali al-Jabir) that hosted U.S. aircraft during the 1990s containment operations against Iraq. As noted previously, Kuwait closed off the entire northern third of the country to serve as host of the U.S.-led invasion force in OIF.
- Even before OEF and OIF, Qatar was building an increasingly close defense relationship with the United States. It signed a defense pact with the United States on June 23, 1992, and accepted the prepositioning of enough armor to outfit two U.S. brigades at a site called As Saliyah site, which was upgraded with U.S. help. (Most of the armor at the site was used in OIF.)[13] The United States built an air operations center (Combined Air Operations Center, CAOC) at Al Udeid air base that, by 2003, had largely supplanted the one in Saudi Arabia and Qatar now hosts U.S. Central Command (CENTCOM) forward headquarters. Qatar publicly acknowledged the U.S. use of Al Udeid in OEF, and it continues to support OEF and OIF, according to the State Department.
- The UAE did not have close defense relations with the United States prior to the 1991 Gulf war. After that war, the UAE determined that it wanted a closer relationship with the United States, in part to deter and balance out Iran. On July 25, 1994, the UAE announced it had signed a defense pact with the United States, although there are still some differences in interpretation of the legal jurisdiction of U.S. military

personnel in the UAE, according to observers. The UAE allows some U.S. pre-positioning, as well as U.S. ship port visits at its large man-made Jebel Ali port, and it hosts U.S. refueling aircraft at Al-Dhafra air base for OEF and OIF. However, wanting to act within an Arab consensus, the UAE limited the United States to conducting support air operations during OIF.

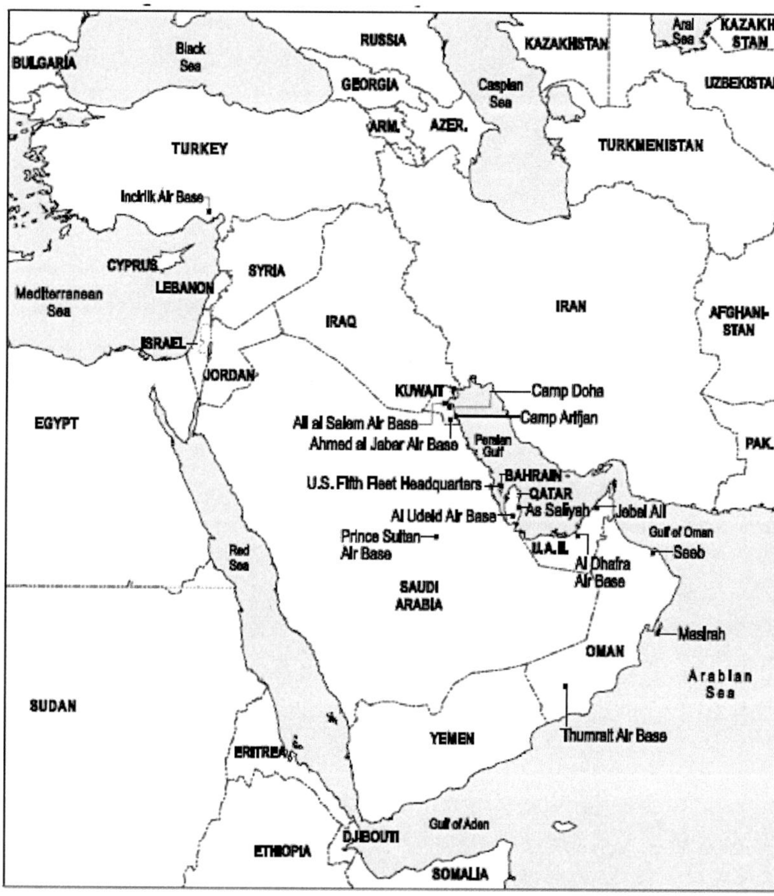

Source: Map Resources. Adapted by CRS. (M.Chin 01/03).

Figure 1. Facilities Used by U.S. Forces in the Gulf.

U.S. Arms Sales and Security Assistance

A key feature of the U.S. strategy for protecting the Gulf states has been to sell them arms and related defense services. Some of the Gulf states, particularly Saudi Arabia, are reportedly contemplating new arms purchases from other suppliers, as well as the United States, to counter the perceived growing threat from Iran.[14] On August 19, 2006, it was announced that Saudi Arabia had agreed to buy 72 Eurofighter Typhoon aircraft in a deal valued at about $18 billion.

Congress has not blocked any U.S. sales to the GCC states since the 1991 Gulf war, although some in Congress have expressed reservations about sales of a few of the more sophisticated weapons and armament packages to the Gulf states in recent years. Some Members believe that sales of sophisticated equipment could erode Israel's "qualitative edge" over its Arab neighbors, if the Gulf states were to join a joint Arab military action against Israel or transfer weapons to "frontline" states, but few experts believe that the Gulf states would do so. Others are concerned that some U.S. systems sold to the Gulf contain missile technology that could violate international conventions. Even if they were to do so, successive U.S. administrations have maintained that the Gulf states are too dependent on U.S. training, spare parts, and armament codes to be in a position to use sophisticated U.S.-made arms against Israel or any other U.S. ally.[15] The Foreign Relations Authorization Act of 1994-1995 (P.L. 103-236, signed April 30, 1994) bars U.S. arms sales to any country that enforces the primary and secondary Arab League boycott of Israel. The provision has been waived for the Gulf states every year since enactment.

Most of the GCC states are considered too wealthy to receive substantial amounts of U.S. security assistance, including Foreign Military Financing (FMF) and excess defense articles (EDA). However, U.S. aid to the GCC states, even the most wealthy among them, has increased recently. It is being used to promote a number of U.S. objectives in the Gulf, including building GCC anti-terrorism capabilities, promoting military-to-military ties and military obedience to civilian rule; enabling the GCC states to maintain U.S.-made weapons and to operate them in concert with U.S. forces; and signaling continued support for their alliance with the United States. Despite its wealth, Saudi Arabia receives a nominal amount of International Military Education and Training funds (IMET) to lower the costs to the Saudi government (approximately a 50% discount) of sending its approximately 400 military officers to U.S. schools each year. A provision of the FY2005 foreign aid appropriations (in Consolidated Appropriations law, P.L. 108-447) cut IMET for Saudi Arabia, but President Bush waived that restriction on September 26, 2005, to provide the aid (PD2005-38).

Table 2. U.S. Assistance to the Gulf States (Amounts in USD)

Country	Aid Type	FY2005	FY2006 est.	FY2007 request
Saudi Arabia	IMET		24,000	20,000
	NADR-CTF	200,000	100,000	
	NADR-ATA	760,000		400,000
Oman	FMF	19.84 million	13.86 mil.	14 mil.
	IMET	1.141 mil.	1.089 mil.	1.135 mil.
	NADR-EXBS	400,000	300,000	325,000
	NADR-ATA	254,000	1.3 mil.	1.045 mil.
Bahrain	FMF	18.847 mil.	15.593 mil.	15.75 mil.
	IMET	649,000	650,000	640,000
	NADR-ATA	1.489 mil.	3.098 mil.	955,000
Kuwait	IMET			20,000
	NADR-ATA	814,000	840,000	1.07 mil.
	NADR-CTF		300,000	
Qatar	NADR-ATA	1.379 mil.	1.274 mil.	1.493 mil.
	NADR-CTF		300,000	
UAE	NADR-ATA	284,000	810,000	1.105 mil.
	NADR-CTF		300,000	
	NADR-EXBS	250,000		230,000

Note: IMET: International Military Education and Training funds; ESF: Economic Support Funds; FMF : Foreign Military Financing; NADR: Nonproliferation, Anti-Terrorism, Demining, and Related Programs. ATA is Anti-Terrorism Assistance; CTF is Counter-terrorism financing; EXBS is Export Control and Related Border Security Assistance.

Excess Defense Articles (EDA)

Of the Gulf states, only the two least financially capable, Bahrain and Oman, are eligible to receive EDA on a grant basis (Section 516 of the Foreign Assistance Act). EDA are U.S. military items declared to be surplus or out of service for U.S. uses, but are still considered usable either as-is or with refurbishment. The UAE is eligible to buy or lease EDA. In 1998-1999, Oman received 30 and Bahrain 48 U.S.-made M-60A3 tanks on a "no rent" lease basis. The Defense Department subsequently transferred title to the equipment to the recipients. Since July 1997, Bahrain has taken delivery of a U.S. frigate and an I-HAWK air defense battery as EDA. Bahrain is currently seeking a second frigate under this program. According to State Department budget documents, in FY2007, both Bahrain and Oman will receive some EDA to assist military mobility and their ability to monitor their borders.

Foreign Military Sales (FMS)

The United States has considered U.S. arms sales (foreign military sales, FMS) to the Gulf states as an integral part of U.S. efforts to cement its alliances with the Gulf states, as well as to promote inter-operability between Gulf and U.S. forces.[16] Some of the recent sales, particularly of combat aircraft, appear intended to deter Iran. The rationale for some land systems might be less clear now that the land threat from Iraq has largely ended and because Iran is judged to lack an ability to move land forces across the Gulf. Some Gulf states might be seeking arms from non-U.S. sources, possible to diversify their defense relationships or perhaps to gain leverage over potential suppliers or allies of Iran.

- The UAE historically has purchased its major combat systems from France, but UAE officials apparently have come to believe that arms purchases from the United States enhance the U.S. commitment to UAE security. In March 2000, the UAE signed a contract to purchase 80 U.S. F-16 aircraft, equipped with the Advanced Medium Range Air to Air Missile (AMRAAM), the HARM (High Speed Anti-Radiation Missile) anti-radar missile, and, subject to a UAE purchase decision, the Harpoon anti-ship missile system. The total sale value, including weapons and services, is estimated at over $8 billion.[17] Deliveries began in May 2005. On November 17, 2004, DSCA notified Congress of a potential sale to UAE of 100 JAVELIN anti-tank missile launchers (plus 1,000 JAVELIN missile rounds) at a potential cost of $135 million. On July 28, 2006, DSCA notified Congress of a sale of up to 26 UH-60M (Blackhawk) helicopters, with a total sale value of up to $808 million. The UAE is also considering buying an anti-ballistic missile system, according to UAE Air Force Commander Maj. Gen. Khalid Al Bu-Ainain in November 2005.
- Saudi Arabia, buoyed by high oil prices, has absorbed about $14 billion in purchases of U.S. arms during the Gulf war, as well as post-war buys of 72 U.S.-made F-15S aircraft (1993, $9 billion value), 315 M1A2 Abrams tanks (1992, $2.9 billion), 18 Patriot firing units ($4.1 billion) and 12 Apache helicopters. It reportedly is now considering major new purchases, including a new generation fighter aircraft to replace aging U.S.-made F-5's and British-made Tornadoes. A *Wall Street Journal Europe* report on December 22, 2005 said Saudi Arabia had signed an agreement to buy up to 48 Eurofighter Typhoon jets. In three notifications on October 3, 2005 DSCA told Congress that Saudi Arabia intends to buy up to $2 billion in U.S.-made armored personnel carriers

(144) and related equipment and services; equipment support; and communications upgrades for the military and National Guard (SANG). In two notifications on July 28, 2006, DSCA notified Congress of a sale of 58 M1A1 new Abrams tanks, as well as upgrades of Saudi Arabia's existing Abrams tanks and upgrades of its U.S.-made Apache helicopters. The total of these sales is up to $3.3 billion.

- In 2005, Kuwait began taking delivery of a long-delayed purchase of 16 U.S.-made AH-64 "Apache" helicopters, equipped with the Longbow fire control system - a deal valued at about $940 million. According to DSCA, Kuwait is considering purchasing an additional 10 F/A-18 aircraft to complement its existing fleet of 40 of those aircraft, but there has been no movement on this recently. Kuwait also bought 5 Patriot firing units in 1992 and 218 M1A2 Abrams tanks in 1993. On April 1, 2004, the Bush Administration designated Kuwait as a "major non-NATO ally" (MNNA), a designation that will facilitate the future U.S. sales of arms to Kuwait.
- President Bush designated Bahrain an MNNA in March 2002, reflecting the close relationship. Among recent sales, in 1998, Bahrain purchased 10 F-16s from new production at a value of about $390 million. In late 1999, the Administration, with congressional approval, agreed to sell Bahrain up to 26 AMRAAMs, at a value of up to $69 million. Among the more controversial sales to a Gulf state, in August 2000 Bahrain requested to purchase 30 Army Tactical Missile Systems (ATACMs), a system of short-range ballistic missiles fired from a multiple rocket launcher. The Defense Department told Congress the version sold to Bahrain would not violate the rules of the Missile Technology Control Regime (MTCR),[18] an effort to allay congressional concerns that the the sale would facilitate the spread of ballistic and cruise missiles in the Gulf.[19] In addition, the Administration proposed a system of joint U.S.-Bahraini control of the weapon under which Bahraini military personnel would not have access to the codes needed to launch the missile.[20] Bahrain accepted that control formula, and delivery began in October 2002. In two notifications on July 28, 2006, DSCA reported to Congress a sale of up to 180 Javelin missiles (and associated launchers and equipment) and nine Blackhawk helicopters, with a total value of up to $294 million.

Table 3. Comparative Military Strengths of the Gulf States, Iraq, and Iran (2006)

Country	Military Personnel	Tanks	Surface-Air Missiles	Combat Aircraft	Surface Ships	Defense Budget (billion dollars)
Saudi Arabia	199,500 (incl. 75,000 Saudi National Guard)	1055 (incl. 315 M-1A2 Abrams)	160 Patriot-2 plus 3,716 other SAM (plus 10 CSS-2 missile)	291 (incl. 155 F-15)	76 (incl. 7 frigate)	21.3
UAE	50,500	545 (incl. 390 Leclerc)	40 + (plus 6 Scud-B missile)	100 + (incl. new F-16)	18 (incl. 2 frigate)	2.65
Oman	41,700	154 (incl. 70 M-60)	54 (incl. 20 Javelin)	32 (incl. 12 F-16)	13	3.0
Kuwait	15,500	368 (incl. 218 M-1A2 Abrams)	84 batteries (incl. 24 I-Hawk and Patriot batts.)	39 F/A-18 C and D	40	4.3
Qatar	12,400	30 AMX-30	75 SAMs (incl. 12 Stinger)	18	21	2.2
Bahrain	11,200	180 M-60A3	8 I-Hawk batteries	33 (incl. 21 F-16)	11 (incl. 1 frigate)	.526
Total GCC	330,800	2,300 +	4,000 +	500 +	179	33.98
Iraq	115,000	77 T-72 other donated armor	?	Negligible. Mostly helos.	10 patrol	?
Iran	545,000 (incl. 125,000 Revolutionary Guard)	1,693 (incl 75 T-72)	76 batteries (incl. I-Hawk) plus some Stinger	280 (incl. 25 MiG-29 and 30 Su-24)	260 (incl. 10 Hudong, 40 Boghammer, 3 frigates) Also has 3 Kilo subs	4.4

Source: International Institute for Strategic Studies, *The Military Balance 2006*. (Note: Figures shown here include materiel believed to be in storage); various press reports. Iraqi aircraft figures include aircraft flown from Iraq to Iran during 1991 Gulf war. Patriot firing unit figures do not include U.S.-owned firing units emplaced in those countries by the United States. U.S. Patriot firing units are emplaced in Qatar, Kuwait, and Saudi Arabia. *Boston Globe*, May 23, 2006.

- Qatar has traditionally been armed by France and Britain, and no major U.S. sales seem imminent, despite Qatar's healthy economy that benefits from burgeoning sales of natural gas. DSCA says that Qatar has expressed interest in a few U.S. systems, including the ATACM, which Bahrain has bought and which the United States has told Qatar it is eligible to buy. Qatar is also expressing active interest in the Patriot (PAC III) missile defense system, according to DSCA. Qatar might be seeking to buy advanced combat aircraft if it finds a buyer for the 12 Mirage 2000s it put up for sale in 2002; a possible sale to India collapsed in August 2005 over pricing issues.[21]
- Oman has traditionally purchased mostly British weaponry, reflecting British influence in Oman's military, and the British military's mentoring and advisory relationship to Sultan Qaboos. In October 2001, in an indication of waning British influence, the United States announced that Oman would buy 12 F-16 A/B aircraft, at an estimated value of $825 million. The first deliveries began in December 2005. In April 2003, Oman decided to purchase a podded airborne reconnaissance system for the F-16's; a sale valued at $46 million. On July 28, 2006, DSCA notified Congress of a possible sale to Oman of up to 250 Javelin missiles and associated launchers and equipment, valued at $48 million.

Other Gulf State Security Initiatives

The United States has continued to encourage the Gulf states to increase military cooperation among themselves. As shown in table 3, the Gulf states could potentially have superiority in equipment over Iran were they to combine their operations in response to a threat, and the Gulf states' military technology purchased from the United States and Europe is likely superior to Iran's mostly Russian and Chinese-supplied arsenal. However, the small (approximately 10,000 personnel) Saudi-based multilateral force known as Peninsula Shield, formed in 1981, has always suffered difficulties in coordination and command. Peninsula Shield, based at Hafar al-Batin in northern Saudi Arabia, did not react militarily to the 1990 Iraqi invasion of Kuwait, exposing the force's deficiencies. After that war, manpower shortages and disagreements over command of the force prevented the GCC states from agreeing to an Omani recommendation to boost Peninsula Shield to 100,000 men. In September 2000, the GCC states agreed in principle to increase the size of Peninsula Shield to 22,000,[22] but no timetable was set for reaching that level. U.S. emphasis on building intra-GCC land force cooperation waned after the fall of Saddam Hussein, not only because Iraq's conventional force was largely eliminated in the 2003 war but because, as noted above, Iran is not considered a major land invasion threat. At the December 2005 GCC summit, the Gulf leaders "endorsed" a Saudi proposal to disperse donated Peninsula Shield forces back to their home countries.[23] These forces would remain available for deployment to the Peninsula Shield force in a crisis.

Sensing growing air and naval threats from Iran and from terrorist infiltration by sea, the United States is reportedly planning to focus on improving GCC state naval and air cooperation. In mid-2006, the Bush Administration, in a series of high-level U.S. visits, began efforts to revive and build on the Clinton Administration's "Cooperative Defense Initiative" to integrate the GCC defenses with each other and with the United States. Under that initiative, in early 2001, the GCC inaugurated its "Belt of Cooperation" network for joint tracking of aircraft and coordination of air defense systems, built by Raytheon. Another part of that initiative, to which Bush Administration officials are attaching new importance, is U.S.-GCC joint training to defend against a chemical or biological attack, as well as more general joint military training and exercises.[24]

The Cooperative Defense Initiative, was a scaled-back version of an earlier U.S. idea to develop and deploy a GCC-wide theater missile defense (TMD) system. However, this missile defense concept reportedly is a focus of the renewed Bush Administration initiative,[25] in response to Iran's growing missile capabilities. The original idea envisioned a system under which separate parts (detection systems, intercept missiles, and other equipment) of an integrated TMD network would be based in the six different GCC states. That concept ran up against GCC states' financial constraints and differing perceptions among the Gulf states of the threat environment.[26] As noted in the table, Kuwait and Saudi Arabia have Patriot antimissile units of their own, and these states, in addition to Qatar, host U.S.-controlled Patriot systems.

The 2006 Bush Administration joint U.S.-GCC security initiative reportedly also focuses on counter-proliferation actions. U.S. officials, in their 2006 visits to the Gulf, are encouraging the GCC states to close Iranian companies in those states, which might be used to procure WMD technology. Another aspect of the initiative is to track shipments to Iran. The Bahrain-based 5th Fleet/Navcent command already plays a major role in patrolling the Gulf to prevent smuggling and the movement of terrorists across the Gulf. The patrols, which also include securing Iraqi oil export platforms, are conducted by about 30 U.S. and (OIF and OEF) allied warships in "Combined Task Force": 150, 152, and 158. On June 28, 2006, CTF-152, responsible for the central and southern Arabian Gulf, came under command of Italy.

Another joint security cooperation idea never extended beyond the concept stage. Gulf state suspicions of Syria and Egypt prevented closer military cooperation with those countries, as envisioned under a March 1991 "Damascus Declaration." Under the Damascus Declaration plan, Egyptian and Syrian forces would have been stationed in the Gulf to bolster the Peninsula Shield force.

Although their manpower constraints continue, many of the political disputes that had hindered cooperation within the GCC have dissipated. Almost all border disputes between GCC states have been settled, although the UAE still claims that Saudi Arabia occupies part of what UAE considers its territory. Bahrain and Qatar resolved their territorial dispute over the Hawar Islands and other territories following a March 2001 decision by the International Court of Justice in favor of Bahrain. The two have now agreed to construct a causeway connecting them.

Potential Cooperation with NATO

There are some indications that the Gulf states might be diversifying their security cooperation relationships with Western powers, while emphasizing such security-related issues as preventing drug trafficking, human trafficking, and proliferation. NATO is increasingly engaged in activities outside its traditional European base, and the NATO summit in Istanbul in 2004 launched an "Istanbul Cooperation Initiative" for greater NATO-Gulf state cooperation on some of these issues. To date, Kuwait, Bahrain, Qatar, and the UAE have joined the Istanbul initiative, but the absence of Saudi and Omani participation could slow development of this concept. Some NATO experts want to see the Istanbul initiative be further developed to allow for cooperation similar to that provided for in NATO's "Partnership for Peace" program. To promote greater NATO interaction with the Gulf states, NATO Secretary General Jaap de Hoop Scheffer attended a ground breaking meeting of high level Gulf defense officials in Qatar on December 1, 2005. During 2005, NATO (including U.S.) naval units, with participation of some Gulf naval forces, held exercises in the Arabian Sea in support of the U.S.-led "Proliferation Security Initiative" (PSI), a program to halt potential WMD-related shipments at sea.

DOMESTIC STABILITY AND POLITICAL LIBERALIZATION[27]

The external threats the Gulf monarchies face have not produced regime-threatening instability within the Gulf states. However, there are domestic forces that, particularly if aggravated by outside Gulf powers such as Iran, could suddenly and unexpectedly prove destabilizing. Bahrain and Saudi Arabia have experienced periodic open unrest since the early 1990s, although both have largely quieted that unrest. The Gulf states are instituting gradual domestic political and economic reform efforts that are intended to satisfy the pro-reform elements of the population while maintaining tradition.

Leadership Transition

Still governed by hereditary leaders, several of the Gulf states also have completed at least interim leadership transitions over the past several years. The transitions have allowed new leaders to move forward on some long-dormant political or economic reforms.

- In Saudi Arabia, King Fahd suffered a stroke in November 1995 but he held the title of King until his death on August 1, 2005. He was immediately succeeded by his half-brother and heir apparent, Crown Prince Abdullah, who had been de-facto ruler of the country. Abdullah is the same age as was Fahd (about 81) but Abdullah appears to be in reasonably good health. Abdullah has been more willing than Fahd to question U.S. policy in the region and U.S. prescriptions for Saudi security, although he has maintained a cooperative relationship with the United States. Together with his image of piety and rectitude, Abdullah's perceived independence accounts for his relative popularity among the Saudi tribes and religious conservatives, giving him the legitimacy he needs to combat Saudi-based Al Qaeda or pro-Al Qaeda militants. The new heir apparent is Prince Sultan, a full brother of the late King Fahd, as expected, but the longer term succession could be clouded by family factional politics. The post-Fahd cabinet has remained largely unchanged; Sultan remains Defense Minister.
- In Bahrain, the sudden death of Amir (ruler) Isa bin Salman Al Khalifa on March 6, 1999 led to the accession of his son, Hamad bin Isa Al Khalifa, who was commander of Bahrain's Defense Forces. In February 2002, he wanted to promote a more limited monarchy and formally changed Bahrain into a kingdom and took the title King instead of Amir. King Hamad is about 57 years old and has named his son Salman, who is about 38 years old and is an avowed economic reformer, as Crown Prince. The two are sometimes said to be at odds with the King's traditionalist uncle, Khalifa bin Salman Al Khalifa, who remains Prime Minister.

- The UAE completed a transition upon the November 2, 2004 death of Shaykh Zayid bin Sultan al-Nuhayyan, ruler of the emirate of Abu Dhabi who helped found and became President of the seven-emirate UAE federation in 1971. His eldest son, Crown Prince Khalifa, who is about 49, succeeded immediately as ruler of Abu Dhabi and President of the UAE. His dynamic younger brother, Shaykh Mohammad, who is about 45, was named Abu Dhabi Crown Prince/heir apparent and he yielded his UAE Armed Forces chief-of-staff position to a non-royal (Lt. Gen. Hamad Al Rumaithi). Further changes occurred on January 4, 2006 when the ruler of Dubai, Shaykh Maktum bin Rashid Al Maktum, died suddenly. He was succeeded as Dubai ruler and UAE Prime Minister by his younger brother, Mohammad bin Rashid Al Maktum, who had been running Dubai de-facto for many years. The UAE is well placed to weather political transition because it has faced the least unrest of any of the Gulf states. Its GDP per capita ($22,000 per year) is among the highest in the Gulf, and there are few evident schisms in the society.
- Qatar's Amir, Hamad bin Khalifa Al Thani, who ousted his father in a bloodless coup in June 1995, sees himself as the leader among the Gulf rulers in instituting political reform and a public role for women. The Amir's reform agenda has been bolstered by the high public profile of his favorite wife, Shaykha Moza al-Misnad. Amir Hamad also has carved out a foreign policy independent from that of Saudi Arabia, has garnered wide support internally and there has been little evidence of unrest. On the other hand, some indications suggest that Qatar could lack dynamic leadership if the Amir were to leave the scene unexpectedly; in August 2003 the Amir suddenly and unexpectedly changed his crown prince/heir apparent from Shaykh Jassim to Jassim's younger brother, Tamim, purportedly perceiving Jassim as insufficiently capable of leadership.
- Kuwait completed a peaceful but troubled transition following the January 15, 2006 death of Kuwait's long serving Amir Jabir al-Ahmad Al Sabah. A succession struggle among Al Sabah factions was resolved in favor of Sabah al-Ahmad Al-Sabah, about 76 years old, who was serving as Prime Minister. Shunted aside was the heir apparent, Sa'd Abdullah Al Sabah, on the grounds that he was too ill to become leader. However, the struggle left lingering tensions within the ruling family and between it and other elites. It also clouded the leadership futures of some younger potential successors, including Foreign Minister Mohammad Al Sabah and Ahmad al-Fahd Al Sabah, the latter of whom was dropped from the cabinet after the June 29, 2006, National Assembly elections in which

government opponents were mostly victorious. Despite the political skirmishing, there is little anti-regime violence in Kuwait; most opposition is expressed within the National Assembly. On the other hand, some Al Qaeda or pro-Al Qaeda activists have carried out attacks against Kuwaiti security personnel, as discussed later.

- The Sultanate of Oman has seen little unrest since Sultan Qaboos bin Said Al Said took power from his father in 1970. Qaboos is about 65 years old, apparently in good health, and widely assessed as highly popular. However, the royal family in Oman is relatively small and there is no heir apparent or clear successor. This could lead to a succession crisis or power struggle if Qaboos were to leave the scene unexpectedly, as almost happened in 1995 when Qaboos was shaken up in a car accident in which one of his ministers was killed. Since an alleged Islamist plot in 1994 that led to a few hundred arrests, there had been little evidence of a radical Islamist element in the Sultanate until a similar wave of arrests on similar charges in January 2005. Thirty-one Omanis were convicted of subversion in the alleged plotting but were pardoned in June 2005.

Political Liberalization

Virtually all the Gulf leaders are opening the political process to some extent, in part to help them cope with the challenges of modernization and globalization. The Bush Administration has expressed strong support for political liberalization in the Gulf and the broader Middle East as a means of addressing what it sees as root causes of the September 11, 2001 attacks - the relative lack of popular influence in governance. However, most Gulf reform efforts predate Bush Administration urging and appear to be continuing without substantial U.S. prodding. Some of the Gulf leaders fear that more rapid liberalization could backfire by providing Islamist extremists a platform to challenge the incumbent regimes. As part of their liberalization efforts, all of the Gulf states except the UAE and Saudi Arabia now allow full female electoral participation, and all except Saudi Arabia have appointed at least one woman to a cabinet post.

- Kuwait has traditionally been at the forefront of political liberalization in the Gulf, but during the 1990s its progress was limited to expanding the all-male electorate for its 50-seat National Assembly. The Assembly has always had more influence in decision-making than any representative body in the Gulf states, consistently exerting its power to review and veto governmental decrees. It played a role in the succession struggle of January 2006 by confirming the accession of Shaykh Sabah as Amir. The appointment of Shaykh Sabah as Prime Minister in May 2005 was the key to finally achieving Assembly approval of legislation to allow female suffrage. It took effect as of the June 29, 2006, Assembly elections, although none of the women who ran were elected. The newly elected Assembly, which has a majority of reformists, has succeeded in persuading the government to accept a major reform: the consolidation of Kuwait's election districts to five (from 25). The reformists believe that the larger districts reduce the potential for vote-buying and other corruption.

- In the start of a series of initiatives to expand public participation, in March 1999 Qatar held elections to a 29-member municipal affairs council. In a first in the Gulf, women were permitted full suffrage and 6 women ran for the council, but all six lost. (One woman won in the 2003 municipal elections.) In April 2003, a constitution was adopted in a national referendum, in which women voted. Its approval (by 97% of the electorate) paved the way for elections to a one-chamber assembly, now planned for early 2007, according to Qatari officials. It would replace a 35 member consultative council in place since independence in 1971. Thirty seats of the 45-seat Assembly are to be elected, with the remaining fifteen appointed. Qatar has one woman minister (Education).
- Oman began holding direct elections to its 83-seat Consultative Council in September 2000. At that time, the electorate consisted of 25% of all citizens over 21 years old - mostly local notables and elites. The process contrasted with past elections (1994 and 1997) in which a smaller and more select electorate chose two or three nominees per district and the Sultan then selected final membership. At the same time, Qaboos appointed new members, including five women, to a 53-seat "State Council." The State Council serves, in part, as a check and balance on the elected Consultative Council; both combined form a bi-cameral "Oman Council." In November 2002, Qaboos extended voting rights to all citizens over 21 years of age, beginning with the October 4, 2003 Consultative Council elections. Those elections produced a body similar to that elected in 2000, including election of the same two women as the previous election (out of 15 female candidates). The Oman Council lacks binding legislative powers and there are no evident groupings or factions within it. Formal parties are banned. Since 2001, Qaboos has expanded

the number of women of ministerial rank to four, with two heading full ministries.

- The King of Bahrain's decision to abandon his late father's refusal to accommodate Shiite Muslim demands to restore an elected national assembly has changed Shiite unrest from the violence of the 1990s to mostly peaceful election competition. In February 2002, Bahrain held a referendum on a new "national action charter," establishing procedures for electing a 40-member national assembly. Those elections (two rounds) were held in late October 2002, and the results were split between moderate Islamists and secular Muslims. None of the eight female candidates was elected. Some Shiite critics of the Sunni-dominated government boycotted the elections, claiming that the formation of an appointed upper body of the same size represented an abrogation of the government's promise to restore the 1973 parliamentary process. (No appointed upper body was established during the 1970s.) However, the major Shiite opposition bloc (Wifaq) says it will take part in the October 2006 National Assembly elections, hoping to use the Assembly to assert their demands and air grievances. The King has appointed two women to cabinet posts, and two others have been given ministerial rank.
- Saudi Arabia, now under King Abdullah, is beginning to accelerate political liberalization.[28] During King Fahd's reign, the Kingdom expanded its national Consultative Council to 90 seats from 60 in 1997, to 120 seats in 2001, and to 150 in April 2005, but Fahd resisted national elections or the appointment of women to the Council. In 2004, the government approved new powers for the Council, including the ability to initiate legislation rather than merely review government proposed laws, and giving the Council increased ability to veto draft governmental laws. Observers in Saudi Arabia say the public is increasingly aware of the Council's activities and its growing role as a force in Saudi politics. In February 2005, Saudi Arabia held elections for half of the seats on 178 local municipal councils around the Kingdom, but women were not allowed to vote. In November 2005, two Saudi women won election to the Jeddah Chamber of Commerce, the first vote of any kind in the country in which women participated. The vote was viewed as a prelude to allowing female suffrage in the 2009 municipal elections, and it could presage a possible move by King Abdullah to allow women to drive.
- To date, the UAE has been the least active on political reform, but movement is now evident. In November 2005, the government

announced that half the seats of the forty seat advisory Federal National Council (FNC) would be selected by a limited electorate in each emirate. Each of the seven emirates of the UAE federation has a fixed number of seats on the FNC, and the size of the electorate will be 100 times the number of seats each emirate has. The UAE constitution permits males or females to sit on the FNC (although no women have been on it to date), indicating that women might be selected to the FNC in the newly opened selection process. Since the November 2004 death of Shaykh Zayid, two women have been appointed to cabinet positions.

Continued Human Rights Concerns

The moves toward political openness in the Gulf states are praised by U.S. officials but still do not give Gulf citizens the right to peacefully change their government. The foreign workers on which the Gulf economies rely have virtually no political rights, although they are slowly acquiring labor rights, particularly in Bahrain, including the right to join unions. Some strikes by foreign workers have taken place in UAE for non-payment and poor working conditions. Almost all the Gulf states are cited by human rights organizations and U.S. human rights reports for varying degrees of religious discrimination, arbitrary arrests and detentions, suppression of peaceful assembly and free expression. Virtually all are criticized by the State Department for abuses against domestic workers who are mostly of foreign, and primarily Asian, origin. On November 28, 2005, the State Department condemned the UAE's arrest of a dozen same-sex couples and the announcement that they would be subjected to hormone treatment.

On religious freedom, Saudi Arabia draws the sharpest U.S. criticism for actively prohibiting the practice of non-Muslim religions on its territory, even in private, with limited exceptions. In 2005, for the second year in a row, it was designated as a "Country of Particular Concern" under the International Religious Freedom Act (IRFA). Qatar prohibits public non-Muslim worship but tolerates it in private, although it has shifted its position in late 2005 and is now allowing church construction. In Kuwait, Bahrain, the UAE, and Oman, there are functioning Christian churches and congregations. Small Jewish communities in some Gulf countries are generally allowed to worship freely, and there is a Jewish member of the upper house of Bahrain's national assembly.

The Gulf states appear to be falling short of U.S. expectations in preventing trafficking in persons, although some have pledged to improve their performance. Several, including Qatar and UAE, have taken steps to end the trafficking of young boys to the Gulf to work as camel jockeys. As of the 2006 State Department Trafficking in Persons report, only Saudi Arabia has remained in "Tier 3," the worst category, indicating it is not making significant efforts to address the problems of human trafficking. The other five Gulf states are designated as "Tier 2 'Watch List'" suggesting they might be placed in Tier 3 if they do not improve efforts to prevent this activity. This designation represents a downgrading of Oman's performance; it was Tier 2 in the 2005 report. Kuwait, Qatar, and UAE were Tier 3 in 2005 and have apparently taken some steps against trafficking since then.

U.S. Democratization Efforts

As the Bush Administration has made political and economic reform a priority, it has expanded the programs and policies used to promote that agenda. As noted in the State Department's "Supporting Human Rights and Democracy: The U.S. Record 2005-2006," released April 5, 2006, the Administration is promoting these reforms not only through diplomatic exchanges between U.S. diplomats in the Gulf and their counterparts but also with new programs run by the U.S. Agency for International Development (USAID), the State Department's Near East Bureau and its Bureau of Democracy, Human Rights, and Labor, and the "Middle East Partnership Initiative" (MEPI).[29]

Recent and ongoing U.S.-funded democratization programs in the Gulf focus on adherence to the rule of law, economic transparency, judicial reform, strengthening civil society organizations, including political societies in some Gulf states, improvement in the education system, media openness, and women's empowerment. Because U.S. diplomats in the region generally seek to maintain good relations with their counterparts and because U.S. interests in the Gulf are broad, most U.S.-funded programs are supported by — or at least not opposed by — the Gulf governments. Many of the programs bring Gulf government officials, students, journalists, and other civil society participants to the United States for training or to see firsthand how various functions are carried out in a democracy. Several programs using MEPI funds were used to help the Gulf countries comply with World Trade Organization and other requirements for the free trade agreements being negotiated with the United States (see below).

Economic Liberalization and Integration

Iran, Iraq, and the GCC states possess about 715 billion barrels of proven oil reserves, representing about 57% of the world's total, and 2,462 trillion cubic feet (tcf) of natural gas, about 45% of the world's proven reserves of that commodity. The countries in the Gulf (including Iran and Iraq) produce about 20 million barrels per day (mbd) of oil, about 30% of the world's oil production, according to the U.S. Energy Information Administration. Saudi Arabia and Iraq are first and second, respectively, in proven reserves. Iraq, which is relatively unexplored, might ultimately be proven to hold more oil than does Saudi Arabia. Iran and Qatar, respectively, have the second and third largest reserves of natural gas in the world; gas is an increasingly important source of energy for Asian and European countries. This resource concentration virtually ensures that the Gulf will remain a major source of energy well into the 21st century. All of the countries of the Gulf, including Iran and Iraq, appear to have an interest in the free flow of oil, but past political conflict in the Gulf has sometimes led to sharp fluctuations in oil prices and increased hazards to international oil shipping. As noted in the below, oil export revenues still constitute a high percentage of GDP for all of the Gulf states. The health of the energy infrastructure of the Gulf producers is also a key concern of the United States — Gulf state oil exports comprise about 20% of the United States' approximately 13 million barrels per day (mbd) net imports.

A sharp oil price decline in 1997-1998 prompted the GCC states to reevaluate their longstanding economic weaknesses, particularly the generous system of social benefits they provide to their citizens. However, the strong expectation in these countries of continued benefits led the Gulf regimes to look to other ways to reform their economies. In the current period of high oil prices (about $70 per barrel in August 2006), the Gulf leaders say they are determined not to discontinue economic reform at a time of high oil prices, as they did in the past to their economic detriment. The cornerstone of GCC economic reform efforts has been to ease underemployment problems by instituting programs, including job training in high-wage industries, to encourage their nationals to work in jobs traditionally held by foreigners. Some of the Gulf states have tried to reduce the percentage of foreign workers by requiring that certain percentages of jobs in some industries be held by nationals as of specified dates.

Table 4. GCC State Oil Production/Exports (2005)

Country	Oil Exports (mbd)	Oil Exports to U.S. (mbd)	Oil Revenues as % GDP
Kuwait	2.2	0.26	50%
Saudi Arabia	8.75	1.558	40%
Qatar	1.02	negligible	30%
U.A.E.	2.33	negligible	33%
Oman	0.763	0.04	40%
Bahrain	0.02	0	30%
Iran	2.55	0	20%
Iraq	1.5	0.665	32%
Total	19.133	2.52	N/A

Source: DOE, Energy Information Agency (EIA), OPEC Revenue Fact Sheet viewed in August 2006, although some EIA data are as of 2004 or 2005, and various press reports. All countries in the table are members of OPEC except Bahrain and Oman.

Several of the Gulf states have made substantial strides to diversify their economies and to attract international capital and needed advanced technology to the energy and other sectors. Several Gulf states have developed relatively dynamic tourism industries, particularly UAE, but increasingly including Qatar and Oman. The Gulf states have passed laws allowing foreign firms to own majority stakes in projects and eased restrictions on repatriation of profits. Some, including UAE and Qatar, are now allowing outright foreign ownership of real estate. U.S. officials have applauded progress by the Gulf states in eliminating the requirement that U.S. firms work through local agents and in protecting the intellectual property rights of U.S. companies.

As a result of the economic liberalization, several Gulf states now host companies that are of global scale and impact, such as the Kingdom Holding Co. established by Prince Walid bin Talal Al Saud in Saudi Arabia, Dubai Ports World of Dubai, and another UAE-based firm, Emaar Properties. Bahrain has largely rebuilt its reputation as a Gulf financial hub since the unrest there in the 1990s. On the other hand, some Arab and other critics say that the UAE emirate of Dubai, in particular, has gone away from its Arab roots by building huge towers, hotels, malls, and other projects designed to cater to Western expatriates. Others say that the need to attract tourism has led to a proliferation of bars and alcohol-serving establishments that has led to crime, drugs, prostitution, human trafficking, and other social ills not previously witnessed to this extent in the Gulf. Of the Gulf states, Saudi Arabia and Kuwait have not to date developed substantial tourist industries; both still prohibit alcohol consumption and do not want to risk the social consequences the other Gulf states are seeing from their tourism drives.

In the oil and gas sector, Qatar has partnered with foreign investors such as Exxon Mobil, Totalfina Elf (France), and others to develop its North Field, the world's largest non-associated gas field, which now has customers in Asia and sells some liquified natural gas (LNG) to the United States. It is also the hub of the "Dolphin Project," in which underwater pipelines are to be constructed to link gas supplies in Qatar and Oman to the UAE, with possible future connections to South Asia. In January 2004, the first Omani supplies under the project began flowing to the UAE emirate of Fujairah; under a swap arrangement, those supplies are replaced by gas shipments from Qatar to Oman. At the same time, both Bahrain and Oman are confronting a declining oil sector; Bahrain and Oman are expected to exhaust their oil supplies in 15 and 20 years, respectively, at current rates of production.

Kuwait and Saudi Arabia have been in discussions with Western oil companies, including several American firms, about further developing their oil and gas reserves. However, internal opposition to opening up this vital asset to foreign investors has significantly slowed the entry of international firms in the two countries. The Kuwaiti government has not, to date, obtained National Assembly approval for its "Project Kuwait," a plan under which foreign investors would develop Kuwait's northern oil fields. The government wants the development to compensate for declining older fields and to increase oil production to 4 million barrels per day by 2020, but the National Assembly wants to ensure that Kuwait retains full sovereignty over its oil sector. Similarly, King Abdullah's 1998 initiative to open the Kingdom's gas reserves to Western development was significantly delayed over commercial issues between the Kingdom and the international energy bidders. After gas development deals collapsed in 2003, the Kingdom signed agreements in June 2005 for the gas investments with Royal Dutch Shell (Netherlands), Totalfina Elf (Italy), Lukoil (Russia), Sinopec (China), ENI (Italy), and Repsol (Spain).

The Dolphin project is an example of growing Gulf economic integration and coordinated action. In December 2002, the Gulf states agreed to implement a "customs union," providing for uniform tariff rate on foreign imports; that union is to be completed by the end of 2007. In October 2005, Saudi Arabia became the last Gulf state to formally join the World Trade Organization (WTO) after protracted negotiations mainly to assuage remaining U.S. concerns.

U.S.-Gulf Free Trade Agreements

As part of its strategy to promote reform and democracy in the Middle East, the Bush Administration has been negotiating bilateral free trade agreements (FTAs) with the Gulf states. The Administration decided that an overall U.S.-GCC FTA would likely take too long to negotiate; a similar joint agreement pursued by the European Union has still not been finalized after about a decade of negotiation. An FTA was signed with Bahrain on September 14, 2004. Legislation to approve and implement the agreement was passed by Congress (H.R. 4340, P.L. 109-169, signed January 11, 2006). In conjunction with congressional review, Bahrain dropped the primary boycott of Israel. In September 2005, the United States and Oman agreed on the provisions of an FTA, and the agreement was signed on January 19, 2006. Implementing legislation on the U.S.-Oman FTA (S. 3569) passed the Senate on June 29, 2006, by a vote of 60-34. Oman also has pledged to drop all Arab boycotts of Israel in conjunction with the FTA. Negotiations on an FTA with the UAE are making progress, according to U.S. negotiators, possibly because the wealthy UAE is unwilling to make many compromises to reach an agreement. Kuwait and Qatar have expressed interest in such FTAs as well.

Other Foreign Policy and Counter-Terrorism Cooperation

The United States has looked to the Gulf states to support U.S. policy on several other regional and international issues. One such issue is the Arab-Israeli dispute, which concerns most citizens in the Gulf countries. Other issues on which the United States seeks Gulf support would include such crises as may arise, such as the July -August 2006 Israel-Hezbollah conflict. Another is counter-terrorism, an issue on which the Gulf states have been increasingly cooperative since their interests in preventing Islamic extremist movements have converged with U.S. goals. In the case of the August 2005 Hurricane Katrina disaster, some Gulf states, particularly Kuwait, have sought to express solidarity with the American public by offering financial disaster assistance to the United States.

Arab-Israeli Peace Process

Since Iran's Islamic 1979 revolution began a period of instability and warfare in the Gulf, the Gulf states have not focused on the Arab-Israeli dispute to nearly the degree that "frontline states" such as Egypt, Syria, Jordan, and Lebanon have. Most of the Gulf states have tried to support U.S. mediation efforts in the Arab-Israeli dispute, but they also have sought to modify and shape U.S. policy on that issue, as well as on other issues such as the July-August 2006 Israel-Hezbollah conflict. In the aftermath of the 1993 Israeli-PLO mutual recognition agreement, the GCC states participated in the multilateral peace talks, even though Syria and Lebanon boycotted those talks. Bahrain, Qatar, and Oman hosted sessions of the multilaterals, and a regional water desalination research center was established in Oman as a result of an agreement reached in that forum. In 1994, all six GCC countries relaxed their enforcement of the secondary and tertiary Arab boycott of Israel, enabling them to claim that they no longer engage in practices that restrain trade (a key WTO condition). Oman and Qatar opened low-level direct trade ties with Israel in 1995 and 1996 and hosted visits by Israeli leaders during that period. In November 1997, at a time of considerable strain in the peace process, Qatar bucked substantial Arab opposition and hosted the Middle East/North Africa economic conference, the last of that yearly event to be held.

At the same time, Saudi Arabia — to which the other Gulf states tend to defer on Arab-Israeli matters — is taking a more active role on this issue now that Abdullah is King. He has always been highly focused on this issue and has often tried to guide and support U.S. policy on this issue; he engineered Arab League approval of a vision of peace between Israel and the Arab states at a March 2002 Arab League summit. The Gulf states all publicly endorsed the Bush Administration's "road map" for Israeli-Palestinian peace. In September 2005, after Israel's unilateral withdrawal from the Gaza Strip, Qatar's foreign minister held a widely publicized meeting with his Israeli counterpart as part of what the Qataris said should be encouragement and praise for Israel's move. The final statement of the GCC summit in December 2005 "hailed" the August 2005 Israeli withdrawal from the Gaza Strip as a "step in the right direction" but expressed the hope it would be followed by a complete Israeli withdrawal from all occupied Palestinian territories. In October 2005, Qatar became the first Arab country to donate money to a town inside Israel, giving $6 million to build a stadium in the ethnically Arab city of Sakhnin in northern Israel. Oman and Bahrain have also dropped the primary Arab boycott in connection with their FTAs with the United States, as discussed above.

On the other hand, the Gulf states, as Arab states, clearly support the Arab position on the dispute. After the latest Palestinian uprising began in September 2000, Oman closed its trade office in Israel and ordered Israel's trade office in Muscat closed. Qatar announced the closure of Israel's trade office in Doha, although observers say the office has been tacitly allowed to continue functioning at a low level of activity. (Qatar did not open a trade office in Israel.) That uprising also prompted the Arab League, with heavy Gulf financial support, to set up funds to support the Palestinian Authority (PA) and the Palestinian people. The funds, called the Al Aqsa fund and the Intifada fund, and managed by the Islamic Development Bank, were to provide up to about $1.2 billion in donated funds to the PA. Saudi Arabia pledged$270 million of that amount, and it has largely fulfilled that commitment. The other Gulf states have mostly been in arrears.[30]

A key difference between the United States and the Gulf states has been on how to treat Palestinian militant groups, particularly Hamas. The differences sharpened in the wake of Hamas' victory in the January 2006 Palestinian legislative elections, which enabled Hamas to form a cabinet for the Palestinian Authority (PA). The United States still sees Hamas as a designated foreign terrorist organization (FTO, as named by the State Department in 1997) that conducts attacks on Israelis and moved to curb aid to the PA in the aftermath of the Hamas win. The Gulf states see Hamas as a legitimate defender of Palestinian interests and resister of Israel's occupation of Palestinian territories. To help the Hamas-led PA cope with the reduction of Western aid, Saudi Arabia and Qatar pledged funds ($92 million and $50 million, respectively) to alleviate a PA budget crisis. In July 2006, Saudi Arabia announced a longer term program of reconstruction aid for the Palestinian territories in the amount of $250 million.

Differences between the United States and the Gulf states was far less pronounced in the Israel-Hezbollah conflict of July-August 2006. Hezbollah is a named FTO and the United States supported Israel's decision to combat Hezbollah following Hezbollah's cross-border raid on July 12, 2006. Viewing the Shiite movement as an ally of Iran, Saudi Arabia criticized the Hezbollah raid as "adventurism," although it and the other Gulf states subsequently denounced Israel's raids on civilian targets and urged an immediate ceasefire. Qatar and the UAE were directly involved in negotiations leading to U.N. Security Council Resolution 1701 (August 11, 2006), which called for a ceasefire and the movement of Hezbollah's militia away from the border with Israel. The UAE flew in humanitarian aid to Lebanon during the crisis, and Saudi Arabia announced a $500 million grant to Lebanon on July 26, 2006 — over and above a $50 million emergency relief grant — to help the country rebuild after the conflict. In August 2006, there reportedly was agreement among the GCC states that, in addition to the Saudi pledge, UAE would help rebuild schools and hospitals and remove landmines in south Lebanon, Qatar would rebuild the town of Bint Jubail, site of heavy Israeli-Hizballah fighting, and Kuwait would donate $800 million in reconstruction funds for Lebanon.

Cooperation Against Al Qaeda

The September 11 attacks stimulated some tensions between the United States and some of the Gulf monarchy states, particularly Saudi Arabia, over allegations that Gulf donors had, wittingly or unknowingly, been contributing to or tolerating groups and institutions linked to Al Qaeda. Many experts believe the Gulf states were tolerant of the presence of militants in order to avoid a backlash among citizens that agree with the militant's anti-U.S., anti-Western stances. Osama bin Laden's Saudi origins, coupled with the revelation that fifteen of the nineteen September 11 hijackers were Saudis, caused substantial criticism of Saudi Arabia among some U.S. experts and opinion-makers. Two of the hijackers were UAE nationals. The September 11 Commission report stated that Khalid Shaykh Mohammad, alleged mastermind of the September 11 plot, lived in Qatar during 1992-1996 at the invitation of Shaykh Abdullah bin Khalid Al Thani, the current Interior Minister and a former Minister of Islamic Affairs, adding that Khalid Shaykh was warned by Qatari officials in 1996 of a U.S. indictment, and fled. Qatar also hosts an outspoken Islamic cleric of Egyptian origin, Shaykh Yusuf al-Qaradawi. In September 2004, in one of his most hardline statements, Qaradawi said that it is a religious duty for Muslims to fight U.S. forces and civilians in Iraq.[31] Despite his statements, Qaradawi meets with and sometimes appears at panel discussions with Qatari senior officials. Some Saudi clerics, and even some Saudi officials, such as Interior Minister Prince Nayef, have earned opprobrium in the United States for similar statements that appear to blame the United States and U.S. policy for Islamic terrorism against the United States.

Others accept the official view of some Gulf states that they hoped to calm regional militancy through negotiations and by working with governments, such as the Taliban, in an effort to keep Al Qaeda militants contained. Saudi Arabia and the UAE were joined only by Pakistan in extending official recognition to the Taliban regime of Afghanistan during 1996-2001, breaking ties with the movement only after the September 11, 2001 attacks. Prior to September 11, the UAE had refused repeated U.S. requests to break ties with the Taliban and to stop hosting Ariana (Afghan national airline) flights to and from Dubai emirate; these flights were one of the few connections between the Taliban and the outside world.[32] The September 11 Commission report on the attacks noted that the hijackers had made extensive use, among other means, of financial networks based in the UAE, in the September 11 plot. There has also been extensive public discussion about the use of Saudi charities and other Saudi-based networks to fund Al Qaeda and other terrorist networks, although the September 11 Commission found no evidence that the Saudi government or Saudi officials funded Al Qaeda.

Since the September 11, 2001, attacks and the start of the Iraq war in March 2003, the Gulf states have been partners of the United States against Al Qaeda and pro-Al Qaeda movements as these militants have posed a threat to the Gulf states themselves. As noted in the table earlier in this paper, the United States has increased U.S. anti-terrorism assistance to almost all of the Gulf states to help them counter Al Qaeda and other terrorist and proliferation threats.

As of mid-2006, the domestic Al Qaeda-related terrorist threat to the Gulf states appears to be receding as these states have moved assertively against the militants. In Saudi Arabia, there have been attacks on Westerners, regime installations, and those perceived as linked to the U.S. military or the U.S.-led war in Iraq. The most well known was the May 12, 2003 attack on a Western housing complex in Riyadh. In December 2004 there was an attack on the U.S. consulate in Jeddah. Saudi authorities have found and captured or killed several successive leaders of the Al Qaeda organization in Saudi Arabia, including Abdul Aziz al-Muqrin and his successor, Saleh al-Oufi, the latter of whom was reputedly killed in August 2005 shoot-out with Saudi authorities. In Kuwait, there have been sporadic attacks on Kuwaiti security personnel in attacks that might have been attempts to disrupt OIF-related U.S. military deployments there, but Kuwaiti authorities have taken actions similar to those of their Saudi counterparts. In addition, in December 2005, Kuwait convicted six men of belonging to a terror group ("Lions of the Peninsula") allegedly planning attacks on U.S. troops in Kuwait. Qatar's tranquility was disrupted in March 2005 when an Egyptian expatriate bombed a theater frequented by Westerners as a purported response to Qatar's hosting of U.S. forces in OIF. No similar incidents have occurred there since.

In its most recent annual report on global terrorism, covering the year 2005 ("Country Reports on Terrorism: 2005, released April 2006), the Bush Administration generally praises Gulf state cooperation against such extremists, although noting some deficiencies:

- All of the Gulf states are credited with enacting at least some new measures to combat terrorism financing, including freezing suspected terrorist assets, requiring approval for charitable transaction, adopting anti-money laundering laws, or instituting laws and procedures to track suspicious financial transactions. Each of the Gulf states has joined the Middle East and North Africa Financial Action Task Force (MENA-FATF), and Bahrain hosted its inaugural meeting. U.S. officials continue to press their Gulf state counterparts to rigorously enforce these new measures, and some U.S. officials have criticized some Gulf governments, particularly Saudi Arabia, for failing to prosecute some individuals suspected of being terrorist financiers.[33]

- Some Gulf states are credited with arrests of suspected Al Qaeda figures. The UAE is praised by U.S. officials for providing assistance in several terrorist investigations; it assisted in the 2002 arrest of at least one senior Al Qaeda operative in the Gulf, Abd al-Rahim al-Nashiri.[34] In August 2004, the UAE emirate of Dubai, in cooperation with Pakistani investigators, arrested an alleged senior Al Qaeda operative, Qari Saifullah Akhtar. Bahrain has on a few occasions in 2003 and 2004 arrested suspected Al Qaeda activists, although it has later released many of them pending trial or because of a lack of legal justification for holding them. Qatar and Oman are generally cited by the 2005 State Department terrorism report for supporting or assisting U.S. counter-terrorism efforts, and the 2004 and 2005 State Department reports did not repeat language from the 2003 report that "Members of transnational terrorist groups and state sponsors of terrorism are present in Qatar."
- Several of the Gulf states are providing assistance on port and container security. In December 2004, the UAE emirate of Dubai, a major Gulf port hub, signed a statement of principles to participate in the U.S. "Container Security Initiative" to screen U.S.-bound container cargo in Dubai. Oman joined that initiative as well in November 2005. On the other hand, some in Congress have expressed concern, including during consideration of the U.S.-Oman FTA, that some GCC or non-GCC firms might try to use U.S.-Gulf FTAs to invest in operations of U.S. ports. The new concerns built on earlier security-related questions that scuttled a February 2006 U.S. decision to allow the Dubai-owned firm, Dubai Ports World, to take over operations at six U.S. ports. U.S. officials say that the FTA agreements with the Gulf countries would permit the United States to block such investments on security grounds.[35]

Figure 2. Map of the Persian Gulf Region and Environs.

APPENDIX 1. GULF STATE POPULATIONS, RELIGIOUS COMPOSITION

Country	Total Population	Number of Non-Citizens	Religious Composition (of total population)
Saudi Arabia	27 million	5.58 million	90% Sunni; 10% Shia
Kuwait	2.42 million	1.29 million	85% Muslim (of which 70% Sunni, 30% Shiite); 15% Christian, Hindu, other
United Arab Emirates	2.6 million	2 million	80% Sunni; 16% Shiite; 4% Christian, Hindu, other
Bahrain	699,000	235,000	81.2% Muslim (of which 70% Shiite, 30% Sunni); 9% Christian; 9.8% other
Qatar	885,000	500,000	95% Muslim, almost all Sunni; 5% other
Oman	3.1 million	577,000	75% Ibadhi Muslim; 25% Sunni and Shia Muslim, and Hindu

Source: *Central Intelligence Agency World Factbook,* updated August 2006, and various press reporting. Most, if not all, non-Muslims in GCC countries are foreign expatriates.

REFERENCES

[1] In May 1987, Iraq hit the U.S.S. Stark with French-supplied Exocet missiles, presumed by most to be a mistake, killing 37 U.S. Navy personnel.

[2] The missiles were supplied by Russia, but Iraq enhanced their range to be able to reach Tehran, which is about 350 miles from the Iraq border. The normal range of the Scud is about 200 miles.

[3] Central Intelligence Agency. "Iraq's Weapons of Mass Destruction Programs." October 2002, p. 8. According to the study, Iraq used mustard gas, tabun, and other "nerve agents." According to the report, the majority of the casualties were Iranian, suffered during major Iranian offensives, including Panjwin (October-November 1983), Majnoon Island (February-March 1984), the Hawizah Marshes (March 1985), Al Faw (February 1986), Basra (April 1987), and Sumar/Mehran (October 1987).

[4] U.N. Security Council. Document S/19823. Report of the Mission Dispatched by the Secretary-General to Investigate Allegations of the Use of Chemical Weapons in the Conflict Between the Islamic Republic of Iran and Iraq. April 25, 1988.

[5] Zarqawi was killed in Iraq by a U.S. air-strike on June 7, 2006.

[6] For further information on developments in and U.S. policy toward Iraq, see CRS Report RL31339, *Iraq: Post-Saddam Governance and Security*; and CRS Report RL32048, *Iran: U.S. Concerns and Policy Responses*, both by Kenneth Katzman.

[7] Krane, Jim. "U.S. Seeks to Bolster Its Gulf Ties." *Boston Globe*, May 23, 2006.

[8] Meyer, Josh. "U.S. Faults Saudi Efforts on Terrorism." *Los Angeles Times*, January 15, 2006.

[9] Provisions of the pacts can be found in Hajjar, Sami. U.S. Military Presence in the Gulf: Challenges and Prospects. U.S. Army War College, Strategic Studies Institute. March 2002, p. 20. Other information in this section derived from unclassified author conversations with U.S. military and diplomatic officials in the Gulf region, 1993-2006.

[10] For more information on these agreements, see CRS Report 94-78, *Saudi Arabia: U.S. Defense and Security Commitments.* February 3, 1994, by Alfred Prados.

[11] Solomon, John. "Saudis Had Wider Role in War." *Philadelphia Inquirer*, April 26, 2004.

[12] Sirak, Michael. "USA looks to Expand Bases in Oman and Qatar." *Jane's Defence Weekly*, April 17, 2002.

[13] U.S. briefing for congressional staff in Qatar, January 2003.

[14] Hammond, Andrew. "Military Expanded in Response to Iran." *Washington Times*, July 24, 2006.

[15] Ratnam, Gopal and Amy Svitak. "U.S. Would Keep Tight Rein on Missile Sold to Bahrain." *Defense News*, September 11, 2000.

[16] Information in this section was provided by press reports, Defense Security Cooperation Agency (DSCA) in *Security Assistance Program Summaries* (unclassified) for each of the Gulf states. March-May 2004; and DSCA arms sales announcements.

[17] See CRS Report 98-436, *United Arab Emirates: U.S. Relations and F-16 Aircraft Sale*. Updated June 15, 2000, by Kenneth Katzman and Richard F. Grimmett. Transmittal notices to Congress, No. DTC 023-00, April 27, 2000; and 98-45, September 16, 1998.

[18] The MTCR commits member states not to transfer to non-member states missiles with a range of more than 300 km, and a payload of more than 500 kilograms. Turkey, Greece, and South Korea are the only countries to have bought ATACMs from the United States.

[19] Ratnam, Gopal and Amy Svitak. "U.S. Would Keep Tight Rein on Missile Sold to Bahrain." *Defense News*, September 11, 2000.

[20] Ibid.

[21] Raghuvanshi, Vivek. "Low Bid Scuttles Deal," Defense News, August 1, 2005.

[22] "GCC States Look to Boost 'Peninsula Shield' Force to 22,000." *Agence France Press*, September 13, 2000.

[23] Khawaji, Riad. "GCC Leaders to Disband Peninsula Shield." *Defense News*, January 2, 2006.

[24] Press Conference with Secretary of Defense William Cohen. Office of the Assistant Secretary of Defense (Public Affairs), April 8, 2000.

[25] Krane, Jim. "U.S. Seeks to Bolster Its Gulf Ties." *Boston Globe*, May 23, 2006.

[26] Finnegan, Philip. "Politics Hinders Joint Gulf Missile Defense." *Defense News*, March 22, 1999.

[27] Much of the information in this section are from the following reports by the State Department: Country Reports on Human Rights Practices - 2005 (March 8, 2006); Supporting Human Rights and Democracy: The U.S. Record 2005-2006 (April 5, 2006); the Trafficking in Persons Report for 2006 (June 5, 2006); and International Religious Freedom report - 2005 (November 8, 2005), as well as recent CRS visits to Gulf states.

[28] For more information on Saudi political reform efforts, see CRS Report RL33533, *Saudi Arabia: Current Issues and U.S. Relations*, August 18, 2004, by Alfred B. Prados and Christopher M. Blanchard. Some of the information in this section is also taken from a CRS staff visit to Saudi Arabia in September 2004, which included several meetings with members of the Saudi Consultative Council.

[29] Funding amounts for each program type can be found at [http://www.mepi.state.gov]. For information on the initiative and funding provided by it, see CRS Report RS21457, *The Middle East Partnership Initiative: An Overview*, by Jeremy M. Sharp.

[30] Kessler, Glenn. "U.S. to Press Arab Nations to Pay Pledges Made to Palestinians." *Washington Post,* February 26, 2005.

[31] "Cleric Says It's Right to Fight U.S. Civilians in Iraq." Reuters, September 3, 2004.

[32] Information in this section from the September 11 Commission final report. pp. 138, 146, and 527. For an extended discussion of this issue, see CRS Report RL32499, *Saudi Arabia: Terrorist Financing Issues*, by Alfred Prados and Christopher Blanchard.

[33] Meyer, Josh. "U.S. Faults Saudi Efforts on Terrorism." *Los Angeles Times*, January 15, 2006.

[34] "U.S. Embassy to Reopen on Saturday After UAE Threat." *Reuters*, March 26, 2004.

[35] See CRS General Distribution Memorandum. "National Security Issues and the Proposed U.S.-Oman Free Trade Agreement." July 19, 2006, by Todd Tatelman.

In: Politics and Economics of the Middle East
Editors: W. Evans & D.J. Harris
ISBN: 978-1-60456-719-9

Chapter 2

EGYPT: BACKGROUND AND U.S. RELATIONS*

Jeremy M. Sharp

ABSTRACT

This report provides an overview of Egyptian politics and current issues in U.S.-Egyptian relations. It briefly provides a political history of modern Egypt, an overview of its political institutions, and a discussion of the prospects for democratization in Egypt. U.S.-Egyptian relations are complex and multi-faceted, and this chapter addresses the following current topics: the Arab-Israeli peace process, Iraq, terrorism, democratization and reform, human rights, trade, and military cooperation. For more information on Egypt, see CRS Report RS22274, *Egypt: 2005 Presidential and Parliamentary Elections*.

U.S. policy on Egypt is aimed at maintaining regional stability, improving bilateral relations, continuing military cooperation, and sustaining the March 1979 Egyptian-Israeli peace treaty. Successive Administrations have long viewed Egypt as a leader and moderating influence in the Middle East, though in recent years, there have been increasing calls for Egypt to democratize.

Congressional views of U.S.-Egyptian relations vary. Some lawmakers view Egypt as stabilizing the region and helping to extend U.S. influence in the most populous Arab country. Others would like the United States to pressure Egypt to implement political reforms, improve its human rights record, and take a more active role in reducing Arab-Israeli tensions.

---

* Excerpted from CRS Report RL33003, dated June 14, 2006.

Among the current issues in U.S.-Egyptian relations are a shared concern about international terrorism. Egypt can claim some experience with the subject, having defeated domestic Islamist terrorists intent on overthrowing the government. As the war on terror continues, the United States relies on Egypt for intelligence cooperation. Egypt provided valuable support during Operation Enduring Freedom in Afghanistan. On the issue of Iraqi reconstruction, Egypt is helping to train Iraqi security forces and has offered to increase its efforts. Egypt and the United States agree on the importance of the Egyptian-Israeli peace treaty and the need to continue current Arab-Israel peace talks. In support of this process, Egypt has been training Palestinian police and has sent 750 Egyptian soldiers to the Egypt-Gaza border in order to prevent weapons smuggling following Israel's recent withdrawal from Gaza.

The United States and Egypt disagree over the speed and depth of, but not the need for, some of Egypt's economic reforms. The two governments differ on Egypt's need to introduce democratic reforms, and many U.S. officials argue that Egypt is not moving quickly enough toward full democracy or in improving the human rights situation. Others caution that movement toward democracy carries a risk of establishment of an Islamist government.

The United States has provided Egypt with an annual average of over $2 billion in economic and military foreign assistance since 1979. The United States will reduce Economic Support Funds (ESF) to about $400 million per year by 2008 in keeping with a plan to reduce aid to both Israel and Egypt. The Administration requested $455 million in economic grants and $1.3 billion in military grants for FY2007 for Egypt.

Most Recent Developments

On June 8, 2006, the House narrowly defeated an amendment (198-225) to H.R. 5522, the FY2007 Foreign Operations Appropriations Bill, which would have reallocated $100 million in economic aid to Egypt and use it instead to fight AIDS worldwide and to assist the Darfur region of Sudan. Many supporters of the amendment were dismayed by the Egyptian government's spring 2006 crackdown on pro-democracy activists in Cairo.

On May 12, 2006, the General Accountability Office, the investigative agency of Congress, released a report on U.S. military assistance to Egypt, recommending that the U.S. State Department and Pentagon assess the potential impact of possible future shifts in U.S. military aid to Egypt and release periodic evaluations of the U.S. Foreign Military Financing program in Egypt.

On May 11-12, 2006, thousands of Egyptian police clashed with protestors in downtown Cairo during demonstrations in support of greater political freedom and judicial independence. The protests were sparked by ongoing disciplinary proceedings against two senior judges who face expulsion from the judiciary for accusing the government of fixing elections. The U.S. State Department said it was "deeply concerned" over police repression of the protesters.

On May 3, 2006, in an amendment to the Senate-passed version of H.R. 4939, the FY2006 Emergency Supplemental bill, the Senate rescinded $47 million in FY2006 economic aid to Egypt (cash grant portion). The June 8, 2006, conference agreement on H.R. 4939 (H.Rept. 109-494) did not include the rescission.

On May 2, 2006, U.S. State Department Spokesman Sean McCormack commented on the the Egyptian parliament's approval of the two-year extension of the nation's 25-year old emergency laws, saying that "It's a disappointment. We understand that Egypt is facing its own issues related to terrorism, but President Mubarak during the presidential campaign had talked about the fact that he was going to seek a new emergency law, but one that would be targeted specifically at fighting terrorism, counterterrorism, and that would take into account respect for freedom of speech as well as human rights. Certainly we would like to see President Mubarak and his government follow through on that pledge."

On April 24, 2006, Egyptian terrorists attacked the Sinai Peninsula resort town of Dahab, killing 21 people and injuring hundreds. Two days later, suicide bombers attacked a police station in the northern Sinai and a base camp of the Multinational Force and Observers, a peacekeeping mission that was created as part of the 1979 peace treaty between Egypt and Israel. Two people were injured in the attacks.

HISTORICAL BACKGROUND

Egypt During the Colonial Era

Egypt's relations with the West, including its current friendly relations with the United States, are colored by a long history of foreign intervention in Egyptian politics, which has made Egypt, along with other Arab states, wary of outside influences on their domestic affairs. In the 19th century, Egypt was a semiautonomous province in the Ottoman Empire, which by then was in decline and being propped up by the British in order to serve as a buffer between it and Czarist Russia. At the time, Egypt was viewed as extremely valuable to the British and French empires and was prized for its agricultural output, large domestic market, and strategic location between the Mediterranean and Red Seas. Most importantly, the British saw Egypt as vital to securing the sea route to its most prized colony, India. Ottoman weakness led its Sultans to grant Europeans certain legal protections and economic advantages in Egypt, which stifled the Egyptian economy by flooding it with European manufactured goods, driving local merchants out of business.[1] Over time, Egypt developed a "cash crop" economy based almost solely on the export of cotton, the price of which constantly fluctuated, leaving the economy vulnerable and dependent on good harvests. Without a strong, diverse economy, Egypt could not generate enough capital to fund its modernization, leading it to become even more financially dependent on the West, as it rulers borrowed huge sums from European banks. Six years after the completion of the Suez Canal in 1869, Egypt was forced to sell all of its shares in the Suez Canal Company, which operated the Canal, in order to make payments on its foreign-owned debt. When Egypt could no longer pay its debts, the British and French became directly involved in Egyptian politics — a trend that would continue until the mid 20th century.[2]

The Constitutional Monarchy and the British

Britain unilaterally declared Egyptian independence in 1922, and for the next three decades, political power in Egypt was contested among three main actors: the British, the Egyptian monarchy, and the nationalist Wafd party, which was the driving force behind the Egyptian independence movement after World War I. Thousands of British troops remained stationed near the Suez Canal, and British officials served in the Egyptian ministries. Egypt's king could appoint a government and dismiss parliament, but ultimately relied on the British for support. The Wafd party dominated parliamentary elections during Egypt's experiment with parliamentary democracy (1922-1952), though the Wafd gradually began to lose popularity to more radical organizations, such as the Muslim Brotherhood.

Nasser and Egypt During the Cold War

By the early 1950s, anti-British sentiment in Egypt had sparked civil unrest, allowing a cabal of Egyptian Army officers, known as the Free Officers Movement, to oust the king in what is referred to as the July 1952 revolution. The

Free Officer Movement ushered in an era of military involvement in Egyptian politics, as all of Egypt's presidents in the post-revolutionary period have been high ranking officers. In the aftermath of the coup, Colonel Gamal Abdul Nasser, the most charismatic of the Free Officers, succeeded in gaining total control over the government. Nasser abolished the monarchy and outlawed the Muslim Brotherhood (1954), which at the time was the only potential rival for power. Nasser would rule Egypt until his death in 1970.

Source: Map Resources. Adapted by CRS. (K.Yancey 7/1/05).

Figure 1. Map of Egypt.

Nasser and Egypt During the Cold War

By the early 1950s, anti-British sentiment in Egypt had sparked civil unrest, allowing a cabal of Egyptian Army officers, known as the Free Officers Movement, to oust the king in what is referred to as the July 1952 revolution. The Free Officer Movement ushered in an era of military involvement in Egyptian politics, as all of Egypt's presidents in the post-revolutionary period have been high ranking officers. In the aftermath of the coup, Colonel Gamal Abdul Nasser, the most charismatic of the Free Officers, succeeded in gaining total control over the government. Nasser abolished the monarchy and outlawed the Muslim Brotherhood (1954), which at the time was the only potential rival for power. Nasser would rule Egypt until his death in 1970.

During the Nasser era, Egypt found itself at the center of superpower competition for influence in the Middle East. Wary of taking sides, Nasser managed, for a short period, to steer Egypt clear of either the Soviet or Western "camp" and was instrumental in helping to establish the non-aligned movement. U.S.-Egyptian relations soured when Nasser turned to the Soviets and the Czechs in 1955 for military training and equipment after the West, frustrated by Nasser's repeated rejections and his support of Algerian independence against the French, refused to provide Egypt with defense assistance. A year later, following a U.S.-British decision to retract an offer of economic assistance and help for the construction of the Aswan Dam, Nasser nationalized the Suez Canal Company to use its revenues to finance the dam project. (Egypt owned the Suez Canal, but the British-French company operated the Canal, and collected the revenues from which it paid a small rent to Egypt.) In October 1956, Israel, France, and Britain invaded Egypt — Israel to stop Palestinian guerrillas from using Egypt as a base for operations against Israel, and France and Britain to occupy the Canal. President Eisenhower persuaded the three countries to withdraw from Egypt in early 1957, which briefly improved U.S.-Egyptian relations.[3]

After the 1956 Suez War, Nasser's popularity soared, as he came to embody Arab nationalism in the post-colonial era. Nasser did not hesitate to brandish his newfound authority and developed a muscular Egyptian foreign policy that attempted to destabilize pro-Western governments in Jordan, Iraq, and Lebanon, support Palestinian guerrilla action against Israel, create a unified Arab state by merging briefly with Syria (the United Arab Republic 1958-1961), and intervene against the Saudi-backed royalists in the Yemeni civil war.[4] However, Egypt's defeat at the hands of Israel in the June 1967 War and other setbacks temporarily deflated Nasser's popularity and crushed his ambitions to spread a pan-Arab ideology across the region.

On the domestic front, Nasser turned Egypt into a socialist dictatorship with absolute power in the hands of the President. All banks and commercial firms were nationalized, large landowning estates were broken up into much smaller parcels and held in a state trust, and all political parties were banned. The precursor to the present National Democratic Party (NDP) was formed by Nasser in 1962 and was called the Arab Socialist Union. It served as the Egyptian republic's first mass party and an extension of the ruling elite. Other movements, such as the Muslim Brotherhood, were forced to go underground, as Nasser arrested thousands of Brotherhood activists after a failed Brotherhood assassination attempt against him in 1954.[5]

Egypt-Israeli Peace

After Nasser's death in 1970, Anwar Sadat, one of the original Free Officers, became President of Egypt. At the time, Egypt was humiliated by its defeat in the June 1967 War and the ensuing loss of the Sinai Peninsula to Israel. In addition, military rebuilding expenditures were absorbing nearly 25% of Egypt's gross domestic product. Under these circumstances, Sadat calculated that a military victory was needed to boost his own legitimacy and improve Egypt's position in any future negotiations with Israel. The October 1973 War, which initially took Israel by surprise, was costly for both sides, but succeeded in boosting Sadat's credibility with the Egyptian people, enabling him to embark on a path which would ultimately sever Egypt's ties to the Soviet Union and bring it closer to the West.

In November 1973, Egypt and the United States restored diplomatic relations (which had been cut off in 1967) and, in December, the two countries participated in the Geneva peace conference. U.S. Secretary of State Henry Kissinger's shuttle diplomacy led to Egyptian-Israeli and Syrian-Israeli disengagement agreements in 1974 and a second set of Egyptian-Israeli disengagements in 1975. The United States resumed economic aid to Egypt in 1975 after an eight-year hiatus.

The United States endorsed Anwar al-Sadat's historic trip to Jerusalem in November 1977, and President Jimmy Carter assisted in the Israeli-Egyptian peace negotiations at Camp David in September 1978 and the Egyptian-Israeli peace treaty of March 1979.[6] The United States helped organize the peacekeeping mission along the Egyptian-Israeli border, the Multi-National Force and Observers (MFO), and still maintains a rotating infantry task force as part of it.[7]

Egypt under Mubarak

Sadat's rule came to an abrupt end in 1981, when he was assassinated during a military parade in Cairo by soldiers who also belonged to the Jamaah Islamiyah (Islamic Group) and Al Jihad, the more radical offshoots of the Muslim Brotherhood. Hosni Mubarak, Sadat's Vice President and former commander of the Egyptian Air Force, immediately ascended to the presidency and has remained in office to the present day. Under Mubarak, Egypt has continued to maintain good relations with the United States, as evident in Egypt's 1991 decision to join the allied coalition against Saddam Hussein in Operation Desert Storm. Following the path laid out by Sadat, Egypt has remained at peace with Israel, although critics have characterized this as a "cold peace." Mubarak has made a number of attempts to serve as a broker for Israeli-Palestinian peace talks, most notably in 1999 and 2000, when Egypt hosted the signing of an Israeli-Palestinian agreement for implementing past commitments and meetings between then Secretary of State Madeleine Albright and former Palestine President Yasir Arafat respectively. During the Mubarak era, the ongoing conflict between Egyptian Islamists and the Egyptian authorities continued, culminating in a period (1992-1997) of violent confrontations between Islamic militants and Egyptian police.

After the September 11, 2001, terrorist attacks and the ensuing U.S. focus on promoting democracy in the Middle East, the Mubarak regime has come under increasing U.S. pressure to accelerate political reforms and make Egypt more democratic. In an effort to control the reform agenda without relinquishing their grip on power, Mubarak and the ruling National Democratic Party (NDP) have instituted some political reforms, while emphasizing the need for economic growth as a precondition for democratic change.

REGIME STRUCTURE

Overview

Since the 1952 revolution, Egypt has officially been a republic, and its political system has developed some aspects of a democracy, though most observers continue to describe Egypt as an authoritarian regime dominated by a strong executive, who draws his support from the ruling National Democratic Party (NDP) and the military. Under the 1971 Constitution, authority is vested in an elected president who must stand for reelection every six years.[8] The President appoints the cabinet, who in turn draft and submit legislation to the legislature, the People's Assembly (lower house) and the Shura Council (upper house). The People's Assembly debates legislation proposed by government ministries and calls for amendments to government-sponsored bills but rarely initiates its own bills. The Shura Council is an advisory body, offering reports and recommendations on important subjects, but the Shura Council does not introduce, consider, or vote on legislation. Overall, analysts consider Egypt's legislative branch to be weak; the ruling party constitutes an overwhelming majority.

Egypt at a Glance

Population:	77 million (est.)
GDP per Capita:	$1,100-$1,400
Religions:	90% Sunni Muslim 10% Coptic Christian
Literacy Rate:	57% (47% female)
Unemployment Rate:	15%-20% (est.)
External Debt: (as % of GDP)	$33 billion 37.8%

Source: U.S. Central Intelligence Agency World Factbook 2005.

In the People's Assembly, 444 members are elected and ten are appointed by the President; 176 members of the Shura Council are elected and 88 are appointed. One half of the elected members of the People's Assembly and the Shura Council must be farmers and laborers (Art. 87 and Art. 196 of the Constitution). People's Assembly members are elected for five-year terms, and Shura Council members for six-year terms (one-half the Council members are elected every three years).

Currently, the ruling National Democratic Party (NDP) controls 324 seats in parliament, Muslim Brotherhood-affiliated members hold 88 seats, and the remaining seats are held by a mix of independents and secular opposition parties. NDP members won 74 of the 88 seats contested in the May/June 2001 Shura Council election, with independents winning the other 14 seats. Religious parties, such as the Muslim Brotherhood, are officially banned.

Presidential Succession

Under Egyptian law, if the President should become incapacitated, the Speaker of the People's Assembly becomes the interim President until the People's Assembly can nominate a new President and the name can be submitted to the people in a referendum. A Vice President plays no special role in the transition, but in practice, recent Egyptian Presidents were succeeded by their Vice Presidents. The health of 78-year old President Hosni Mubarak, who has not named a Vice President, has been questioned. Some analysts believe that Egyptian intelligence chief, Omar Suleiman, who has recently been an interlocutor between Palestinians and Israelis, could be a potential successor to Mubarak.

The Rise of Gamal Mubarak

Though President Hosni Mubarak has vehemently denied that he is grooming his 42-year old son Gamal to succeed him, the younger Mubarak has had a meteoric rise to the highest levels of the Egyptian government in a short period of time, suggesting to many observers that his accession to the presidency may be imminent. According to a March 2006 *Washington Post* article, Gamal Mubarak was recently named as one of three Deputy Secretary Generals of the NDP party, and many of his associates now fill the cabinet and party leadership.[9] In press interviews, Gamal Mubarak himself has refuted rumors that he will run for president in any future election, saying "I don't have the intention or the desire to be a candidate. I repeat and emphasize again I don't have this intention or desire, this is clear talk for those who want to understand."[10] In May 2006, Gamal Mubarak secretly traveled to Washington for meetings with Vice President Cheney and other high-level U.S. officials. Many commentators have speculated over the purpose of the meetings, which came amid social unrest and demonstrations in Cairo. Some analysts believe that Gamal's trip signifies his eventual ascension to the presidency.

The Role of the Military in Egyptian Society

Although military officers no longer play a direct role in the affairs of the civilian-run Egyptian government, the military is the preeminent institution in Egyptian society, and has been called on by successive governments to maintain internal security and regime stability.[11] From an economic standpoint, the military also provides employment and social services for hundreds of thousands of young people in a country with annual double digit unemployment rates. Military experts have often asserted that Egypt's armed forces are bloated and maintain manpower at unnecessary levels for peacetime. In response, Egyptian officials and some scholars assert that the large size of Egypt's military is justified based on the services it provides to soldiers and their families. Some estimate that the military trains 12% of young Egyptian males and that Egypt's defense industries employ over 100,000 people.[12] The Egyptian military has its own companies, which produce consumer products, pharmaceuticals, and manufactured goods. The Egyptian officer corps also benefit from higher salaries, better housing, and high quality healthcare, which help ensure their loyalty to the government. Some members of the opposition have criticized these special benefits and the military's fiscal autonomy, asserting that there is little civilian control over the military's budget.

The National Democratic Party (NDP)[13]

As the ruling party, the NDP dominates the political scene in Egypt, controlling well over 80% of the seats in parliament. In the 2000 parliamentary election, popular dissatisfaction with the status quo led to the defeat of many NDP incumbents, though the party maintained its supra-majority in parliament after a number of "independents" who had been NDP members rejoined the party. Thereafter, NDP officials embarked on a campaign to improve the party's public image, holding the first party congress in 10 years in 2002. Since then, the NDP has held conferences in each successive year, touting a number of political reforms under the slogan of "new thinking." More importantly, the President's son, Gamal Mubarak, was appointed to the NDP's higher policy council, and other young reformers have become more visible in the party. Many analysts speculate that the NDP is undergoing a generational struggle between an "old guard" linked to tradition and deliberate change and young reformers who want rapid, far-reaching change. Others believe that even if a "new guard" were to gain control of the party, they would make no dramatic departures from previous NDP policies.

The Judiciary and Calls for Judicial Independence.

Although Articles 64 and 65 of the Constitution guarantee the independence of the judiciary, the state continues to hold sway over most judges and courts.[14] However, many analysts consider this branch of government to hold the most potential for exercising greater "checks and balances" on the regime. Some judges have spoken openly about election abuses allegedly committed by pro-government forces in 2005. In April and May 2006, there were a number of demonstrations against the Mubarak regime. The protests were sparked by the state's disciplinary proceedings against two of Egypt's most senior judges, Mahmoud Mekki and Hisham Bastawisi, who were stripped of their judicial immunity and detained after publicly charging electoral fraud during parliamentary elections late last year. Bastawisi, who suffered a heart attack before his hearing, was warned that another offense would lead to his dismissal from the judiciary, while Mekki was cleared of all charges.

Opposition Parties and Movements

Political opposition in Egypt is divided among legal opposition parties approved by the government, the outlawed Muslim Brotherhood, considered the most powerful opposition force, and a small array of new movements, such as *Kefaya* ("Enough"), composed of civil society activists, academics, and intellectuals. By law, political parties must be approved by the seven-member Political Parties Committee (PPC). Since 1977, the Committee has approved 18 political parties and rejected almost 50. The current make-up of the PPC consists of the Shura Council chairman, three former senior judges, and the ministers of interior, parliamentary affairs and justice. In September 2004, NDP officials announced plans to amend the 1977 political parties law by adding three non-partisan public figures to the committee, though its members would still be chosen by the President.

Legal Opposition Parties

Most experts regard Egypt's legal opposition parties as divided with limited popular support. In the 2000 parliamentary elections, the principal opposition parties secured just 17 seats, despite widespread popular dissatisfaction with the ruling NDP. In 2005, these parties fared even worse, winning just 12 seats. Most recognized opposition parties publish their own newspapers, which frequently criticize the government and often expose human rights abuses. Most parties receive government subsidies and, in some cases, subsidies from foreign interests.

The Al Ghad Party (Tomorrow) and Ayman Nour

Ayman Nour, a former member of the Egyptian parliament and second place finisher in Egypt's first multi-candidate presidential election in 2005, is currently serving a five-year sentence for forgery in a prison hospital. On May 19, 2006, Egypt's highest appeals court rejected Ayman Nour's appeal for a retrial. He cannot file another appeal. Nour's imprisonment is considered a stumbling block in U.S.-Egyptian bilateral relations, though opinions differ on how much of an impact his imprisonment will have over the long term. Most analysts believe that improvements in the relationship, such as announcing the United States' intention to negotiate a U.S.-Egyptian free trade agreement, has been put on hold in part due to the treatment of Nour. In addition, Nour's imprisonment could bolster efforts to alter Egypt's foreign assistance package in Congress. In 2002, the Administration and Congress rejected $134 million in new economic assistance for Egypt to protest the imprisonment of Saad Eddin Ibrahim. In many ways, Nour's case is a trial balloon for the Administration's larger efforts to promote democracy in the region, and many observers are curious as to how far the Bush Administration will push Egypt on the Nour issue. Experts note that political reform is just one of a number of U.S. policy goals with Egypt and that other priorities, including security cooperation, intelligence-sharing, and promoting peace in the region, could influence U.S.-Egyptian relations.

The Muslim Brotherhood

The Muslim Brotherhood (MB) was founded in Egypt in 1928 to turn Egypt away from secularism and toward an Islamic government based on *Sharia* (religious) law and Muslim principles.[15] The Muslim Brotherhood operates as a religious charitable and educational institution, having been banned as a political party in 1954; however, many Muslim Brotherhood members run for parliament as independents. In the 2000 parliamentary elections, 17 independent candidates, who were regarded as Brotherhood sympathizers, were elected. In 2005, Brotherhood-affiliated candidates won 88 seats in parliament. Over the years, the Egyptian government has alternated between tolerating and suppressing the Muslim Brotherhood, sometimes arresting and jailing its members, and other times allowing its members to operate almost without hindrance.

Many foreign observers agree that the organization has renounced the use of violence as a political tactic, while many Egyptian officials continue to perceive the Brotherhood as a threat and are unwilling to legalize the movement. In the West, the issue of whether or not to recognize the Muslim Brotherhood as a legitimate political actor continues to perplex policymakers, particularly after the September 11, 2001 terrorist attacks. On the one hand, there has been a general reluctance to push for Islamist inclusion in politics, out of concern that, once in power, groups such as the Muslim Brotherhood will pursue policies counter to Western interests in the region or will transform states into theocracies. On the other hand, some experts believe that if these groups are not brought into the political mainstream, they will eventually resort to violence out of frustration.

Most analysts believe that, from an organizational standpoint, the Brotherhood is the only movement capable of mobilizing significant opposition to the government, though opinions vary on how much mass support the Brotherhood commands. As is typical for Islamist groups across the region, the Muslim Brotherhood is strongest among the professional middle class, controlling many of the professional syndicates (associations), including those representing engineers, doctors, lawyers and academics.[16]

The Egyptian Movement for Change — *Kefaya* (Enough)

In December 2004, a group of political activists, most of whom are secular in orientation and hail from Egyptian universities, formed the Egyptian Movement for Change, or what has been referred to in Arabic as *Kefaya* (enough), their primary slogan which refers to their opposition to a further term for President Mubarak. Since its formation, the movement has held a number of small demonstrations, and some of the group's members have been detained. In May 2005, female *Kefaya* activists accused Egyptian police officers of sexually assaulting female protesters, which led to widespread condemnation of the government by both secular and Islamic opposition forces. *Kefaya*, which encompasses a mix of opposition groups, boycotted the 2005 presidential election.

Civil Society in Egypt

Although political opposition continues to be stymied, observers note that, over the past two decades, Egypt has developed a vibrant civil society, which some development experts hope will further democratization in the country. The term "civil society" generally refers to the growing number of non-governmental organizations (NGO), charities, and advocacy groups that openly operate in Egyptian society. Many of these groups pursue so-called "safe issues," such as women's rights, human rights, and social equality, as a way to work toward the much broader goal of democratization. Often times, the Egyptian government has created its own associations in order to boost its reform image at home and abroad, such as the government-sponsored National Council on Human Rights.

In Egypt, NGOs are required to apply for legal status and, according to Association Law 84-2003, NGOs must be registered with the Ministry of Social Affairs. There are an estimated 16,000 registered civic organizations in Egypt. In some cases, it may take years before the ministry rules on an application, and many groups are routinely rejected. If an NGO's application is rejected, it has few legal rights and can be shut down. Its members can be imprisoned. However, even registered NGOs must tread carefully when engaging in sensitive political issues, as some groups have been periodically closed or have had their legal status revoked. NGO's also must report all foreign donations to the Ministry of Social

Affairs. Overall, tolerance for the activities of non-registered groups varies, and many NGOs operate without any legal protection.[17]

Saad al-Din Ibrahim

In 2000, authorities closed the internationally-recognized Egyptian NGO known as the Ibn Khaldun Center for Development Studies and arrested its director, Saad al-Din Ibrahim, a sociology professor at American University of Cairo. Ibrahim, who also holds U.S. citizenship, was arrested for defaming Egypt by describing discrimination against Coptic Christians and for not reporting a foreign donation from the European Union for a voter education project. The international community condemned Ibrahim's detention and conviction, and the United States withheld extra foreign assistance in protest.[18] On March 18, 2003, an Egyptian court acquitted Ibrahim, and he was released. Analysts note that Ibrahim is not a popular figure in Egyptian politics but is respected at home and abroad for his work to promote reform. During the September 2005 presidential election, Ibrahim helped organize election monitors to observe the voting process and report violations.

CURRENT ISSUES IN U.S.-EGYPTIAN RELATIONS

Hamas

With the recent electoral victory of Hamas, Egypt, Israel, and the United States all have a shared interest in attempting to moderate and isolate a Hamas-led Palestinian government and prevent it from further exacerbating conflict in the region. Though Egypt has often tried to steer a neutral course in dealing with the Palestinians, most observers believe that Hamas's rise to prominence poses a number of challenges for Egyptian diplomacy in the region, since the Egyptian government has traditionally been at odds with its own domestic Islamist groups. On March 13, 2006, President Hosni Mubarak stated after a meeting with European Union (EU) officials that the EU should not cut off aid to the Palestinian Authority, remarking, "the aid is used by the man-in-the-street to buy medicine and to send his children to school. If this money is cut, terrorism will grow and all the [Palestinian] people will suffer."

Arab-Israeli Peace

The 1979 Egyptian-Israeli peace treaty has served as the basis for good relations between Egypt and the United States. Although Israel and Egypt have maintained cool relations since then, both parties have maintained the peace, and the United States has continued to underwrite the "costs" of peace by providing high amounts of annual economic and military aid to both parties. One "cost" for Egypt was the diplomatic isolation it suffered following the peace treaty. In 1979, Egypt was expelled from the Arab League, an organization it had helped found.[19] At the time, the rest of the Arab world had felt betrayed by Egypt for making a separate peace with Israel.

Despite the treaty, the development of close economic, political, and diplomatic relations between Israel and Egypt has been limited since 1979. Although there have been some initiatives in recent years, such as President Mubarak's attendance at the funeral for former Israeli Prime Minister Rabin and recent energy cooperation agreements,[20] overall relations remain cool. In 1995, relations were strained when Egypt advocated Israeli signature of the Nuclear Non-Proliferation Treaty. Tensions arose again when Egypt withdrew its ambassador to Tel Aviv in November 2000 to protest Israeli actions against the Palestinians at the start of the latest *intifada*. Prime Minister Ariel Sharon sent two envoys to Cairo shortly after his February 6, 2001 election, reportedly to request the return of the Egyptian ambassador and to seek Egyptian assistance in moderating Arab League reactions to Israeli policies. Egypt announced that it would return its ambassador to Tel Aviv at the February 8, 2005 Palestinian-Israeli summit meeting at Sharm al-Shaykh.

Most experts believe that progress in the Israeli-Palestinian peace process is the key to improved Egyptian-Israeli relations, as well as Israel's wider relationships with the Arab world. In light of the continued stalemate on the peace process, President Mubarak has attempted to act as a broker, advisor, messenger, and arbitrator in the hopes of galvanizing both sides to take the necessary risks for peace. In addition, Egypt's intelligence chief, Omar Suleiman, has met with Hamas and Palestinian Authority figures in order to secure ceasefire arrangements with Israel. Since the resumption of negotiations in the early 1990s, Egypt has taken the following major actions to support the peace process, among other steps:

- Endorsed the Declaration of Principles signed by the PLO and Israel in Washington on September 13, 1993;
- Hosted the September 4, 1999 Sharm al-Shaykh signing of an Israeli-Palestinian agreement for implementing past commitments;

- Hosted the meetings between then Secretary of State Madeleine Albright and Palestine President Arafat at Sharm al-Shaykh on October 4, 2000, and also hosted the Arab League meetings that began on October 21; and
- Hosted the February 8, 2005 meeting between Israeli Prime Minister Sharon and Palestinian President Abbas at Sharm al-Shaykh.

Egypt's Role in the Gaza Withdrawal

Israel unilaterally dismantled its settlements and withdrew its troops from the Gaza Strip in August and September 2005. In order to facilitate a smooth transition and take an active role in Israeli-Palestinian peace, Egypt offered to post border guards on the Gaza-Egyptian border, increase its efforts to reorganize and train Palestinian security forces, and halt smuggling of contraband into Gaza. After extensive negotiations with Israeli officials, Egypt deployed 750 border guards to secure "the Philadelphi Route," a strip of land in Egypt immediately adjacent to the Gaza Strip that is notorious for tunnels used for smuggling weapons and narcotics. The memorandum of understanding between Israel and Egypt delineates the type of equipment the Egyptians may use (small arms and jeeps, no heavy armor) and the length of the patrol area (14km on the ground and 3 km into the sea).[21] Most importantly, Egypt is said to have promised not to provide weapons to Palestinian forces in order to allay Israeli concerns that such weapons may be used in terrorist attacks.

After the last Israeli soldiers withdrew, Egyptian border guards began allowing some Gazans to cross the border into Egypt despite Israeli calls for the temporary closing of the border. Reports indicate that there was an initial surge in Palestinians crossing and that Egyptian officials may have been reluctant to enforce a strict closure of the border for fear of sparking a violent confrontation. On October 26, 2005, Israel accepted an Egyptian proposal to reopen the Rafah border crossing between Egypt and the Gaza Strip. Under the terms of the arrangement, the Rafah terminal will be operated under joint Palestinian-Egyptian management, with European inspectors monitoring all entrants. The Rafah terminal will be used for the movement of people only; merchandise will be moved through a new terminal built in Kerem Shalom, Israel on the Israeli-Egyptian-Palestinian border.

Egyptian officials share the opinion of other governments in the region that the unilateral Israeli withdrawal from Gaza should be the first step toward a general withdrawal of all Israeli forces from Palestinian territory. The Egyptians and others point out that Israeli withdrawal is called for in U.N. resolutions, particularly 242, and the recent "Road Map" approach to peace, and that many Israelis also favor withdrawal. Egyptian leaders believe that the United States should be less inclined to accept and support Israeli positions and more inclined to support what they view as an even handed approach that will ensure Palestinian rights. Egyptians also point out that the Road Map calls for Israel to stop building and expanding settlements in the occupied territories, and argue that the United States should be more forceful in compelling Israel to meet those commitments.

Recent Developments in Egyptian-Israeli Relations

In June 2006, Israeli soldiers killed two Egyptian infiltrators who were identified as policemen responsible for guarding the Israeli-Egyptian border in the Sinai. The Egyptians had crossed into Israel and opened fire against an Israeli tank crew. The incident occurred two days before Israeli Prime Minister Ehud Olmert traveled to Sharm al-Shaykh for a meeting with Egyptian President Hosni Mubarak. During the talks, Olmert praised Mubarak stating that "The relationship between Egypt and Israel is very qualitative and very central to our world view and to the types of relations we want to build in the region. The leadership of Hosni Mubarak is an important key to the success of this process." Reportedly, Olmert sought Mubarak's approval of Israel's planned withdrawal from parts of the West Bank.

Depiction of Israel and Jews in the Egyptian Media

Egypt, like other Arab states, has received much criticism for allowing state-owned media outlets to publish unsubstantiated conspiratorial theories regarding Israel and the Jewish people, which likely contribute to detrimental or negative views of Israel by the Egyptian people. Although some Egyptian intellectuals have called for an end to anti-Israeli incitement, Egyptian publications continue to publish stories that perpetuate allegations of Jewish involvement in blood libels, deny the existence of the Holocaust, and portray anti-Semitic publications, such as the Protocols of the Elders of Zion, as truth.[22] U.S. officials and Members of Congress have urged the Egyptian government to speak out against anti-Semitism in media and society. Egyptian officials claim that they do not control the "free press."

Iraq

Egyptian Position on the 2003 Iraq War

The Egyptian public's opposition to the Iraq war precluded the government from publicly supporting the United States. Egypt advised against the March 2003 U.S. intervention in Iraq and continues to question an extended presence of U.S. forces there. In response to U.S. efforts to secure Arab participation in stabilizing Iraq, Egypt informed the United States that it would not participate in any international security arrangements involving force deployments in Iraq unless they were under United Nations auspices.[23] In the past, Egypt did cooperate with U.S.-led international military and peacekeeping operations, such as the 1991 Kuwaiti liberation, Operation Restore Hope in Somalia, Afghanistan,[24] and the Balkans. Egypt has allowed U.S. overflights and waived the 30-day prior notification to pass nuclear-armed U.S. warships through the Suez canal. At a June 2005 conference on Iraq reconstruction, Iraqi Foreign Minister Hoshyar Zebari announced that Egypt and Jordan were the first Arab countries sending ambassadors to Iraq. In July 2005, Egypt's top diplomat in Iraq was kidnaped by terrorists and executed several days later.

Training Iraqi Security Forces

Egypt has been active in helping to train Iraq's new security forces, and some U.S. lawmakers have demanded that the Administration further utilize Egypt's offer of assistance.[25] In late 2004, an Iraqi infantry company was invited to Egypt to participate in a joint training program with the Egyptian army. According to the Egyptian government, 134 soldiers from Iraq's 5th Infantry Division trained alongside Egypt's 3rd Infantry Division at the Mubarak Military City in northern Egypt. No plans for future joint Iraqi-Egyptian training exercises have been announced, although Egyptian officials have expressed their willingness to expand their training program for Iraqi military officers.[26]

Terrorism

Egyptian security forces have long been engaged in their own war on terror against several radical Islamic groups, that have called for the violent overthrow of Egypt's secular government and its replacement with an Islamic state. Two radical offshoots of the aforementioned Muslim Brotherhood, the Jamaah Islamiya (Islamic Group) and Al Jihad,[27] have been responsible for several attacks on high-ranking Egyptian officials, including Al Jihad's 1981 assassination of President Anwar Sadat and Jamaah Islamiya's 1990 killing of the speaker of the Egyptian People's Assembly. Both groups also have attacked tourist sites popular with Western visitors, bombed Coptic Christian churches, and attacked Egyptian banks and other centers of commerce. The Islamic Group also has a non-violent arm which recruits and builds support openly in poor neighborhoods in Cairo, Alexandria, and throughout southern Egypt, and runs social service programs. Al Jihad has operated only clandestinely, focusing almost exclusively on assassinations.

1992-1997 Terror Campaign

Jamaah Islamiya began a terror campaign in 1992 that in six years resulted in 1,300 deaths (90 of whom were foreign tourists) and several thousand injuries. The group also assassinated several Egyptian officials. The government responded with an all-out campaign that included what some viewed as harsh measures that abused human rights. Egyptian authorities used arrest, search, and seizure without warrant, detention without trial, conviction without appeal, and, according to some, physical torture in their drive to stop the Jamaah terrorists. Some Egyptians defend the use of such measures as necessary to eliminate terrorists and stop terrorism from threatening an even larger segment of the Egyptian populace. President Mubarak and other Egyptian officials claimed that the extremists were financed, trained, and directed by Iranian and Sudanese religious militants and returning Egyptian volunteers from the Soviet-Afghan war.

Jamaah leaders inside Egypt announced in 1997 and again in1998 that they were ending the armed attacks.[28] In the interim, six men claiming to be Jamaah members attacked tourists at the Hatshepsut tomb near Luxor in southern Egypt in November 1997, killing 58 foreign tourists and four Egyptians before committing suicide.

Previously, Jamaah members involved in terror attacks tried to escape and did not commit suicide, which led to some speculation that the Luxor attack was the desperate act of a few members rather than an action of the whole group. There have been no major incidents involving Jamaah since the Luxor attack and in June 2000, Jamaah leaders inside Egypt repeated their claim that they had abandoned violence and terrorism. Some observers suggest that harsh and persistent police pressure has greatly reduced if not eliminated the Jamaah threat to Egypt.

Recent Terrorist Activity in Egypt

Over the past two years, there has been a resumption of terrorist activity in Egypt, in what some suggest could be a revival of earlier, more violent periods.

- In October 2004, bombs exploded at two major resorts that cater to Israelis and other Western tourists in the Sinai Peninsula, 34 people were killed and over 120 were wounded in the attack.
- On April 7, 2005, an explosion in the Khan al-Khalili market area of Cairo killed three, including one U.S. citizen. A group called the al-Ezz Islamic Brigade claimed responsibility for the attack.
- On April 30, 2005, a man exploded a suicide bomb near the Egyptian museum while being pursued by police, wounding seven; and two women, the fiancé and sister of the suicide bomber, fired at a tourist bus before committing suicide. No one was injured in the bus attack. Two groups claimed responsibility for the attacks, but neither claim was confirmed.
- On July 23, 2005, two car bombs and a set of explosives concealed in a backpack exploded at various tourist destinations in the Egyptian resort town of Sharm al-Shaykh. As many as 88 people, including one American, were killed in the blasts. Investigations into the attacks have focused on the possible link to a local terrorist cell who may have committed the October 2004 bombings.
- On April 24, 2006, Egyptian terrorists attacked the Sinai Peninsula resort town of Dahab, killing 21 people and injuring hundreds. Two days later, suicide bombers attacked a police station in the northern Sinai and a base camp of the Multinational Force and Observers, a peacekeeping mission that was created as part of the 1979 peace treaty between Egypt and Israel. Two people were injured in the attacks.

Egypt has suffered through a new wave of attacks emanating from previously unknown groups in the Sinai Peninsula. After each attack, Egyptian authorities identified some of the perpetrators as members of local Bedouin tribes. Egyptian security forces have launched several operations in the Sinai and have arrested hundreds of Bedouin suspects, leading some to speculate that police heavy-handedness may be further exacerbating tensions between Bedouin and the state.

The extent of outside involvement in the recent wave of terrorism in Egypt is still uncertain. The Bedouin/Palestinian terrorist network in the Sinai that has claimed credit for the bombings in Dahab, Sharm al-Shaykh, and Taba calls itself Al-Tawhid w'al-Jihad. Israeli officials have suggested that Al Qaeda or another international group operating in the Sinai may have supported the Bedouin operatives. Egyptian intelligence officials have publicly stated that some members of Al-Tawhid w'al-Jihad were sent to the Gaza Strip to receive training from Hamas. Other observers discount the possibility of outside involvement and believe that the Bedouin, who have historically kept their distance from the state, have grown frustrated with poor living conditions in the Sinai and sought revenge for the mass detentions that followed the October 2004 bombings. Some experts postulate that, although the terrorists may have acted on their own, members of Al-Tawhid w'al-Jihad may have drawn their inspiration from Al Qaeda.

Source: Map Resources. Adapted by CRS. (K.Yancey 5/19/06).

Figure 2. The Sinai Peninsula.

Political and Economic Reform in Egypt

Overview

International and domestic pressure for reform in Egypt reached an apex in 2005, as Egyptian civil society groups and Islamist activists held a number of anti-government demonstrations calling for greater political freedom in Egypt. U.S. officials, including Secretary of State Condoleezza Rice, also called on Egypt to abrogate draconian emergency laws,[29] hold free and fair elections, and reform its Constitution. At the same time, the political elite of Egypt, recognizing that its popular support was on the decline and President Mubarak's health was questionable, was undergoing its own internal reformation in order to modernize the ruling National Democratic Party's (NDP) image and restore its popular appeal and credibility. With pressure coming from both outside and within the ruling clique, President Mubarak took action in February 2005 by launching a process to amend Egypt's Constitution to allow for multi-candidate presidential elections for the first time in its history.

For a complete overview of the recent presidential and parliamentary elections and their implications for U.S. policy toward Egypt and U.S. efforts to promote democracy in the region, see CRS Report RS22274, *Egypt: 2005 Presidential and Parliamentary Elections*, by Jeremy M. Sharp.

Despite vibrant campaign seasons for both presidential and parliamentary elections in 2005, the results, which saw President Mubarak receiving 88% of the popular vote and the NDP maintaining its supra-majority in parliament, led many analysts to conclude that the elections had been merely a symbolic show of reform and that the underlying power structure in Egypt remains firmly intact. Though Muslim Brotherhood affiliates made noticeable gains during parliamentary elections, the organization remains outlawed and, by law, cannot field a candidate in any future presidential election. Furthermore, with the election season concluded, the government has cracked down on reformists, journalists, and independent judges in 2006.

U.S. Policy to Promote Reform in Egypt

Although the United States has long advocated the promotion of human rights and political freedom in Egypt, most experts agree that, prior to the terrorist attacks of September 11, 2001, economic reform superseded political reform in the West's relations with Egypt. However, with the recent push for democracy in the Middle East seen as a counterweight to Islamic militancy and intellectual and social stagnation, U.S. policy regarding Egypt has been reinvigorated, as policymakers seek to balance U.S. security interests with U.S. democracy promotion policies.

U.S. officials have employed a variety of diplomatic tools to push for reform in Egypt, including speeches on democratization given by high level visiting officials such as Secretary of State Condoleezza Rice, foreign aid to pro-democracy organizations to assist local efforts to monitor elections and train activists, and withholding U.S.-Egyptian free trade talks as a protest to the recent conviction of Ayman Nour.

Nevertheless, some analysts have questioned the depth of the U.S. commitment to democratization in Egypt, particularly after the recent Hamas victory in Palestinian parliamentary elections earlier this year. With Hamas poised to take over most of the Palestinian Authority, Egypt, the United States, and Israel all have a shared purpose in containing Hamas and the spread of political Islamist influence into neighboring states. In this changed atmosphere, in which Egyptian security cooperation on the Gaza-Egyptian border also is valued, some observers have speculated that U.S. policy makers may tone down their rhetoric on reform in Egypt.

Through annual foreign operations and State Department appropriations legislation, Congress provides funding for reform in Egypt through the following programs: the United States Agency for International Development's (USAID) Egypt Office;[30] the Middle East Partnership Initiative (MEPI), a State Department program designed to encourage reform in Arab countries by strengthening Arab civil society, encouraging micro-enterprise, expanding political participation, and promoting women's rights;[31] the State Department's Human Rights and Democracy Fund (HRDF), an account that funds human rights promotion in Muslim-majority countries; and the National Endowment for Democracy's (NED) Muslim Democracy Program.

Many in the Egyptian government appear to feel threatened by the current thrust of U.S. policy and resist some U.S. advocated changes that seek to empower opposition movements. In June 2006, the Egyptian government accused the local head of the International Republican Institute's (IRI) Egypt program of meddling in Egypt's internal affairs and demanded that the organization temporarily halt its activities there.

Congress seeks to ensure that U.S. foreign assistance for Egypt is being appropriately used to promote reform. In conference report language accompanying P.L. 108-447, the FY2005 Consolidated Appropriations Act, conferees specified that "democracy and governance activities shall not be subject to the prior approval of the GoE [government of Egypt]. The managers intend this language to include NGOs and other segments of civil society that may not be registered with, or officially recognized by, the GoE. However, the managers understand that the GoE should be kept informed of funding provided pursuant to these activities."[32]

Economic Reform

As a developing country with the largest population (and the second largest economy) in the Arab world, Egypt faces a number of economic and environmental challenges, including a lack of arable land, high unemployment, rampant corruption, rapid urbanization, and extreme poverty (30% of the population lives below the poverty line). Egypt's economy revolves around several sectors: the state; the production of oil and natural gas; the tourism industry; remittances from over 2 million Egyptians working abroad; revenues from the Suez Canal; agriculture; clothing and textile manufacturing; pharmaceuticals; and foreign aid. Since the early years of Anwar Sadat's rule, Egypt has been evolving from a centrally controlled, socialist economy to a free market, capitalist society — a gradual process that has created difficult decisions for the Egyptian government, income inequality, and hardships for the Egyptian people.[33]

In order to increase foreign investment and qualify for development loans from international lending institutions, Egypt has had to demonstrate that it is making tangible progress in liberalizing its economy. In recent years, the government has reduced public subsidies for basic foodstuffs, privatized many state-owned corporations, and removed trade barriers.[34] Although analysts remain cautious as to what effect reforms may have on the economy, the government has recently streamlined the tax system, canceled many customs duties, and forced smaller banks to merge with the country's four largest banks.

Corruption

Egypt, like other developing nations, has struggled to overcome high levels of corruption, which many analysts consider the biggest obstacle to achieving economic growth. Corruption in Egypt is found in all sectors of the government as, in recent years, a number of high level officials (including several former ministers) has been indicted for fraud and influence peddling. Moreover, Egypt's bloated, cumbersome bureaucracy is infamous for making bribery a common practice, as poorly-paid government workers seek additional money and citizens seek ways to circumvent the maze of public regulations and overlapping agencies. Some analysts believe that the corruption issue enhances the popularity of the Muslim Brotherhood, which frequently invokes Islam to rally against the moral corruption in society. The Egyptian press also has been active in exposing corruption scandals.

U.S.-Egyptian Trade

Trade Overview

The United States is Egypt's largest bilateral trading partner, while Egypt is the United States' 54th largest trading partner.[35] According to the Department of Commerce's 2004 Country Commercial Guide for Egypt, Egypt is the largest single market worldwide for American wheat and is a significant importer of other agricultural commodities, machinery, and equipment.[36] The United States also is the second largest foreign investor in Egypt, primarily in the oil and gas sector.

Table 1. U.S.-Egyptian Trade Statistics 2004

Selected commodities	$ amount (estimated)
U.S. Exports to Egypt	($3.1 billion total in 2004)
Cereals	$808 million
Machinery	$514 million
Aircraft	$350 million
Vehicles	$229 million
U.S. Imports from Egypt	($1.3 billion total in 2004)
Apparel	$422 million
Mineral Fuel, Oil	$262 million
Iron and Steel	$254 million

Source: Trade Stat Express, U.S. Department of Commerce.

Since the mid-1990s, Egyptian officials have sought to negotiate a free trade agreement (FTA) with the United States, claiming that an Egyptian-American FTA could boost Egypt's economy by as much as 3%. The two parties signed a Trade and Investment Framework Agreement (TIFA) in 1999. The TIFA established a Council on Trade and Investment (TIFA Council) composed of representatives of both governments and chaired by the United States Trade Representative (USTR) and Egypt's Minister of Economy and Foreign Trade. However, on January 17, 2006, the *New York Times* reported that the United States had put on hold its intention to announce free trade talks with Egypt. The decision to table such an announcement was reportedly done in protest to the sentencing of secular opposition figure Ayman Nour to five years in prison for his alleged fraud in registering his political party.

Nour, who placed second in Egypt's 2005 presidential election, is appealing the decision and remains in prison. In October 2005, Rob Portman, the United States trade representative, had told Congress that the Administration was considering negotiating trade agreements with Egypt and three other Middle Eastern countries.

In 1996, Congress authorized the creation of Qualified Industrial Zones (QIZ) in order to entitle goods jointly produced by Israel and either Jordan or Egypt to enter the United States duty free.[37] In December 2004, Egypt finally reached an agreement with Israel to designate several Qualified Industrial Zones (QIZ) in Egypt under the mandate of the U.S.-Israeli Free Trade Agreement. Goods produced in Egyptian QIZs allow Egyptian-made products to be exported to the United States duty-free if the products contain at least 11.7% input from Israel. On November 1, 2005, the USTR designated a new Qualified Industrial Zone (QIZ) in the central Nile delta region, bringing the total number of QIZs in Egypt to four.

Human Rights, Religious Freedom, and Women's Rights

Egypt consistently ranks poorly in its human rights record, as the U.S. State Department and international human rights organizations have long documented instances of torture, arbitrary detainment, and discrimination against women, homosexuals, and Coptic Christians. According to Human Rights Watch, Egyptian security forces and police routinely torture and mistreat detainees, particularly during interrogations. The government has long restricted freedom of assembly, though recent opposition protests have been permitted and, in some cases, police were absent from public demonstrations. In recent years, press freedom and general freedom of speech have expanded in Egypt, though legal restrictions, such as a 1996 press law which can lead to jail terms for journalists convicted of defamation, continue to foster a high degree of self-censorship in the media. However, Arab satellite televisions, like Al Jazeera and others, have challenged Egyptian state-owned media by broadcasting, among other programs, opposition demonstrations and interviews with Muslim Brotherhood members.

The 1981 Emergency Laws

After Islamic militants assassinated former President Anwar Sadat in 1981, officials reinstated a set of laws granting the state and security forces sweeping powers in order to curb the outbreak of further violence. Over time, these laws, which were extended for three years in February 2003, have come under heavy scrutiny from reformers and human rights advocates for their arbitrary application to non-security cases. In 2006, the Egyptian government announced its intention to abrogate these laws and replace them with new anti-terrorism legislation. According to the 2004 State Department Report on Human Rights Practices in Egypt, the Emergency Laws:

- authorize incommunicado detention for prolonged periods,
- restrict or deny access to counsel for detainees in state security facilities,
- permit the state to refer any criminal case to the Emergency Courts, in which the accused does not receive most of the constitutional protections of the civilian judicial system,
- suspend the constitutional provisions regarding the right to privacy.

Religious Freedom

There is no official government policy of discrimination against the 9 million Coptic Christians in Egypt, and the Constitution provides for equal rights without regard to religion. Nevertheless, critics note that there are no Christians serving as governors, police commissioners, city mayors, public university presidents, or deans.[38] Converts to Christianity in Egypt may face bureaucratic obstacles in registering their new religious status with the state. In addition, there have been reports of periodic discrimination against small minority communities of Baha'is, Shiites, and Jews (200 remain in Egypt). In an effort to promote tolerance, President Mubarak in December 2003 recognized the Coptic Christmas, January 6, as a national holiday.

Despite government efforts to improve Muslim-Christian relations, a number of obstacles remain. For example, the 10 articles of "Humayun," or the Humayun Code, a portion of Ottoman legislation from 1856, still controls the building or repair of churches in Egypt and is a source of great aggravation to Coptic Christians. Under this law, a license is required to erect a church. In addition, there are ten restricting conditions for the construction of churches, including a minimum distance between churches and between a church and the nearest mosque, as well as the absence of objection on the part of Muslim neighbors. In December 2004, President Mubarak issued a new decree that devolved church repair and reconstruction decisions to the provincial level and stipulated that churches would be permitted to proceed with rebuilding and repair without legal hindrance. However, permits for construction of new churches require a presidential decree.

On April 14, 2006, clashes broke out between Muslims and Coptic Christians in Alexandria, Egypt after a Muslim man attacked Christian worshipers with a machete at three churches during Palm Sunday services. The rioting continued for three days after the initial attack, though religious leaders organized peaceful demonstrations to help quell the violence. The sectarian violence was the latest manifestation of growing Muslim-Christian tension in Egypt, which has seen several similar incidents over the past two years.

Women's Rights

Although Egyptian women have played major roles in the country's drive for independence and many women currently serve in prestigious public posts, women face a number of obstacles at the legal, religious, and cultural levels. For example, according to the U.S. State Department's 2004 Human Rights Report on Egypt, female genital mutilation (FGM) remained a serious problem due to widespread cultural acceptance, despite the government's attempts to eliminate the practice.[39] Moreover, personal status laws governing marriage, divorce, custody, and inheritance discriminate against women, particularly when it comes to divorce, as there is much societal resistance to breaking up the family unit. Domestic violence also is a major issue, as some estimate that as many as a third of all married Egyptian women have faced some form of physical abuse.[40] In recent years, new nongovernmental organizations have started to provide services and counseling to women, who may be too afraid to go to the authorities.

Military Cooperation

"Bright Star" and other Joint Military Operations

The United States and Egypt conducted the first "Bright Star" joint military exercise in August 1983, and continue to hold periodic "Bright Star" exercises for infantry, airborne, artillery, and armored forces. The 1983 Bright Star was more than a training exercise: President Mubarak asked the United States to send Airborne Warning and Control System aircraft (AWACS) to monitor Libya's activity toward Sudan in February 1983. President Reagan sent AWACS planes and crews to monitor Libyan flights and the AWACS remained to take part in the first Bright Star. AWACS returned to Egypt in March-April 1984 to monitor Libyan flights toward Sudan after an incident in which a Libyan plane allegedly bombed Khartoum. On August 11, 2003, the United States announced that it was canceling the October 2003 Bright Star exercise because U.S. armed forces were over-committed in Afghanistan, Iraq, and other areas. In 2005, Bright Star exercises took place in Egypt with over 9,000 U.S. troops reportedly participating.

"Desert Storm"

In the week prior to the August 2, 1990, Iraqi invasion of Kuwait, President Mubarak traveled to Iraq, Kuwait, and Saudi Arabia in an attempt to negotiate a peaceful end to the crisis. After the invasion, Mubarak advised President Bush to withhold sending armed forces to allow Egypt more time to work out a peaceful resolution. On August 7, when the United States announced that it was deploying troops to Saudi Arabia, Mubarak denied a U.S. request to allow U.S. forces use of Egyptian military bases on their way to the Arabian Peninsula so that he would have time to negotiate (he later granted the request). Mubarak and other Egyptian officials continued their peacemaking efforts in the Arab League, the Organization of the Islamic Conference (OIC), and through personal contacts and visits with Arab leaders. On August 10, Egypt voted for an Arab League resolution to send armed forces to defend Saudi Arabia against a possible Iraqi invasion. The first contingent of Egyptian troops, a commando unit and a paratrooper unit, joined U.S. forces along the Saudi-Kuwaiti border the next day, on August 11. Egypt stated that its forces would assist in liberating Kuwait but would not attack or occupy Iraq. In February 1991, an Egyptian reinforced infantry division of some 30,000 troops took part in Desert Storm, advancing into western Kuwait in a corridor between U.S. Marines to the east and U.S. Army forces to the west in Iraq. Egypt suffered 9 killed and 74 wounded in action in Desert Storm.[41]

Egyptian and U.S. military officers state that cooperation in Bright Star exercises facilitated the U.S.-Egyptian cooperation and military compatibility in Desert Storm, and Egyptian officers claim that Bright Star and Desert Storm serve as precedents for future U.S.-Egyptian cooperative ventures. Moreover, Egyptian participation in Desert Storm provided benefit to the U.S.-led operation in that it helped broaden the allied coalition that liberated Kuwait. Later, Egyptian troops served as peacekeeping forces in Somalia and Yugoslavia.

Egyptian Participation in International Peacekeeping

In the Sudan, Egypt has provided soldiers for peacekeeping operations in southern Sudan. Egypt has sent relief supplies and police forces to the strife-ridden Darfur region to bolster humanitarian efforts there. In Afghanistan, Egypt maintains a field hospital at Bagram Air Base.

Intelligence Cooperation

Although it is difficult to discern the extent of U.S.-Egyptian intelligence cooperation, there is a sense among many U.S. security officials that Egypt's long struggle against domestic Islamic radicals has made it a valuable partner in the global war on terrorism. Since the September 11, 2001 terrorist attacks, there have been several reports suggesting that the U.S. Central Intelligence Agency has deported several suspected Al Qaeda operatives to Egypt (along with other Arab countries) in order to be interrogated.[42] In May, Egyptian Prime Minister Ahmed Nazif said the United States has dispatched 60 to 70 Egyptian detainees to their home country since the September 11 attacks.[43] More recently, an Italian prosecutor has asked a judge to issue arrest warrants for 13 Americans accused of kidnaping an Egyptian cleric off the streets of Milan and bringing him to Egypt in 2003. The cleric reportedly has been held in prison for more than two years without formal charges, though Egyptian officials have accused him of having ties to Jamaah Islamiya.[44]

U.S. Foreign Assistance to Egypt

Since 1979, Egypt has been the second largest recipient, after Israel, of U.S. foreign assistance, receiving an annual average of over $2 billion in economic and military aid. Congress typically earmarks foreign assistance for Egypt in the foreign operations appropriations bill. The annual earmark has included a statement that Egypt should undertake further economic reforms in addition to reforms taken in previous years.

Economic Aid

Annual bilateral economic assistance to Egypt is typically provided in three different ways: (1) as a direct cash transfer to the Egyptian government; (2) as part of the Commodity Import Program, which provides hard currency to the Egyptian private sector to purchase U.S. agricultural goods; and (3) as funds for USAID programming in Egypt. In recent years, Congress has sought to specify how Egypt's economic aid would be spent, prioritizing funding for USAID's democracy and education programs. Egypt claims that U.S. assistance programs must be jointly negotiated and cannot be unilaterally dictated by the United States.

As part of the FY2007 request, USAID plans on spending $255 million in ESF. The Administration intends to provide $183 million of Egypt's $455 million total ESF package as a direct cash transfer. There is no request for CIP funds in the FY2007 Administration budget.

U.S. economic assistance to Egypt has been decreasing since 1998, when the United States began reducing economic assistance to Egypt and Israel. In January

1998, Israeli officials negotiated with the United States to reduce economic aid and increase military aid over a 10-year period. A 3 to 2 ratio similar to U.S. aid to Israel and Egypt was applied to the reduction in aid ($60 million reduction for Israel and $40 million reduction for Egypt), but Egypt has not received an increase in military assistance. Economic aid has dropped in annual $40 million increments from $815 million in FY1998 to $455 million in ESF for the FY2007 request.[45]

The cash transfer portion of annual ESF to Egypt is conditioned on Egyptian efforts to implement necessary economic reforms. USAID has withheld the disbursement of several hundred million dollars in ESF to Egypt until certain benchmarks have been met. These benchmarks were outlined in a March 2005 financial sector reform agreement between USAID and the Egyptian government.

Military Aid

The Administration has requested $1.3 billion in FMF for Egypt in FY2007 —the same amount it received in FY2006. FMF aid to Egypt is divided into three general components: (1) acquisitions, (2) upgrades to existing equipment, and (3) follow-on support/ maintenance contracts. According to the General Accountability Office, over the life of Egypt's FMF program, Egypt has purchased 36 Apache helicopters, 220 F-16 aircraft, 880 M1A1 tanks, and the accompanying training and maintenance to support these systems, among other items.[46] According to the U.S. and Egyptian defense officials, approximately 30% of annual FMF aid to Egypt is spent on new weapons systems, as Egypt's defense modernization plan is designed to gradually replace most of Egypt's older Soviet weaponry with U.S. equipment. That figure is expected to decline over the long term due to the rising costs associated with follow-on maintenance contracts. Egyptian military officials have repeatedly sought additional FMF funds to offset the escalating costs of follow-on support. Egypt is currently committed to payments on a multi-billion dollar arms sale involving the purchase of U.S. F-16 aircraft, M-1 tanks, and a Patriot missile battery. Egypt also receives Excess Defense Articles (EDA) worth hundreds of millions of dollars annually from the Pentagon. Egyptian officers also participate in the IMET program ($1.2 million requested for FY2007) in order to facilitate U.S.-Egyptian military cooperation over the long term.

In addition to large amounts of annual U.S. military assistance, Egypt also benefits from certain aid provisions that are available to only a few other countries. Since 2000, Egypt's FMF funds have been deposited in an interest bearing account in the Federal Reserve Bank of New York and have remained there until they are obligated. By law (P.L. 106-280), Congress must be notified if any of the interest accrued in this account is obligated. Most importantly, Egypt is allowed to set aside FMF funds for current year payments only, rather than set aside the full amount needed to meet the full cost of multi-year purchases. Cash flow financing allows Egypt to negotiate major arms purchases with U.S. defense suppliers.

Recent U.S. Military Sales to Egypt

As stated earlier, Egypt uses its FMF funds to purchase U.S. defense equipment. By law, Congress must be notified of any new purchase agreement. Israel has protested U.S. sales of certain military technologies to Egypt; the Egyptians insist that all U.S. weaponry is used for defensive purposes and is intended to upgrade or replace its aging Soviet hardware. The Department of Defense's Defense Security Cooperation Agency (DSCA), is charged with managing U.S. arms sales to Egypt. Recent sales include one reported on July 29, 2005, when the Defense Security Cooperation Agency notified Congress of a possible Foreign Military Sale to Egypt of 200 M109A5 155mm self-propelled howitzers as well as associated equipment and services. The total value, if all options are exercised, could be as high as $181 million.

FY2006 Foreign Operations Appropriations Bill

The conference report (H.Rept. 109-265) on H.R. 3057, the FY2006 Foreign Operations Appropriations Bill, provides the full request for Egypt ($495 million in ESF, $1.43 billion in FMF); however, it designates $100 million in economic aid for USAID education and democracy and governance programming and conditions another $227.6 million on economic reform benchmarks set out in a March 2005 memorandum of understanding between the United States and Egypt. In addition, conferees stated that "not less than 50 percent of the funds for democracy, governance and human rights be provided through non-governmental organizations for the purpose of strengthening Egyptian civil society organizations, enhancing their participation in the political process and their ability to promote and monitor human rights."[47] Finally, conferees did not include a Senate provision conditioning U.S. assistance to Egypt on the construction of an FM transmitter tower for Radio Sawa.

U.S. Assistance to Egypt: Possible Changes

Some lawmakers believe that U.S. assistance to Egypt has not been effective in promoting political and economic reform and that foreign assistance agreements must be renegotiated to include benchmarks that Egypt must meet to continue to qualify for U.S. foreign aid. Others have periodically called for restrictions on U.S. aid to Egypt on the grounds that Egypt indirectly supports Palestinian terrorism, suppresses its own population, including minority Christians, and continues to allow Egyptian state-owned media outlets to publish unsubstantiated conspiracy theories regarding Israel and the Jewish people.

The Administration and Egyptian government assert that reducing Egypt's military aid would undercut peace between Israel and Egypt. Overall, many U.S. observers believe that U.S. support for Egypt stabilizes the region and extends U.S. influence in the most populous Arab country. Supporters of continued U.S. assistance note that Egypt helps train Iraqi and Palestinian security forces, cooperates with the U.S. military, provides access and facilities to U.S. forces in the Middle East, and is helping patrol the Egyptian-Gaza border after Israel's 2005 withdrawal from the Gaza Strip.

For years, Congress has specified in annual foreign operations appropriations legislation that ESF funds to Egypt are provided with the understanding that Egypt undertake certain economic reforms and liberalize its economy. USAID believes that its programs have helped contribute to Egypt's economic growth and macroeconomic stability. Others note that Egypt still has a bloated public sector, and assert that U.S. economic aid mainly helps subsidize Egypt's social welfare and education budget. U.S. policymakers have repeatedly suggested that trade with and investment in Egypt may be as effective as aid in reforming the Egyptian economy. In 1994, then-Vice President Al Gore and Egyptian President Hosni Mubarak launched the United States-Egyptian Partnership for Economic Growth and Development, a council of private and public sector officials dedicated to enhancing trade between the two countries. The United States has withheld announcing its intention to launch U.S.-Egyptian free trade negotiations . Some have speculated that this has been in response to the December 2005 prosecution of Ayman Nour, the runner-up in the 2005 presidential election.

Legislative Proposals and Congressional Action on Aid to Egypt

An amendment offered on July 15, 2004, to the House FY2005 foreign operations bill (H.R. 4818) would have reduced U.S. military aid to Egypt by $570 million and increased economic aid by the same amount, but the amendment failed by a vote of 131 to 287. An amendment offered on June 28, 2005, to the

House FY2006 foreign operations bill (H.R. 3057) would have reduced U.S. military aid to Egypt by $750 million and would have transferred that amount to child survival and health programs managed by USAID. The amendment failed by a recorded vote of 87 to 326.

The FY2005 Consolidated Appropriations Act (P.L. 108-447) stipulates that U.S. funds for democracy and governance activities in Egypt are no longer subject to the prior approval of the Egyptian government. At this point, it is unclear how this provision will affect USAID programming in Egypt. USAID completed a $32 million NGO Service Center in order to facilitate the growth of independent, nongovernmental organizations in Egypt.

H.R. 2601, the FY2006/FY2007 House Foreign Relations Authorization bill, would reduce U.S. military assistance to Egypt by $40 million for each of the next three fiscal years, while using the funds to promote economic changes, fight poverty, and improve education in Egypt. There is no comparable provision in the Senate's Foreign Relations Authorization bill (S. 600).

On May 25, 2006, the House Appropriations Committee in a voice vote rejected an amendment to cut $200 million in military aid to Egypt during markup of H.R. 5522, the FY2007 Foreign Operations Appropriations Bill. In June 2006, the House narrowly defeated an amendment (198-225) to H.R. 5522 that would have reallocated $100 million in economic aid to Egypt and used it instead to fight AIDS worldwide and to assist the Darfur region of Sudan. Many supporters of the amendment were dismayed by the Egyptian government's spring 2006 crackdown on pro-democracy activists in Cairo.

Table 2. Recent U.S. Aid to Egypt (millions of dollars)

Year	Economic	Military	IMET	Total
1948-1997	23,288.6	22,353.5	27.3	45,669.4
1998	815.0	1,300.0	1.0	2,116.0
1999	775.0	1,300.0	1.0	2,076.0
2000	727.3	1,300.0	1.0	2,028.3
2001	695.0	1,300.0	1.0	1,996.0
2002	655.0	1,300.0	1.0	1,956.0
2003	911.0	1,300.0	1.2	2,212.2
2004	571.6	1,292.3	1.4	1,865.3
2005	530.7	1,289.6	1.2	1,821.5
2006	490.0	1,287.0	1.2	1,778.2
Total	29,459.2	34,022.4	37.3	63,518.9

Note: FY2004 totals reflect the .59% across-the-board reduction.

Table 3. U.S. Foreign Assistance to Egypt, 1946-1997 (millions of dollars)

Year	Total	Military Loan	Military Grant	I.M.E.T Grant	Misc. Economic Grant	D.A. Loan	D.A. Grant	ESF Loan	ESF Grant	P.L. 480 I	P.L. 480 II
1946	9.6	—	—	—	9.3 Surplus 0.3 UNWRA	—	—	—	—	—	—
1948	1.4	—	—	—	1.4 Surplus	—	—	—	—	—	—
1951	0.1	—	—	—	0.1 Tech Asst	—	—	—	—	—	—
1952	1.2	—	—	—	—	—	0.4	—	—	—	0.8
1953	12.9	—	—	—	—	—	12.9	—	—	—	—
1954	4	—	—	—	—	—	3.3	—	—	—	0.7
1955	66.3	—	—	—	—	7.5	35.3	—	—	—	23.5
1956	33.3	—	—	—	—	—	2.6	—	—	13.2	17.5
1957	1	—	—	—	—	—	0.7	—	—	—	0.3
1958	0.6	—	—	—	—	—	0	—	—	—	0.6
1959	44.8	—	—	—	—	—	2	—	—	33.9	8.9
1960	65.9	—	—	—	—	15.4	5.7	—	—	36.6	8.2
1961	73.5	—	—	—	—	—	2.3	—	—	48.6	22.6
1962	200.5	—	—	—	—	20	2.2	20	—	114	44.3
1963	146.7	—	—	—	—	36.3	2.3	10	—	78.5	19.6
1964	95.5	—	—	—	—	—	1.4	—	—	85.2	8.9
1965	97.6	—	—	—	—	—	2.3	—	—	84.9	10.4
1966	27.6	—	—	—	—	—	1.5	—	—	16.4	9.7
1967	12.6	—	—	—	—	—	0.8	—	—	—	11.8
1972	1.5	—	—	—	—	1.5	—	—	—	—	—
1973	0.8	—	—	—	—	—	—	—	—	—	0.8
1974	21.3	—	—	—	—	—	—	—	8.5	9.5	3.3

Table 3. (Continued).

Year	Total	Military Loan	Military Grant	I.M.E.T Grant	Misc. Economic Grant	D.A. Loan	D.A. Grant	ESF Loan	ESF Grant	P.L. 480 I	P.L. 480 II
1975	370.1	—	—	—	—	—	—	194.3	58.5	104.5	12.8
1976	464.3	—	—	—	—	—	5.4	150	102.8	201.7	4.4
TQ	552.5	—	—	—	—	—	—	429	107.8	14.6	1.1
1977	907.8	—	—	—	—	—	—	600	99.2	196.8	11.7
1978	943.2	—	—	0.2	0.1 Narc.	—	—	617.4	133.3	179.7	12.5
1979	2588.5	1500	—	0.4	—	—	—	250	585	230.7	22.4
1980	1167.3	—	—	0.8	—	—	—	280	585	285.3	16.1
1981	1681.2	550	—	0.8	—	—	—	70	759	272.5	28.9
1982	1967.3	700	200	2.4	—	—	—	—	771	262	31.9
1983	2332	900	425	1.9	—	—	—	—	750	238.3	16.8
1984	2470.8	900	465	1.7	—	—	—	—	852.9	237.5	13.7
1985	2468.7	—	1175	1.7	—	—	—	—	1065.1	213.8	13.2
1986	2539.1	—	1244.1	1.7	—	—	—	—	1069.2	217.5	6.6
1987	2317	—	1300	1.8	—	—	—	—	819.7	191.7	3.9
1988	2174.9	—	1300	1.5	—	—	—	—	717.8	153	2.6
1989	2269.6	—	1300	1.5	—	—	1.5	—	815	150.5	1.2
1990	2397.4	—	1294.4	1.6	—	—	—	—	898.4	203	—
1991	2300.2	—	1300	1.9	—	—	—	—	780.8	165	52.5
1992	2235.1	—	1300	1.8	—	—	—	—	892.9	40.4	—
1993	2052.9	—	1300	1.8	—	—	—	—	747.0	—	4.1
1994	1868.6	—	1300	0.8	—	—	—	—	561.6	35	6.2

Table 3. (Continued).

Year	Total	Military Loan	Military Grant	I.M.E.T Grant	Misc. Economic Grant	D.A. Loan	D.A. Grant	ESF Loan	ESF Grant	P.L. 480 I	P.L. 480 II
1995	2414.5	—	1300	1	—	—	0.2	—	1113.3	—	—
1996	2116.6	—	1300	1	—	—	—	—	815	—	0.6
1997P	2116	—	1300	1	—	—	—	—	815	—	—
Total	45669.4	4550	17803.5	27.3.0	11.2	80.7	82.8	2620.7	15923.8	4,114.3	455.1

Notes: Totals may not add due to rounding. No U.S. aid programs for years 1947, 1949, 1950, 1968, 1969, 1970, and 1971. P.L. 480 II Grant for 1993 includes $2.1 million in Sec. 416 food donations.

TQ = Transition Quarter; change from June to September fiscal year

* = less than $100,000

I.M.E.T. = International Military Education and Training

UNRWA = United Nations Relief and Works Agency

Surplus = Surplus Property

Tech. Asst. = Technical Assistance

Narc. = International Narcotics Control

D. A. = Development Assistance

ESF = Economic Support Funds

P.L. 480 I = Public Law 480 (Food for Peace), Title I Loan

P.L. 480 II = Public Law 480 (Food for Peace), Title II Grant

P = Preliminary

REFERENCES

[1] Library of Congress, Federal Research Division, *Egypt: A Country Study*, accessible at [http://lcweb2.loc.gov/frd/cs/egtoc.html].

[2] Napoleon invaded Egypt in 1798. The British invaded in 1882 and established a de facto protectorate. They would keep a sizeable military force in Egypt until the 1950s.

[3] M.E. Yapp, *The Near East Since the First World War*, London: Longman, 1991, p. 409.

[4] During the Yemeni Civil War of 1963 through 1967, Egypt reportedly used mustard bombs in support of South Yemen against Saudi-backed royalist troops in North Yemen. See Federation of American Scientists (FAS) Egypt Special Weapons Guide, available online at [http://www.fas.org/nuke/guide/egypt/index.html].

[5] One of the Brotherhood activists arrested was Sayyid Qutb, a writer and former government official whose writings provided a philosophical foundation for Islamic radicalism. Qutb spent years in prison and, after being briefly released in 1964, was rearrested and hanged in 1966. See Daniel Benjamin and Steven Simon, *The Age of Sacred Terror* (New York: Random House, 1966), p. 62.

[6] A copy of the 1979 Egyptian-Israeli peace treaty is available online from MidEast Web Gateway at [http://www.mideastweb.org/ egyptisraeltreaty.htm].

[7] The MFO is an independent (non-UN) peacekeeping mission, created as a result of the 1979 peace treaty. The MFO's expenses are funded in equal parts by Egypt, Israel, and the United States with additional contributions from Germany, Japan, and Switzerland. For more information on the MFO, see [http://www.mfo.org/Default.asp?bhcp=1].

[8] In 1980, the Constitution was amended to allow the President to run for an unlimited number of terms, rather than one as was stipulated in the 1971 Constitution. An English language version of the Constitution is available at [http://www.parliament.gov.eg/EPA/ en/sections.jsp?typeID=1 and levelid=54 and parentlevel=6 and levelno=2].

[9] "Clearing the Path For Scion of Egypt," *Washington Post*, March 10, 2006.

[10] "Gamal Mubarak Says He Has No Intention to Run for Presidency to Succeed His Father," *Associated Press*, January 24, 2006.

[11] In 1986, President Mubarak called on the military to put down riots in Cairo, sparked by the protests of Central Security conscripts who were angry with their low pay and poor working conditions. The military also

was deployed in 1977 during riots over a temporary reduction in food subsidies.

[12] Imad Harb, "The Egyptian Military in Politics: Disengagement or Accommodation?," *The Middle East Journal*, Washington, spring 2003. vol. 57, Issue 2, p. 269.

[13] The NDP's website is available at [http://www.ndp.org.eg/index_en.htm].

[14] According to Egyptian law #47 (1972), the Egyptian Justice Ministry controls the pay and promotion scales for judges, thereby making many judges hesitant to rule against the government out of concern for their own careers and livelihoods.

[15] The Muslim Brotherhood is generally considered as the parent organization for Brotherhood branches throughout the Middle East region. Former Brotherhood members also have formed a number of radical and extremist off-shoots, including Hamas. See Gilles Kippel, *Jihad: The Trail of Political Islam* (Cambridge: Harvard University Press, 2002), p. 151.

[16] John Walsh, "Egypt's Muslim Brotherhood," *Harvard International Review* (Cambridge: winter 2003), vol. 24, issue 4, p. 32.

[17] Human Rights Watch, "Margins of Repression: State Limits on Non-Governmental Organization Activism," July 2005. Available online at [http://hrw.org/english/docs/2005/ 07/04/egypt11217.htm].

[18] In August 2002, the Bush Administration rejected an Egyptian request for economic assistance as part of the FY2002 Supplemental Act (P.L. 107-206) in order to protest the arrest and conviction of Ibrahim. The House Appropriations Committee had already considered and rejected an amendment to the FY2002 supplemental appropriations bill (H.R. 4775) to provide $134 million in economic assistance for Egypt. The proposed funds for Egypt would have maintained the three-to-two ratio of aid to Israel and Egypt; Israel was slated to receive $200 million in ESF in the supplemental bill.

[19] Egypt was readmitted to the Arab League in 1989 during a period of renewed international interest in Arab-Israeli peace.

[20] In June 2005, Egypt and Israel signed a long-delayed $2.5 billion agreement on sales of Egyptian natural gas to Israel. Under the terms of the agreement, Israeli state-owned utility Israel Electric Corp will purchase gas from Eastern Mediterranean Gas (EMG), a private Israeli-Egyptian firm. A pipeline from Egypt to Israel is being built.

[21] For a summary of the Israeli-Egyptian border agreement, see [http://www.washington institute.org/templateC05.php?CID=2374].

[22] For a report on instances of anti-Semitism in Egypt, see the Anti-Defamation League's website at [http://www.adl.org/main_Arab_World/default.htm].

[23] "Friction Over Egypt's Role in Regional Issues Strains Relations With U.S.," *Washington Post*, May 25, 2003.

[24] In helping to rebuild Afghanistan, Egypt built a field hospital at Bagram Air Base. It has declined to send peacekeeping forces there.

[25] "Mubarak insists Palestinian, Iraqi Solutions Linked," *Washington Times*, April 14, 2004.

[26] See CRS Report RL32105, Post-War Iraq: Foreign Contributions to Training, Peacekeeping, and Reconstruction, by Jeremy M. Sharp and Christopher M. Blanchard.

[27] Over a period of three decades following the 1952 revolution, there were a number of defections from the Muslim Brotherhood, which had chosen to work within the Egyptian political system after being crushed by former President Nasser. In the early 1970's, radicals broke away from the Brotherhood and formed Jamaah Islamiya (Islamic Group) and Al Jihad.

[28] Experts note that Jamaah and Al Jihad members who fled Egypt never renounced the use of violence against the Egyptian government, as both groups ultimately merged with Al Qaeda. Ayman Al-Zawahiri, the leader of Al Jihad, has long been known as Al Qaeda's "second-in-command" to Osama bin Laden. See "Jihad Militant Leader Calls for Change to Non-violence," *Dow Jones Newswires*, February 6, 2000.

[29] On March 23, 2006, Egyptian Prime Minister Ahmad Nazif announced to Parliament that the government would abrogate the 25-year old Emergency Laws and replace them with new anti-terror legislation. At this time, it is unclear how such proposed legislation would differ from existing law.

[30] For a list of USAID's democracy and good governance programs in Egypt, see the USAID website at [http://www.usaid.gov/locations/ asia_near_east/countries/egypt/egypt.html].

[31] It was recently reported that, for the first time, MEPI has issued several small grants to political activists and human rights organizations in Egypt. See "Tentative Steps: Democracy Drive By America Meets Reality in Egypt," *Wall Street Journal*, April 11, 2005.

[32] Conference report (H.Rept. 108-792) to accompany H.R. 4818, November 20, 2004.

[33] It is estimated that the public sector in Egypt still employs nearly a third of the population. See American Chamber of Commerce in Egypt, Egypt Key

Economic Indicators, online at [http://www.amcham.org.eg/BSAC/EconomicIndicators/EcIndicators.asp].

[34] In 1977, there were mass demonstrations throughout Egypt following the government's decision to cut public subsidies on flour, rice, and cooking oil in order to demonstrate to international lenders, such as the International Monetary Fund, that Egypt was making necessary macroeconomic reforms. Over the course of two days, several hundred were killed and hundreds more arrested, as the Egyptian army was called into the streets to restore order.

[35] The European Union is Egypt's largest multilateral trading partner.

[36] U.S. Department of Commerce, *Egypt Country Commercial Guide FY2004*, October 2003.

[37] See CRS Report RS22002, Qualified Industrial Zones in Jordan: A Model for Promoting Peace and Development in the Middle East?, by Mary Jane Bolle, Alfred Prados, and Jeremy Sharp.

[38] Egypt's Minister of Finance, Yusef Boutros-Ghali, hails from a prominent Christian family.

[39] According to the report, an estimated 97% of Egyptian women who have ever been |married had undergone FGM. See U.S. State Department, Country Report on Human Rights Practices: Egypt, February 2005. Available at [http://www.state.gov/g/drl/rls/hrrpt/ 2004/41720.htm].

[40] Human Rights Watch, "Divorced from Justice: Women's Unequal Access to Divorce in Egypt,"June 2004. Available online at [http://hrw.org/reports/2004/egypt1204/].

[41] On September 14, 1990, then President George H.W. Bush asked Congress to transfer Egypt's $6.7 billion military debt from the Federal Financing Bank of the Treasury Department to the Department of Defense, and to cancel the debt. President Bush was rewarding Egypt for cooperating with the Desert Shield operations against the Iraqi invasion of Kuwait and was relieving Egypt of part of its debt repayment burden. Section 592 of P.L. 101-513, signed into law on November 5, 1990, provided for canceling Egypt's military debt to the United States.

[42] This practice is known as "extraordinary rendition." "US Ships Al Qaeda Suspects to Arab States," *Christian Science Monitor*, July 26, 2002.

[43] "Abductee Still Jailed, Lawyer Says; Egyptian Cleric Was Seized in Milan in Alleged CIA Action," *Washington Post*, July 21, 2005.

[44] Ibid.

[45] Egypt has periodically received supplemental aid. The FY2003 Emergency Supplemental Appropriations Act (P.L. 108-11) included $300 million in

ESF for Egypt, which could be used to cover the costs of up to $2 billion in loan guarantees. The loan guarantees are to be issued over three years.

[46] See [http://www.gao.gov/new.items/d06437.pdf].

[47] Conference report (H.Rept. 109-265) on H.R. 3057, Foreign Operations, Export Financing, and Related Programs Appropriations Act, 2006, November 2, 2005.

In: Politics and Economics of the Middle East
Editors: W. Evans & D.J. Harris
ISBN: 978-1-60456-719-9

Chapter 3

EGYPT-UNITED STATES RELATIONS*

Jeremy M. Sharp

ABSTRACT

U.S.-Egyptian relations are aimed at maintaining regional stability, improving bilateral relations, continuing military cooperation, and sustaining the March 1979 Egyptian-Israeli peace treaty. Experience gained from Egyptian-U.S. joint military exercises proved valuable in easing coordination during the February 1991 Desert Storm operation to reverse Iraqi aggression against Kuwait. Egypt is seen by U.S. policy makers as a leader and moderating influence among many Arab, African, Islamic, and Third World states.

Among the current issues in U.S.-Egyptian relations are a shared concern about international terrorism. Egypt can claim some experience with the subject, having defeated domestic Islamic terrorists intent on overthrowing the Egyptian government. The two countries disagree over the speed and depth, but not the need for some of Egypt's economic reforms. Egypt and the United States agree on the importance of the Egyptian-Israeli peace treaty, the need to continue current Arab-Israel peace talks, and the need for regional stability. The two nations agree on Egypt's need to introduce democratic reforms in Egypt, although critics argue that Egypt is not moving quickly enough toward full democracy or in improving the human rights situation. The United States has provided Egypt with an annual

* Excerpted from CRS Report IB93087, dated June 15, 2005.

average of over $2 billion in economic and military foreign assistance since 1979. The United States will reduce Economic Support Funds (ESF) to about $400 million per year by 2008 in keeping with a plan to reduce aid to Israel. The Administration requested $575 million in economic grants and $1.3 billion in military grants for FY2004 for Egypt.

Egypt in Brief

Area = 385,229 sq. miles (equal to Wisc., Mich., Ohio, Ind., Ill., Ky, and Tenn. combined)
Population = 74.7 million (2003 est.)
Pop. Growth rate = 1.88% per yr. (2003)
Religion = 94% Muslim, 6% Christian
Labor Force = 17.4 million (1996)
Unemployment = 12% (2001)
Literacy Rate = 57.7% (2003)
GDP = $92 billion (2000)
GDP per cap. = $1420 (2000)
GDP Growth Rate = 4% (2000)
Inflation = 4.3% (2002)
Exports = $7 billion (2000)
Imports = $15.2 billion (2000)
Gov't. Revenues = $17.4 billion (1995 est.)
Gov't. Expend. = $18.8 billion (1995 est.)
Foreign Debt = $30.5 billion (2000)

Most Recent Developments

On May 25, 2005, the Egyptian public approved (in a public referendum) the amending of Article 76 of the Egyptian constitution to permit direct and pluralistic elections for the presidency. Some members of the opposition boycotted the referendum, calling the amendment insufficient in that it sets difficult requirements for independent candidates to run in future elections, does not guarantee freedom of assembly for political parties, and does not provide for independent judicial oversight of elections. The ruling National Democratic Party has called the approval of the amendment a step forward for Egyptian democracy.

Over the past several weeks, Egyptian authorities have arrested hundreds of Muslim Brotherhood protestors, including several of the groups leaders. In addition, activists from the *Kifaya* ("Enough") movement have accused Egyptian police officers of sexually assaulting female protesters on the day of the constitutional referendum.

Background and Analysis

Egypt-U.S. Relations

Historical Background

The United States endorsed the 1952 Revolutionary Command Council military coup led by Gamal Abd al-Nasir that overthrew King Faruk and the monarchy. The military reformers appeared to have Egypt's best interests at heart and, although not pro-Western, at least were not pro-Soviet. But, U.S.-Egyptian relations soured when the Colonels turned to the Soviets and the Czechs in 1955 for military training and equipment after the West refused defense assistance. That same year, Egypt, Yugoslavia, and India led the third world nations at the Bandung Conference in establishing the non-aligned movement independent of the Eastern and Western blocs, an act that further alienated Egypt and the United States.

In July 1956, following a U.S.-British decision to retract an offer of economic assistance and help for the Aswan Dam, Egypt nationalized the Suez Canal Company to use its revenues to finance the dam. (Egypt owned the Suez Canal, but the British-French company operated the Canal, and collected the revenues from which it paid a small rent to Egypt.) In late October 1956, Israel, France, and Britain invaded Egypt, Israel to stop Palestinian guerrillas from using Egypt as a base for operations against Israel, and France and Britain to occupy the Canal. President Eisenhower persuaded the three invaders to withdraw from Egypt in early 1957, which improved U.S.-Egyptian relations briefly. (According to persistent but unconfirmed reports, Eisenhower's persuasion included threats to cut U.S. aid to Israel and to withdraw support for the British and French currencies.)

Many in the West believed Egypt fomented the 1958 anti-Western unrest in Jordan and Lebanon and coup in Iraq that led to the U.S. intervention in Lebanon and the British intervention in Jordan, and relations between Egypt and the United States remained strained. Egypt broke formal diplomatic relations during the June 1967 Arab-Israeli war following Egyptian charges that the United States had provided direct assistance to Israel. Anwar al-Sadat became President of Egypt upon the death of al-Nasir in September 1970, and it was al-Sadat who expelled

Soviet advisors in July 1972, an act that some in the United States considered a harbinger of better Egyptian-U.S. relations. Egypt attacked Israeli forces occupying the Sinai Peninsula and Syria attacked the Golan Heights in October 1973. In November 1973, Egypt and the United States restored diplomatic relations, and in December, the two countries participated in the Geneva peace conference. U.S. Secretary of State Henry Kissinger's so-called shuttle diplomacy led to Egyptian-Israeli and Syrian-Israeli disengagement agreements in 1974 and a second set of Egyptian-Israeli disengagements in 1975. The United States resumed economic aid to Egypt in 1975 after an eight-year hiatus.

The United States endorsed Egyptian President Anwar al-Sadat's dramatic and courageous trip to Jerusalem in November 1977, and President Jimmy Carter assisted in the Israeli-Egyptian peace negotiations at Camp David in September 1978 and the Egyptian-Israeli peace treaty of March 1979. The United States organized the peacekeeping regime along the Egyptian-Israeli border, the Multi-National Force and Observers (MFO), and maintains a rotating infantry battalion in the force. President al-Sadat was assassinated in October 1981 and was replaced by Husni Mubarak.

U.S. Interests in Egypt

A primary U.S. interest in continued good relations with Egypt is to capitalize on Egypt's historic leadership role in the Arab world. Often, other Arab states look to Egypt to initiate action or set an example on regional problems. For example, in the past, other Arab states followed the Egyptian lead in turning to the Soviet Union for weapons, in nationalizing foreign interests, in land reform programs, in introducing democratic institutions, and in many other areas. In a current example, the United States appreciates Egypt's active opposition to terrorism and welcomes Egyptian influence in convincing other Arab states to cooperate in the war on terrorism.

Another U.S. interest in good relations with Egypt is to sustain Egypt's moderate voice in Arab councils, and in some cases to rely upon Egypt to persuade less moderate Arab states of the wisdom of compromise. President Mubarak serves as a conduit carrying the various peace proposals among the Syrian, Lebanese, U.S., Israeli, Jordanian, and Palestinian negotiators and has counseled leaders of Libya, Sudan, and Iraq.

A third U.S. interest is to maintain the Egyptian-Israeli peace treaty.

A fourth reason for maintaining good U.S.-Egyptian relations is defense cooperation in opposing threats or aggression against regional friends, as was demonstrated in Egypt's active participation in the 1991 liberation of Kuwait and in Egypt's military cooperation with U.S. forces in the 2003 invasion of Iraq. Cooperation between U.S. and Egyptian armed forces in joint military exercises over the previous decade (the "Bright Star" exercises) prepared the way for the 1990-1991 defense of the Arabian Peninsula ("Operation Desert Storm"). The most recent Bright Star exercise took place in October and November 2001.

The United States, Egypt, and Israel

Beginning after World War II, the United States opposed all aspects of Egypt's belligerency toward Israel, including military posturing, arms purchases, the economic boycott, use of Soviet military advisors, attempts to exclude Israel from international fora, providing haven for guerrilla attacks against Israel, refusal to negotiate, and other gestures or positions considered unfriendly. As a result of Egypt's cooperation with the 1974-1975 disengagement agreements, President al-Sadat's 1977 trip to Jerusalem, the 1978 Camp David agreements, and the 1979 Egyptian-Israeli peace treaty, Egypt's policy toward Israel changed from belligerency to cooperation, and U.S. policy toward Egypt changed as well. At first, U.S. friendly gestures toward Egypt appeared to be intended as guarantees for Israeli security and the Egyptian-Israeli peace treaty, but in the 25 years since the peace treaty signing, U.S.-Egyptian relations have evolved, moving beyond the limited connection to Israel and toward an independent bilateral friendship. The United States provides foreign assistance, cooperates in economic development, shares military equipment and technology, participates in joint military exercises, and includes Egypt among its advisors and confidants on Middle Eastern affairs.

Role of Congress in Egyptian-U.S. Relations

Congress typically earmarks foreign assistance for Egypt in the foreign aid appropriation bills. (See table 1, and section on Issues in Egyptian-U.S. Relations below. The annual earmark includes a statement that Egypt should undertake economic reforms in addition to reforms taken in previous years. The proviso appears in the foreign operations appropriations act for FY2004, P.L. 108-199.

During June 2004 hearings, some Members of Congress questioned Egypt's need for U.S. military assistance, the speed with which Egypt was implementing economic and political reforms, and the absence of Egyptian support for the U.S.

presence in Iraq. During the July debate on the foreign operations appropriations bill, H.R. 4818, House Members voted down an amendment that would have converted U.S. military assistance to Egypt to economic assistance. The issue surfaced again in February 2005 discussions of aid to Egypt.

Issues in Egyptian-U.S. Relations

Iraq

Egypt advised against the March 2003 U.S. intervention in Iraq and continues to question an extended U.S. occupation. In July 2003, the Egyptian President's office issued a statement praising the formation of the interim governing council in Iraq and repeated the hope that Iraq would draft a new constitution, hold elections, and quickly install a permanent Iraqi government.[1] Egypt informed the United States that it would not participate in any international security arrangements unless such peacekeeping operations were under United Nations auspices.[2] In the past, Egypt did cooperate with U.S.-led international peacekeeping efforts, such as the Kuwaiti liberation, Somalia, Afghanistan, and the Balkans. Egypt allows U.S. overflights and Suez Canal passages in support of the U.S. military efforts in Iraq.

Arab-Israel Peace Process

In 1977, President Anwar al-Sadat announced that he would go to Jerusalem to discuss peace with the Israelis. Israeli Prime Minister Menachem Begin extended an invitation, al-Sadat accepted, and the visit led to the 1978 Camp David meetings and the March 1979 Egyptian-Israeli peace treaty. Egypt benefitted from the peace treaty by redirecting resources from defense to development, but Egypt suffered by being ostracized by other Arab states for six years.

President Mubarak has acted as a broker, advisor, messenger, and arbitrator for the continuing peace talks. Mubarak offered Cairo as a venue for the talks, offered compromise positions on returning 415 Palestinian deportees in Lebanon in December 1992, encouraged other Arab nations to continue the talks, and endorsed the Declaration of Principles signed by the PLO and Israel in Washington on September 13, 1993. Egypt hosted the September 4, 1999 Sharm al-Shaykh signing of an Israeli-Palestinian agreement for implementing past commitments, and President Mubarak was in contact with the Palestinian and Israeli negotiators at the Camp David summit in late July 2000. President Mubarak hosted the meetings between then Secretary of State Madeleine Albright and Palestine President Arafat at Sharm al-Shaykh on October 4, 2000, and also hosted the Arab League meetings that began on October 21. In November 2000, Egypt recalled its ambassador to Tel Aviv to protest Israeli actions against the Palestinian demonstrators in the intifadah, the uprising against Israeli occupation that began in late September. On April 3, 2002, President Mubarak cut all contacts with Israel except those dealing with the Palestine issue; the President was protesting Israel's treatment of the Palestinians and the Israeli re-occupation of Palestinian areas. On June 3, 2003, Mubarak hosted a meeting of U.S. and Arab leaders in preparation for the June 4 meeting in Jordan of President Bush, Israeli Prime Minister Sharon, and Palestinian Prime Minister Abbas. Egypt hosted the February 8, 2005 meeting between Israeli Prime Minister Sharon and Palestinian President Abbas at Sharm al-Shaykh, and has invited Palestinian leaders to Egypt in March to discuss extending the cease-fire and the Israeli withdrawal from Gaza.

Relations with Israel

Many in Israel, and some in the U.S. Congress, interpreted the letter attached to the 1979 Egypt-Israel peace treaty as an Egyptian commitment to negotiate on behalf of the Palestinians, or at least advise Palestinian negotiators to reach a Palestinian-Israeli peace treaty. But, it was never Egypt's intention or place to negotiate on behalf of the Palestinians, regardless of what the Israelis may have believed or wished. Those Israelis and Members of Congress who claimed that Egypt reneged on a commitment cited the Egyptian "failure" is part of the Egyptian "cold peace" with Israel. Israel also complains that Egypt has not established the close economic, political, and diplomatic relations that Israel envisioned would emerge from the peace treaty. Despite the recent Egyptian-Israeli cooperation on the peace process, relations were strained in early 1995 when Egypt pushed for an Israeli signature on the Nuclear Non-Proliferation Treaty, and remained strained following August 1995 disclosures that Israeli soldiers killed Egyptian prisoners of war and civilians during the 1956 and 1967 wars. Relations improved when President Mubarak attended the funeral of Israeli Prime Minister Rabin in November 1995. Relations declined further after Prime Minister Netanyahu's election in May 1996, because Egyptians believed Netanyahu slowed the peace process, but relations improved after the May 17, 1999, election of Ehud Barak as Prime Minister of Israel. Egypt withdrew its ambassador to Tel Aviv in November 2000 to protest Israeli actions against the Palestinians. Prime Minister Ariel Sharon sent two envoys to Cairo shortly after his February 6, 2001, election, reportedly to request the return of the Egyptian ambassador and to seek Egyptian assistance in moderating Arab League reactions to Israeli policies. Egypt announced that it would return its ambassador to Tel Aviv at the February 8, 2005 Palestinian-Israeli meeting at Sharm al-Shaykh.

Human Rights

According to State Department human rights reports, there is "convincing evidence" that the Egyptian police use torture to extract confessions, and detain suspects without charge or trial. Freedom of assembly has been constricted because the government fears violence associated with some public demonstrations. Many newspapers are partially government-owned and tend to follow the government line, although even some government-owned newspapers will voice anti-government opinions. Journalists oppose the 1995 law that places a greater burden on the press in libel cases, although the two-year jail sentence for libel was repealed in March 2004. According to the State Department reports, some judges are becoming more independent and are deciding cases against the government, but cases against the Islamic militants were held in military courts where the government prevailed and opportunity for appeal was nil. There appears to be little restriction on freedom of religion, speech, movement, occupation, or trade union association. Egypt has executed more than 60 of the 90 Islamists sentenced to death since 1992.

In June 2003, the Peoples' Assembly approved a bill creating a National Council for Human Rights. The Council, formed in January 2004, consists of 25 members, headed by former U.N. Secretary-General Butrus Butrus Ghali, all appointed by President Mubarak. The Council is to survey and document human rights conditions in Egypt and to coordinate human rights activities among other Egyptian human rights organizations. President Mubarak created the National Council for Women by decree in February 2000.

Saad al-Din Ibrahim

One human rights case that drew international attention involved Saad al-Din Ibrahim, a sociology professor at American University of Cairo and a critic of the Egyptian government's human rights and democracy record. Ibrahim, who also holds U.S. citizenship, was arrested for defaming Egypt by describing discrimination against Copts and for not reporting a foreign donation from the European Union for a voter education project. Egyptian officials closed Ibrahim's Ibn Khaldun Center for Development Studies and arrested some 20 of its staff.

Ibrahim was convicted and sentenced to seven years on May 21, 2001, but the conviction was overturned on appeal in February 2002. A second trial completed on July 29, 2002, produced the same result — conviction and a seven-year sentence. On December 3, 2002, the Court of Cassation overturned the second verdict and announced that the Court of Cassation would conduct a new trial. On March 18, 2003, the Court of Cassation acquitted Ibrahim of the charges.

Ayman Nur

(alternate spelling Nour) On January 29, 2005, Egyptian authorities arrested Ayman Nur, a member of the Peoples' Assembly, allegedly for forging names on petitions required to get his political party authorized in October 2004. Nur was a co-founder of the liberal, secular Ghad (Tomorrow) party that advocates constitutional reforms to open the presidential election to multiple candidates, limit presidents to two five-year terms, and other democratic reforms. Nur was released from jail on March 12, and announced that he would be a candidate for president in the elections scheduled for autumn 2005. Nur's supporters claim he is a target of the government for advocating reforms, but his opponents claim that the forgery charges are valid, and that Nur is a minor political figure who is using his new found fame for political gain.

Coptic Christians

The Department of State Human Rights report for 2002 and the International Religious Freedom Report for 2002 point out that there is no official government policy of discrimination against the 4.5 million Coptic Christians in Egypt but that some Egyptian people do discriminate against the Copts. From 1992 through 1997, Islamic terrorists attacked Coptic churches, Coptic-owned businesses, and Coptic villagers in southern Egypt because the Islamists believed the Christians were a conduit for foreign influence. In December 2003, President Mubarak recognized the Coptic Christmas, January 6, as an Egyptian national holiday.

Democracy

In keeping with a goal of the 1952 revolution, Egypt has been moving away from the totalitarian regimes of the monarchy and the early years of the Revolutionary Command Council toward democracy, although some would argue that the progress toward democracy has been slow. Under Egypt's parliamentary system, the President appoints the cabinet, who in turn draft and submit legislation to the legislature, the People's Assembly (lower house) and the Shura

Council (upper house). The People's Assembly debates legislation proposed by Government Ministries and calls for amendments to government-sponsored bills but rarely initiates its own bills. The Shura Council is an advisory body, offering reports and recommendations on important subjects, but the Shura Council does not introduce, consider, or vote on legislation.

In the People's Assembly, 444 members are elected and ten are appointed; 176 members of the Shura Council are elected and 88 are appointed. One half of the elected members of the People's Assembly and the Shura Council must be farmers and laborers (Art. 87 and Art. 196 of the Constitution). People's Assembly members are elected for five-year terms, and Shura Council members for six-year terms (one-half the Council members are elected every three years). The National Democratic Party (NDP) won 388 seats in the October-November 2000 People's Assembly elections, independents won 37 seats, (17 of whom were Muslim Brotherhood supporters), the Wafd Party won 7, Tagammu won 6, the Nasserites won 3, and al-Ahrar won one seat. NDP members won 74 of the 88 seats contested in the May/June 2001 Shura Council election, with independents winning the other 14 seats. Religious parties, such as the Muslim Brotherhood, are banned.

Some observers fret over President Mubarak's failure to name a vice president and fear that there would not be an orderly transition if something should incapacitate the President. Under Egyptian law, the Speaker of the Peoples' Assembly becomes the interim president until the Peoples' Assembly can nominate a new President and the name can be submitted to the people in a referendum. A vice president plays no direct role in the transition.

Political Reforms

Led by political reformers at the 2002 National Democratic Party convention, Egypt began implementing some political reforms, such as ending the state security courts, some military decrees issued under the emergency laws, and hard labor sentences. The 2003 and 2004 NDP conventions considered more reforms, such as ending the emergency laws entirely, calling for direct election of the President, introducing proportional representation, allowing more political parties to operate by changing the political party committee that approves the formation of new parties, and others. But political reform is becoming a contest between an "old guard" linked to tradition and deliberate change and young reformers who want rapid, far reaching change. On February 26, 2005, President Husni Mubarak announced that he would seek a constitutional amendment to replace the current nominating and referendum process with a direct election for the office of president.

Economic Issues

Egypt comprises 387,000 square miles (about the size of Wisconsin, Michigan, Illinois, Indiana, Ohio, Kentucky, and Tennessee combined), but of that total only 3% is arable (or 11,600 sq. mi., a little less than the size of Maryland). There are 65 million people, growing at a rate of 1.89% per year. Cairo is estimated to contain between 12 and 20 million people, making it one of the most populous cities on Earth. Forty-two percent of the people are engaged in agriculture, but Egypt cannot feed itself and must import two-thirds of its food. The official unemployment rate for 2000 was estimated at 12%, but some economists estimate the figure may be higher. Egypt needs to find as many as 600,000 jobs each year to employ the country's high schools and college graduates. Estimates of per capita income range from $1420 up to $3,900. There are 1 million Egyptians working in Europe and another 1 million in the Persian Gulf, according to Egyptian officials.

Economic Reforms

The transition from a centrally controlled socialist economy to a free market economy has created difficult decisions for the Egyptian government, and hardships for the Egyptian people. Egypt signed agreements with the International Monetary Fund (IMF) and the International Bank for Reconstruction and Development (IBRD) in 1991 stipulating that Egypt implement a series of economic reforms in order to qualify for a structural adjustment loan and for debt reductions. Among the IMF/IBRD reforms are eliminating subsidies and liberalizing prices on consumer goods, eliminating export/import non-tariff barriers, privatizing Egyptian government-owned industries, reducing budget deficits, deregulating some industries, implementing fiscal and monetary reforms, and developing human resources.

Since 1991, Egypt has eliminated subsidies on essential consumer goods, such as sugar, cooking oil, and dairy products — only the subsidy on bread remains — and allowed other prices to rise to world market levels. Egypt reduced the budget deficit, reduced many non-tariff barriers, and deregulated some industries (cement and fertilizer, for example). Since 1994, Egypt has sold 119 government-owned companies of the 314 targeted for privatization. The Egyptian government has contracted public credit and expanded private credit, floated the Pound, increased taxes, and witnessed a decrease in inflation from 22.5% in 1988 to 3.67% in 1998 (but creeping back up to 4.3% in 2000). The IMF and the IBRD have convinced Egypt's creditors to reduce Egypt's $30 billion external debt by 15%, and have targeted another 15% reduction. The reforms have placed Egypt firmly on the road to a free market economy. (See CRS Report RL30686, *Egypt's Economy: U.S. Interests and Market Reforms*, by Jeannie Sowers, September 18, 2000.)

At the National Democratic Party convention in September 2004, the Ministers of Finance, Investment, and Industry and Trade recommended reforms to be considered by the party and the Government, including revised tax codes, tariff and custom reform, new banking laws, more rapid privatization, government financial transparency, adopting modern business practices, and others.

Previous Issues

EgyptAir Flight 990

On October 31, 1999, EgyptAir flight 990 en route from New York to Cairo crashed shortly after takeoff, killing 271 passengers and crew. Investigators reported that there was no evidence of mechanical failures or explosions on the plane but that a co-pilot was heard repeating a prayer prior to sending the plane into a steep dive that resulted in the crash. The implication of the investigators' report was that the co-pilot purposely had committed suicide and killed the passengers and crew. The National Transportation Safety Board (NTSB) issued its final report on March 21, 2002, concluding that the co-pilot purposely crashed the plane but did not offer an explanation for the copilot's actions. Egyptian officials rejected the NTSB report because they viewed blaming the co-pilot as an insult to Egypt and EgyptAir.

Militant Islamic Movement in Egypt

The Muslim Brotherhood was founded in Egypt in 1928 to turn Egypt away from secularism and toward an Islamic government based on Sharia (religious) law and Muslim principles.[3] The Muslim Brotherhood exists as a religious charitable and educational institution, having been banned as a political party in 1954. But, offshoots of the Brotherhood, the Jemaah Islamiyah (Islamic Group) and Egyptian Islamic Jihad, were more militant and used violence in an attempt to overthrow the government. Both were implicated in the 1981 assassination of President Anwar al-Sadat, and in the attacks beginning in 1992 against foreign, and therefore in their view anti-Islamic, influences, Coptic Christians, tourists and tourist sites, and the police. Between October 1992 and November 1997, the confrontation between the police and the Islamic militants killed 1,200, 90 of whom were foreign tourists. The Islamic militant forces called a cease-fire in 1997 and since have been relatively quiet. President Mubarak and other Egyptian officials claimed that the Islamic reformers were financed, trained, and directed by Iranian and Sudanese religious militants and returning Egyptian volunteers from the Soviet-Afghan war.

Some have expressed concern that the Egyptian police did not conform to international human rights standards in pursuing and bringing to justice Islamists suspected of terror attacks. Ayman al-Zawahiri, leader of the Jihad group, Muhammad Atif, and other Egyptians who escaped from Egypt to avoid arrest have been associated with Osama bin Laden. The press reported that Muhammad Atif was killed during a mid-November 2001 U.S. bombing attack in Afghanistan.

Shaikh Umar Abd al-Rahman

Shaikh (an honorific title for a learned religious or tribal leader) Umar Abd al-Rahman, a cleric and Islamic scholar associated with the Jemaah movement, was arrested six times in Egypt on various charges, and served prison time although he was acquitted of involvement in the al-Sadat assassination. In 1989, Abd al-Rahman went to Sudan, where, one year later, he acquired a U.S. visitors visa despite his name being on a list of undesirables. On June 24, 1993, the FBI arrested eight men in New York suspected of plotting to assassinate several prominent people and to bomb several targets in New York. Reportedly, the accused were associated with Shaikh Abd al-Rahman and his New Jersey mosque. Abd al-Rahman and 14 others were indicted for conspiracy in the assassination and bombing schemes on August 25, 1993. The United States rejected an Egyptian request for Abd al-Rahman's extradition on July 3, 1993, and he went on trial with nine other men on January 9, 1995. The trial ended on October 1, 1995, with guilty verdicts for all, including a life sentence for Abd al-Rahman. Some observers speculated that the United States served Egypt's best interests by refusing extradition and trying Shaikh Abd al-Rahman in U.S. courts because the Shaikh may have become a martyr and rallying symbol for the militant Islamists at an Egyptian show trial.

U.S. Foreign Assistance to Egypt

Some Members of Congress hold that U.S. relations with and assistance for Egypt guarantees continued Egyptian adherence to the 1979 Egypt-Israel peace treaty, thereby helping to secure Israel. Other Members of Congress believe that U.S. assistance for and good relations with Egypt extend U.S. influence in Egypt and among Egypt's moderate Arab, Islamic, and African friends, which contributes to regional stability. And, some Members of Congress believe U.S. aid to Egypt ensures U.S. access to the region's oil reserves, trade opportunities, or military bases. For these and other reasons, a majority of the Members of Congress approve aid to Egypt. Members opposed to U.S. aid to Egypt often base their opposition on their belief that Egypt has failed to establish the close economic, political, and cultural relations with Israel expected after the 1979 peace treaty, or because they believe that the U.S. is financing the wrong kinds of projects. In June 1997, a subcommittee of the Senate appropriations committee dropped the earmark for Egypt because, in the subcommittee's judgement, Egypt was hindering the peace process and Egypt was improving its relations with Libya, thereby encouraging the Libyan quest for chemical weapons and the Libyan programs to assist terrorists. The Senate agreed later to restore the earmark.

In March 2001, Members of Congress reportedly considered legislation to cut military assistance to Egypt because Egypt recalled its ambassador to Israel. An amendment offered on July 15, 2004, to the FY2005 foreign operations bill (H.R. 4818) would have reduced U.S. military aid to Egypt by $570 million and increased economic aid by the same amount, but the amendment failed by a vote of 131 to 287.

U.S. Economic Assistance

From 1993 through 1998, Egypt received from the United States $815 million in Economic Support Funds (ESF) annually, $200 million of which was designated for the Commodity Import Program, and an equal amount was direct transfer not associated with any specific program. In the past, Egypt also received food aid, but the food aid has been reduced in recent years. In January 1998, Israeli officials negotiated with the United States to reduce economic aid and increase military aid over a 10-year period. A similar formula for reducing economic aid was applied to Egypt but Egypt did not receive an increase in military assistance. Economic aid has dropped in annual $40 million increments from $815 million in FY1998 to $535 million requested for FY2005.

In early January 2002, the United States agreed to release $655 million in FY2002 ESF and $304 million in funds in the foreign aid "pipeline" to help Egypt overcome economic problems exacerbated by the fall in tourism after September 11, 2001. The House Appropriations Committee considered but rejected an amendment to the FY2002 supplemental appropriations bill (H.R. 4775) to provide $134 million in economic assistance for Egypt. The proposed funds for

Egypt would have maintained the three-to-two ratio of aid to Israel and Egypt; Israel was slated to receive $200 million in ESF in the supplemental bill.

The President's March 25, 2003, request to Congress for supplemental appropriations included $300 million in Economic Support Funds (ESF) and $2 billion in loan guarantees for Egypt. The President also announced that $379.6 million in Commodity Import Program funds and other programs in the pipeline would be converted to cash grant. The loan guarantees are to be issued over three years, and Egypt will pay the fees and subsidy costs. The aid to Egypt was included in P.L. 108-11 of April 16, 2003, the FY2003 supplemental appropriations.

U.S. Military Assistance

The United States has provided $12.992 billion in military grants, and $10.2 million in International Military Education and Training funds over the past 10 years, an average of just over $1.3 billion per year.

On September 14, 1990, then President George H.W. Bush asked Congress to transfer Egypt's $6.7 billion military debt from the Federal Financing Bank of the Treasury Department to the Department of Defense, and to cancel the debt. President Bush was rewarding Egypt for cooperating with the Desert Shield operations against the Iraqi invasion of Kuwait and was relieving Egypt of part of its debt repayment burden. Section 592 of P.L. 101-513, signed into law on November 5, 1990, provided for canceling Egypt's military debt to the United States.

Military Cooperation

U.S.-Egyptian Military Industrial Cooperation

In addition to the FMF purchases and excess defense articles, Egypt co-produces the U.S. M1A1 "Abrams" tank under a 1988 Memorandum of Understanding. Beginning in mid-1992, Egypt started assembling M1A1 tank components imported from the United States. Egypt manufactured about 40% and imported 60% of the components for the 555 tanks produced. Egypt also repairs and overhauls U.S. M60-A3 and M60-A1 tanks, trucks, jeeps, and armored personnel carriers, and is involved in a rehabilitation program to re-fit some older Soviet T-62 tanks. The Egyptians propose contracting for depot level maintenance and repairs for U.S. and NATO armored forces and some cargo aircraft. Under the

1999 agreement mentioned above, Egypt will assemble an additional 200 M1 Abrams tanks.

"Bright Star" and other Joint Military Operations

The United States and Egypt conducted the first "Bright Star" joint military exercise in August 1983, and continue to hold periodic "Bright Star" exercises for infantry, airborne, artillery, and armored forces. The 1983 Bright Star was more than a training exercise: President Mubarak asked the United States to send Airborne Warning and Control System aircraft (AWACS) to monitor Libya's activity toward Sudan in February 1983. President Reagan sent AWACS planes and crews to monitor Libyan flights and the AWACS remained to take part in the first Bright Star. AWACS returned to Egypt in March-April 1984 to monitor Libyan flights toward Sudan after an incident in which a Libyan plane allegedly bombed Khartum. 70,000 troops from 10 nations participated in the October 7 through 31, 2001, Bright Star exercises. On August 11, 2003, the United States announced that it was canceling the October 2003 Bright Star exercise because U.S. armed forces were over committed in Afghanistan, Iraq, and other areas. The next Bright Star is scheduled for autumn 2005.

Egypt and the United States conducted their first joint naval exercise in August 1986 and followed with other naval exercises in subsequent years. Earlier, in August 1984, the U.S. Navy cooperated with the Egyptians in clearing Libyan mines from the Suez Canal, the Gulf of Suez, and the Red Sea. And in 1974, the U.S. Navy and private U.S. companies had assisted in clearing the Suez Canal of sunken ships, military ordnance, and other obstacles from the 1967 and 1973 wars.

"Desert Storm"

In the week prior to the August 2, 1990, Iraqi invasion of Kuwait, Egyptian President Husni Mubarak traveled to Iraq, Kuwait, and Saudi Arabia in an attempt to negotiate a peaceful end to the crisis. After the invasion, Mubarak advised President Bush to withhold sending armed forces to allow Egypt more time to work out a peaceful resolution. On August 7 when the United States announced that it was deploying troops to Saudi Arabia, Mubarak denied a U.S. request to allow U.S. forces use of Egyptian military bases on their way to the Arabian Peninsula so that he would have time to negotiate (he later granted the request). Mubarak and other Egyptian officials continued their peacemaking efforts in the Arab League, the Islamic Conference Organization (ICO), and through personal contacts and visits with Arab leaders. On August 10, Egypt voted for an Arab League resolution to send armed forces to defend Saudi Arabia against a possible

Iraqi invasion. The first contingent of Egyptian troops, a commando unit and a paratrooper unit, joined U.S. forces along the Saudi-Kuwaiti border the next day, on August 11. Egypt stated that its forces would assist in liberating Kuwait but would not attack or occupy Iraq. In February 1991, an Egyptian reinforced infantry division of some 30,000 troops took part in Desert Storm, advancing into western Kuwait in a corridor between U.S. Marines to the east and U.S. Army forces to the west in Iraq. Egypt suffered 9 killed in action and 74 wounded in action in Desert Storm.

Egyptian and U.S. military officers state that cooperation in Bright Star exercises facilitated the U.S.-Egyptian cooperation and military compatibility in Desert Storm, and Egyptian officers claim that Bright Star and Desert Storm serve as precedents for future U.S.-Egyptian cooperative ventures. Egyptian troops served as peacekeeping forces in Somalia and Yugoslavia, and an Egyptian contingent has been designated to serve with the Gulf Cooperation Council armed forces.

Bases

United States interest in a military base in Egypt followed the renewed interest in the late 1970s in a "Rapid Deployment Force" (now Central Command) and the need for overseas staging, support, and material storage areas. According to press reports, the United States has shown an interest in an air facility, such as Cairo West or the air base near Nag Hamadi, or an air and sea base, such as the small Egyptian base at Ras Banas on the Red Sea. Egypt denied rumors that the United States used Egyptian air fields during the April 1980 attempted hostage rescue in Iran. In 1981, Egypt agreed to allow the United States use of Ras Banas if an Arab state were threatened, but the negotiations to upgrade the facility collapsed in 1984 because of disagreements over managing the facility and the U.S. Congress' insistence on a formal agreement. Since the mid-1980s, there has been less talk of a U.S. base in Egypt. Under a reported but unconfirmed understanding, Egypt will allow U.S. access to military facilities after mutual discussion and agreement in time of crisis.

Table 1. Recent U.S. Aid to Egypt (millions of dollars)

Year	Economic	Military	IMET	Total
1948-1997	23,288.6	22,353.5	27.3	45,669.4
1998	815.0	1,300.0	1.0	2,116.0
1999	775.0	1,300.0	1.0	2,076.0
2000	727.3	1,300.0	1.0	2,028.3
2001	695.0	1,300.0	1.0	1,996.0
2002	655.0	1,300.0	1.0	1,956.0
2003	911.0	1,300.0	1.2	2,212.2
2004	571.6	1,292.3	1.4	1,865.3
2005	530.7	1,289.6	1.2	1,821.5
Total	28,969.2	32,735.4	36.1	61,740.7

Notes: FY2004 totals reflect the .59% across-the-board reduction. The Administration has requested $1.3 billion in FMF, and $495 million in ESF for FY2006.

Table 2. U.S. Foreign Assistance to Egypt, 1946-1997 (millions of current dollars)

Year	Total	Military Loan	Military Grant	I.M.E.T Grant	Misc. Economic Grant
1946	9.6	—	—	—	9.3 Surplus 0.3 UNWRA
1948	1.4	—	—	—	1.4 Surplus
1951	0.1	—	—	—	0.1 Tech Asst
1952	1.2	—	—	—	—
1953	12.9	—	—	—	—
1954	4.0	—	—	—	—
1955	66.3	—	—	—	—
1956	33.3	—	—	—	—
1957	1.0	—	—	—	—
1958	0.6	—	—	—	—
1959	44.8	—	—	—	—
1960	65.9	—	—	—	—
1961	73.5	—	—	—	—
1962	200.5	—	—	—	—
1963	146.7	—	—	—	—
1964	95.5	—	—	—	—
1965	97.6	—	—	—	—
1966	27.6	—	—	—	—
1967	12.6	—	—	—	—
1972	1.5	—	—	—	—
1973	0.8	—	—	—	—
1974	21.3	—	—	—	—
1975	370.1	—	—	—	—
1976	464.3	—	—	—	—

Year	Total	Military Loan	Military Grant	I.M.E.T Grant	Misc. Economic Grant
TQ	552.5	—	—	—	—
1977	907.8	—	—	—	—
1978	943.2	—	—	0.2	0.1 Narc.
1979	2,588.5	1,500.0	—	0.4	—
1980	1,167.3	—	—	0.8	—
1981	1,681.2	550.0	—	0.8	—
1982	1,967.3	700.0	200.0	2.4	—
1983	2,332.0	900.0	425.0	1.9	—
1984	2,470.8	900.0	465.0	1.7	—
1985	2,468.7	—	1175.0	1.7	—
1986	2,539.1	—	12,44.1	1.7	—
1987	2,317.0	—	1,300.0	1.8	—
1988	2,174.9	—	1,300.0	1.5	—
1989	2,269.6	—	1,300.0	1.5	—
1990	2,397.4	—	12,94.4	1.6	—
1991	2,300.2	—	1,300.0	1.9	—
1992	2,235.1	—	1,300.0	1.8	—
1993	2,052.9	—	1,300.0	1.8	—
1994	1,868.6	—	1,300.0	0.8	—
1995	2,414.5	—	1,300.0	1.0	—
1996	2,116.6	—	1,300.0	1.0	—
1997P	2,116.0	—	1,300.0	1.0	—
Total	45,669.4	4,550.0	17,803.5	27.3.0	11.2

Year	D.A. Loan	D.A.Grant	ESF Loan	ESF Grant	P.L. 480 I	P.L. 480 II
1946	—	—	—	—	—	—
1948	—	—	—	—	—	—
1951	—	—	—	—	—	—
1952	—	0.4	—	—	—	0.8
1953	—	12.9	—	—	—	—
1954	—	3.3	—	—	—	0.7
1955	7.5	35.3	—	—	—	23.5
1956	—	2.6	—	—	13.2	17.5
1957	—	0.7	—	—	—	0.3
1958	—	0	—	—	—	0.6
1959	—	2.0	—	—	33.9	8.9
1960	15.4	5.7	—	—	36.6	8.2
1961	—	2.3	—	—	48.6	22.6
1962	20.0	2.2	20.0	—	114	44.3
1963	36.3	2.3	10.0	—	78.5	19.6
1964	—	1.4	—	—	85.2	8.9
1965	—	2.3	—	—	84.9	10.4
1966	—	1.5	—	—	16.4	9.7
1967	—	0.8	—	—	—	11.8
1972	1.5	—	—	—	—	—

Table 2. (Continued).

Year	D.A. Loan	D.A.Grant	ESF Loan	ESF Grant	P.L. 480 I	P.L. 480 II
1973	—	—	—	—	—	0.8
1974	—	—	—	8.5	9.5	3.3
1975	—	—	194.3	58.5	104.5	12.8
1976	—	5.4	150.0	102.8	201.7	4.4
TQ	—	—	429.0	107.8	14.6	1.1
1977	—	—	600.0	99.2	196.8	11.7
1978	—	—	617.4	133.3	179.7	12.5
1979	—	—	250.0	585.0	230.7	22.4
1980	—	—	280.0	585.0	285.3	16.1
1981	—	—	70.0	759.0	272.5	28.9
1982	—	—	—	771.0	262.0	31.9
1983	—	—	—	750.0	238.3	16.8
1984	—	—	—	852.9	237.5	13.7
1985	—	—	—	1065.1	213.8	13.2
1986	—	—	—	1069.2	217.5	6.6
1987	—	—	—	819.7	191.7	3.9
1988	—	—	—	717.8	153.0	2.6
1989	—	1.5	—	815.0	150.5	1.2
1990	—	—	—	898.4	203.0	—
1991	—	—	—	780.8	165.0	52.5
1992	—	—	—	892.9	40.4	—
1993	—	—	—	747.0	—	4.1
1994	—	—	—	561.6	35.0	6.2
1995	—	0.2	—	1113.3	—	—
1996	—	—	—	815.0	—	0.6
1997P	—	—	—	815.0	—	—
Total	80.7	82.8	2,620.7	15923.8	4,114.3	455.1

Notes: Totals may not add due to rounding No U.S. aid programs for years 1947, 1949, 1950, 1968, 1969, 1970, and 1971 P.L. 480 II Grant for 1993 includes $2.1 million in Sec. 416 food donations

TQ=Transition Quarter; change from June to September fiscal year

*=less than $100,000

I.M.E.T.=International Military Education and Training

UNRWA=United Nations Relief and Works Agency

Surplus=Surplus Property

Tech Asst=Technical Assistance

Narc.=International Narcotics Control

D. A.=Development Assistance

ESF=Economic Support Funds

P.L. 480 I=Public Law 480 (Food for Peace), Title I Loan

P.L. 480 II=Public Law 480 (Food for Peace), Title II Grant

P=Preliminary

REFERENCES

[1] "Egypt Welcomes Iraqi Council as 'Step in the Right Direction,'" *Financial Times*, July 14, 2002.

[2] "Egypt said to Reject Iraq Role Without UN Mandate at Talks With US," *BBC Monitoring Newsfile*, July 12, 2003.

[3] The Muslim Brotherhood has spawned militant Islamic groups in other countries, such as Hamas and Palestine Islamic Jihad in Palestine, or the anti-government Islamic groups in Syria and Jordan.

In: Politics and Economics of the Middle East ISBN: 978-1-60456-719-9
Editors: W. Evans & D.J. Harris

Chapter 4

QUALIFYING INDUSTRIAL ZONES IN JORDAN AND EGYPT

Mary Jane Bolle, Alfred B. Prados and Jeremy M. Sharp

ABSTRACT

In 1996, Congress authorized the creation of *Qualifying Industrial Zones* (QIZs), thereby entitling goods jointly produced by Israel and either Jordan or Egypt to enter the United States duty free. The QIZ creation vehicle was an amendment to the *United States-Israel Free Trade Area Implementation Act of 1985* (P.L. 99-47), and its purpose was to promote peace and development between Israel and her Arab neighbors. Although Israeli-Palestinian violence has continued, some observers have praised QIZs for helping to spark Jordan's economic growth. Others note that QIZs, while promoting U.S.-Jordanian trade, have had modest impact on promoting job growth in Jordan. In 2005, Egypt began participating in the QIZ program. This chapter provides an overview of QIZs in the context of promoting regional development and peace. For more information on Jordan, see CRS Issue Brief IB93085, *Jordan: U.S. Relations and Bilateral Issues*, by Alfred Prados. For more information on Egypt, see CRS Report RL33003, *Egypt: Background and U.S. Relations*, by Jeremy M. Sharp.

QIZ Authorizing Legislation

The 1996 *West Bank and Gaza Strip Free Trade Benefits Act* (P.L.104-234) amended and extended the *U.S.-Israel Free Trade Area Implementation Act* to permit certain products from *qualifying industrial zones* (QIZs) to enter the United States duty free. QIZs were designed to: (1) help broaden support for the Middle East peace process, since Jordan and Egypt were the two Arab countries that had signed peace treaties with Israel; and (2) produce tangible economic benefits for Jordan, Egypt, the West Bank, and the Gaza Strip by stimulating their economies and increasing employment. (S.Rept. 104-270, p.3.)

During the first eight years after the QIZ amendment was adopted, Jordan, but not Egypt, entered an agreement with Israel to take advantage of QIZ benefits offered. Subsequently, the United States Trade Representative (USTR), on behalf of the President, designated 13 QIZs (one was later expanded) in Jordan. Finally, in December of 2004, following an agreement between Israel and Egypt, the USTR designated the first three QIZs in Egypt, and in 2005 expanded two of these and added a fourth.[1]

QIZs in a Nutshell

QIZs can be compared to free trade zones. QIZs are typically industrial parks housing manufacturing operations. They simplify cooperative production between countries because they: 1) are enclaves of infrastructure in developing countries where infrastructure may be sparse; and 2) are fiscally outside the customs territory of a country. Thus, on raw materials flowing into and goods moving out of zones, customs procedures are streamlined and tariffs do not apply until the item formally enters a country as an import for consumption. QIZs are distinguished from other trade zones as follows: Trade zones in general: (a) are stand-alone entities within *one* country (not directly connected to *other* countries); (b) produce for export to or domestic consumption in *any* country; and (c) operate solely under the authority of and conditions determined by the host government. QIZs, however: (a) have operations in two countries (Israel and either Jordan or Egypt); (b) produce goods solely for export to the United States; and (c) operate under both the authority of the host countries and the oversight authority of the United States, which determines conditions for and authorizes tariff relief for QIZ imports.

P.L. 104-234 requires that articles eligible for QIZ status must: (1) be wholly the growth, product, or manufacture of, and must be imported directly from, the West Bank/Gaza Strip (administered by the Palestinian Authority), or a QIZ; and (2) meet the following rules-of-origin requirements: At the time the product enters the United States, material and processing costs incurred in a QIZ[2] must total not less than 35% of the appraised value of the product. Of this 35%, 20% must come from Israel and Jordan or Egypt, and 15% may be either U.S. materials or materials from Israel, the West Bank/Gaza Strip, and/or Jordan or Egypt, depending on the participating QIZ program. The remaining 65% can come from anywhere in the world. In addition, the article must have been "substantially transformed in the manufacturing process."[3] The importer must certify that the article meets the conditions for the duty exemption. Details of the Jordanian-Israeli and Egyptian-Israeli QIZ programs (including exact shares comprising the minimum 20% from Israel and either Jordan or Egypt) differ slightly, based on the QIZ agreements between Israel and Jordan and Israel and Egypt, respectively, and on U.S. approval.[4]

QIZs in Jordan

For Jordanian-Israeli QIZs, a Jordanian-Israeli joint committee with two co-chairmen, each appointed by the respective government, and an American Observer must approve all eligible products. Product approval is renewed every 12 months.[5]

Both the public and private sectors in Jordan have a role in the industrial activity taking place in Jordan's QIZs. Of Jordan's 13 QIZs, three are publicly operated industrial estates and function under the supervision of the Jordan Industrial Estates Corporation (JIEC). A semi-governmental corporation with financial and administrative autonomy, the JIEC was created by law in 1985 to promote the establishment of industrial estates in Jordan. Subsequently, JIEC spearheaded the development of QIZs after President Clinton inaugurated the program in 1996.

IMPACT OF THE QIZS ON TRADE AND THE JORDANIAN ECONOMY

U.S. trade with Jordan has grown substantially in recent years — from both the QIZ program and, to a substantially lesser extent, from the U.S.-Jordan free trade agreement which went into effect in 2001. Between 1998 and 2005 Jordan moved up from the United States' 13th to 8th largest trading partner among the 20 Middle-East-North African (MENA) entities.[6] In 2005, U.S. exports to and imports from Jordan totaled an estimated \$1.9 billion: U.S. exports, at an estimated \$646 million, were 1.8 times their 1998 level; U.S. imports, at \$1.3 billion, were 80 times their 1998 level (USITC Dataweb). (See figure 1.) Despite the 2001 FTA between the United States and Jordan, most Jordanian articles still enter the United States through the QIZ program (75%). The apparel industry dominates both Jordan's QIZs and total exports to the United States, accounting for 99.9% of all QIZ exports and 86% of all Jordanian exports to the United States. The reason for continuing QIZ dominance is that QIZ products enter the United States free of duty, whereas, under the U.S.-Jordan FTA, tariffs will not be fully eliminated until the end of the ten-year phase-in period, in 2011. Nevertheless, in 2005, the growth in QIZ exports from Jordan leveled off to only a 2% growth over 2004 exports. This growth slowdown could have been affected by the removal of textile and clothing quotas (but not tariffs) that occurred with the January 2005 expiration of the 1995 *WTO Agreement on Textiles and Clothing*.

Trade in general and QIZ trade in particular has been a major engine of growth for Jordan's economy in the past few years. The Economist Intelligence Unit (EIU) projects that from an average annual rate of around 20% in 2000-2004, export earnings growth is expected to slow to a more modest 9% for 2005-2007 as the initial impact of the special trade agreement with the United States wanes, and competition from Asian textile producers toughens. The gains in export earnings have been overwhelmed by a surge in import spending, which was driven sharply upward in 2005 by rapid growth in international oil prices.[7]

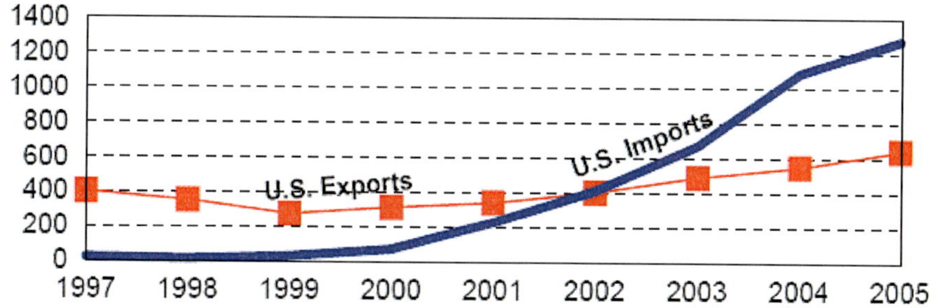

Data source: U.S. International Trade Commission Dataweb.

Figure 1. U.S. Trade with Jordan, 1997-2005, in $Millions.

Jobs

An important ancillary effect of the QIZ program in Jordan has been the creation of jobs to ease generally high rates of unemployment. In late 2003, the State Department estimated that QIZs had created more than 40,000 new jobs in Jordan, mainly for women.[8] According to local Jordanian press reports and international economists, however, close to half of these jobs have been filled by expatriates, mainly from southern Asia.[9] A breakdown of the number of workers employed at each of the 13 QIZs is not available.

QIZs in Egypt

On December 14, 2004, after an agreement between Israel and Egypt (which has the largest economy of the Middle East countries), the USTR designated three QIZs in Egypt: the Greater Cairo Zone, the Alexandria Zone, and the Suez Canal Zone (69 CFR 78094). On November 4, 2005, the USTR designated a fourth zone in the Central Delta region and expanded the Greater Cairo and Suez Canal zones. Several factors contributed to Egypt's desire for QIZ participation at this time. First was the January 1, 2005 end of quotas on textiles and apparel (which dominate Egypt's as well as Jordan's exports to the United States) under a WTO agreement. This meant that the flood of similar articles from China and India to the United States could crowd out Egyptian exports, and could result in the loss of 150,000 job opportunities in the industry,[10] and some of the $3.2 billion U.S. foreign direct investment in Egypt. In addition, Egypt was in search of sources for increased economic growth and trade to provide jobs for its rapidly growing labor force, to contain the fiscal deficit, to arrest the growth of public debt, and to address the trade deficit with the United States, and bolster ties with Israel in order to improve regional relations. The United States, on the other hand, views Egypt's interest in QIZ participation as an opportunity to press for desired economic reforms in Egypt.[11] Negotiations toward a U.S.-Egyptian free trade agreement have recently been suspended over human rights issues.[12]

Among the 20 MENA entities, Egypt is the United States' 7th largest trading partner, with U.S. imports for 2005 at an estimated $2.1 billion and exports at an estimated $3.1 billion for the first 11 months of 2005. For 2005, Egypt's first full year of QIZ participation, Egypt exported $230 million dollars worth of goods to the United States through the QIZ program. This represents 12% of Egypt's total exports to the United States. As with the Israel-Jordan QIZ program, textiles and apparel exports dominated Egypt's QIZ exports to the United States: 89% of those exports were apparel and 5% were textiles.

QIZs: Broader Implications

Although the creation of QIZs has been a positive step toward Jordan's and Egypt's economic growth, Jordan, like other non oil-producing Middle East countries, faces enormous challenges to its long term economic well being. For some countries in the region, lack of adequate water resources impedes growth (Jordan is one of the ten most water-deprived countries in the world). Beyond natural resources, the region's human resources also need to be further developed in order to spur economic development. For example, most experts note that Jordan's workforce is still largely unskilled, which hinders the economy's transformation from one based on small-scale agriculture and pastoral grazing to a labor-intensive, industrialized economy. Despite recent government investment in higher education and vocational training, Jordanian workers, according to one Jordanian businessman, "lack vocational experience and a strong work ethic."[13] Some factories located in QIZs have high numbers of more productive foreign workers from China and Southeast Asia.[14] In order to increase the competitiveness of Jordanian labor, the Ministry of Labor has launched several programs aimed at recruiting skilled rural workers, particularly women.

The Social Impact of QIZs

Although most experts note that companies based in QIZs continue to hire foreign laborers, thousands of Jordanians, particularly women from the rural countryside, have found jobs at garment factories in QIZs. In a traditional society such as Jordan, many of these women had little previous work experience and were largely caretakers of their home. Despite the low wages paid by apparel factories in the QIZs, some women have been able to support their families where the father or husband had fallen sick or died, and others have been able to supplement the income of the male breadwinner. However, traditional attitudes toward a woman's place in the home persist, and many families continue to prohibit female members from working in QIZs. In response, the Jordanian Ministry of Labor has worked to ease the adjustment of women moving from the home to a new job by providing free transportation to work, subsidizing the cost of food in QIZs, and paying for dormitories near factories to cut commuting times. According to the Jordanian Trade Minister, "a new sort of culture is being established where girls are going to work, they are supporting their families and they are raising the standard of living in their villages."[15] The long term effect of female employment in QIZs has yet to be measured, and there is some concern that over time, Jordanian women may have difficulty in achieving higher wages in a global economy where apparel manufacturers can easily relocate to cheaper labor markets.

Impact on the Arab-Israeli Peace Process

When the QIZ program came into being in 1996, many observers regarded it as a vehicle to support the development of peaceful relations and normalization of commercial ties between Israel and the two Arab states (Jordan and Egypt) with which it had signed peace treaties. In both cases, however, a "cold peace" continues to prevail between Israel and the two Arab states. Since the conclusion of the Jordan-Israel peace treaty in October 1994, large numbers of Jordanians, particularly Islamic fundamentalists, those of Palestinian origin, and members of the professional unions continue to oppose normalization with Israel and resist the expansion of commercial relations. With the establishment of 13 QIZs in Jordan, there has been an increase in the volume of bilateral trade, though the overall totals remain modest. Trade between Israel and Jordan in 2004 were nearly six times what they were in 1997. Israel's exports to Jordan in 2004 were roughly $133 million (up from about $21 million in 1997). Israel's imports from Jordan were roughly $51 million (up from about $12.5 million in 1997.)[16] It is possible that some incremental improvement in bilateral relations could occur over time as a result of increased commercial contacts and joint participation in mechanisms related to the QIZ program.

RECENT ISSUES

In May of 2006, the National Labor Committee (NLC), a human rights advocacy group, issued a 161-page report alleging sweatshop-like conditions in 28 out of 100 QIZ plants in Jordan. The report, *U.S.-Jordan Free Trade Agreement Descends into Human Trafficking and Involuntary Servitude*, was compiled from interviews with over 100 foreign guest workers in Jordan and workers forcibly returned to Bangladesh. In response to the allegations, the USTR raised the matter with the Jordanian Government. Jordan's trade minister Sharif Zu'bi subsequently indicated that the report incorrectly identified three sweatshops that are not even in Jordan, and that three others had been closed before the report was released in May. In addition, he noted that the Jordanian government had formed nine inspections teams to investigate the entire garment trade in the country, and is working with the International Labor Organization, U.S. labor committees, the USTR, the State Department, and U.S. and Jordanian apparel companies to address the challenges and improve their monitoring system.

REFERENCES

[1] The President gave this power to the USTR through Proclamation 6955 on Nov. 13, 1996 (61CFR 58761).
[2] xxamples of such costs are originating materials, wages and salaries, design research and development, depreciation of capital investment, and overhead.
[3] Section 1 of P.L. 104-234, amending Section 9 of P.L. 99-47.
[4] For example, the manufacturer from the Jordanian side must contribute at least 11.7% of the final produce and the manufacturer on the Israeli side must contribute 8% (7% on high tech products); and under the Israeli-Egyptian agreement, 11.7% of the inputs must be made in Israel.
[5] Export and Finance Bank, Jordan. *Qualifying Industrial Zones*. Sector Report, June 10, 2003.

[6] Middle East entities are: Bahrain, Cyprus, Egypt, Gaza Strip/West Bank, Iran, Iraq, Israel, Jordan, Kuwait, Lebanon, Oman, Qatar, Saudi Arabia, Syria, United Arab Emirates, and Yemen. North African Countries are: Algeria, Libya, Morocco, and Tunisia.

[7] *The Economist.* Economist Intelligence Unit (EIU) Country Outlook: Jordan, Dec. 2005.

[8] U.S. Department of State, International Information Programs, "U.S.-Jordan Free Trade Agreement Spurs Jordan's Economic Growth," Oct. 16, 2003.

[9] According to the Jordanian press in late 2003, QIZs were employing 21,486 local workers and 15,078 expatriates. Sahar Aloul, "QIZ investors voice concerns at workshop," *The Jordan Times*, Sept. 23, 2003.

[10] Embassy of Egypt. Qualifying Industrial Zones (QIZ) Protocol and the Potential Impact on the Egyptian Economy, 2004, p. 16.

[11] U.S. to Consider Egypt FTA after next TIFA, wants Further Reforms. *Inside U.S. Trade.* January 14, 2005.

[12] The Realities of Exporting Democracy. *The Washington Post*, January 25, 2006, p. A-1.

[13] "Jordan's Peace Dividend," *Jerusalem Post*, October 26, 2004.

[14] Some estimate that approximately 20% of companies based in QIZs are wholly owned by Jordanians. See, "Trade Without Consent - Choosing Between Free Trade and Democracy in Jordan," Daily Star, July 14,2003.

[15] "Jordan's Peace Dividend," op. cit.

[16] Source of data: U.S. Department of Commerce. Trade Policy Information System (TPIS).

In: Politics and Economics of the Middle East
Editors: W. Evans, et al., pp. 119-148
ISBN: 978-1-60456-719-9

Chapter 5

PROPOSED U.S.-OMAN FREE TRADE AGREEMENT*

Mary Jane Bolle
Specialist in International Trade
Foreign Affairs, Defense, and Trade Division

ABSTRACT

In aiming to fight terrorism with trade, the United States has negotiated and the President signed on January 19, 2006, the U.S.'s fifth bilateral free trade agreement (FTA) in the proposed 20-entity Middle East Free Trade Area (MEFTA). This proposed FTA is with Oman. Other U.S.-FTAs are with Israel, Jordan, Morocco, and Bahrain. A sixth is being negotiated with the United Arab Emirates. Oman is a small oil-exporting U.S. trade partner that has been supportive of U.S. policies in the Middle East and is strategically located at the mouth of the Persian Gulf. Because its oil reserves could be exhausted within 15-20 years, Oman is trying to liberalize and diversify its trade regime beyond oil and gas to provide economic opportunities for its fast growing workforce. Supporters of the agreement typically cite political and economic reasons. Opponents typically point to labor and human rights issues.

The proposed FTA with Oman is similar to other MEFTA FTAs and has three basic parts: new tariff schedules, broad commitments to open markets and provisions to support those commitments, and protections for labor and the environment. It would provide immediate duty-free access for almost all

* Excerpted from CRS Report RL33328, dated August 1, 2006.

consumer and industrial goods, with special provisions for agriculture and textiles and apparel.

Among all U.S. trade partners, Oman ranks 88th for the United States, while the United States ranks third for Oman (after the United Arab Emirates and Japan). U.S.-Oman trade at about $1 billion for 2005 represents 0.04% (four-one hundredths of one percent) of total U.S. trade. In 2005, the most important U.S. imports from Oman were oil and natural gas (75%), and apparel (10%). The most important U.S. exports to Oman were transport equipment (56%), and machinery (24%). The U.S. International Trade Commission (USITC) predicts that the economic effect of the proposed U.S.-Oman FTA is likely to be minimal since trade levels are low; and any increase in U.S. imports of apparel would come at the expense of workers elsewhere in the world, not in the United States. Total U.S. foreign direct investment in Oman was $358 million in 2003, up from $193 million in 2002.

Supporters argue that a U.S.-Oman FTA would contribute to bilateral economic growth and trade, generate export opportunities for U.S. companies, farmers, and ranchers, and help create jobs in both countries. Critics argue that labor protections are inadequate for Omani workers, compared to those they receive under the Generalized System of Protections, and that the proposed FTA would not help level the playing field for Omani and U.S. workers. Critics also argue that a provision in Annex II of the FTA could obligate the United States to open up landside aspects of its port activities to operation by companies doing business in Oman — the very activities about which Congress expressed national security concerns during the Dubai Ports World debate. (See sections on "Current Labor Issues," and "Current Issues on Port Security.") After the President submits the agreement and the implementing legislation to Congress, relevant committees have 45 days to consider (or not consider) it, and either chamber has 15 more days to vote the legislation up or down without amendment to the agreement itself or the legislation. The Senate passed implementing legislation for the U.S.-Oman FTA on June 29, 2006; and the House passed it on July 20.

A proposed U.S. free trade agreement (FTA) with Oman was concluded on October 13, 2005, after seven months of negotiation, and was signed by U.S. Trade Representative (USTR) Bob Portman and Omani Minister of Commerce and Industry Maqbool bin Ali Sultan on January 19, 2006. The proposed U.S.-Oman (FTA) is the fifth U.S. bilateral free trade agreement with a country in the proposed Middle East Free Trade Area (MEFTA). MEFTA would consist of 16 entities in the Middle East and four in North Africa. The entire proposed MEFTA is included in the map in figure 1, with Oman, heavily shaded, in the lower right hand corner.

Completion of a MEFTA by 2013 was proposed by President George W. Bush in 2003, as part of a plan to fight terrorism by supporting Middle East economic growth and democracy through trade.[1] To date, besides Oman, the Administration has negotiated and Congress has implemented free trade agreements with four other MEFTA political entities: Israel and Jordan (before MEFTA was announced), Morocco, and Bahrain. A sixth FTA is being negotiated with the United Arab Emirates (UAE).[2]

About Oman
(for 2005 except as indicated)

Location: mouth of the Persian Gulf (see map)
Size: slightly smaller than Kansas
Religion: Ibadhi Muslim 75%, Sunni Muslim, Shi'a Muslim Hindu
Government: monarchy
GDP: $40 billion (similar to that of Idaho)
Labor force: about 1 million (2002)
Unemployment rate: 15% (2004)
Population: roughly 3 million (43% under age 14) growing at 3.3% per year
Per-capita income: $13,400
Industries: crude oil production and refining, natural and liquefied natural gas production, construction, cement, copper, steel, chemicals, optic fiber.
Primary source: CIA The World Factbook, 2006.

Congressional consideration of the proposed U.S.-Oman FTA, which is expected to occur some time this year, is governed by the timeline set forth in the *Trade Act of 2002*, (P.L. 107-210). Under this law, which lays out the President's trade promotion authority (TPA), the President must give Congress a 90-day prenotification of his intent to enter into the trade agreement.[3] After that, the President must submit to Congress — under no particular time constraints, but on a day when both houses of Congress are in session — both the agreement itself and the implementing legislation. Any House or Senate committees to which the legislation is referred will have 45 days to report (or not report) the bill; and each house has 15 days after the bill is reported (or the 45 days expire) to consider the legislation. If the House passes its bill to the Senate, the Senate has an additional 15 days to consider the legislation. Floor debate in either house is limited to 20 hours, divided equally between supporters and opponents. For final passage, both houses must vote the legislation up or down by a simple majority, and neither the implementing legislation nor the agreement itself may be amended.[4]

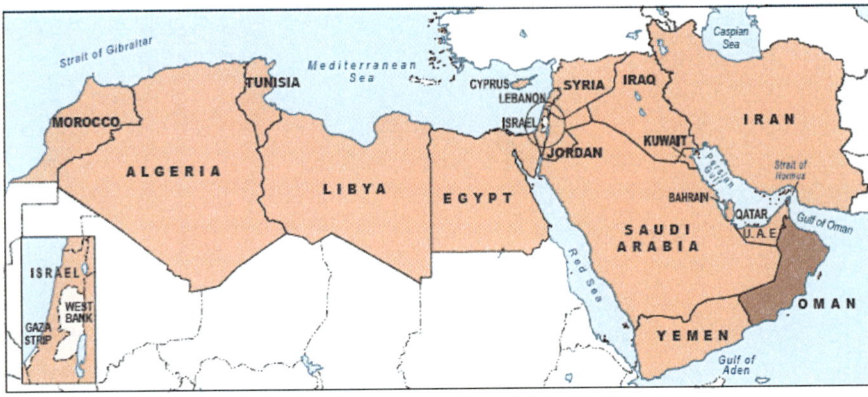

Source: Map Resources. Adapted by CRS. (K.Yancey 12/5/05)

Figure 1. Oman's Geographic Location in the Proposed MEFTA.

WHY OMAN? WHY NOW?

U.S. interest in Oman stems from a number of factors. Oman is a small exporter of oil and natural gas that is strategically located at the entrance to the Persian Gulf, 35 miles directly opposite Iran. It is not a member of the Organization of the Petroleum Exporting Countries (OPEC). Oman is a moderate Islamic country which has sought to maintain good relations with all Middle East countries. It also has a 170 year history of political and economic cooperation with the United States, and has supported the U.S. war on terrorism.[5] Oman is an important gateway to the Persian Gulf region.

Oman has many reasons for wanting to negotiate an FTA with the United States. It is a country whose proven oil reserves could be exhausted within 15 or 20 years; yet, almost 40% of the country's GDP, two-thirds of its export earnings and three-fourth of its government revenues currently come from oil revenues. It is therefore trying to liberalize and diversify its trade regime as it seeks to broaden economic opportunities for a fast-growing workforce. As a result, it is looking to expand its economy beyond oil and gas exports. It sees the United States as an important ally in the venture to prepare itself for a time when its economic and social challenges intersect.[6]

U.S.-OMAN BILATERAL TRADE AND INVESTMENT

Oman is a small U.S. trade partner, ranking 88th among all U.S. trade partners. Total U.S.-Oman trade at $1 billion in 2005 ($593 million in U.S. exports and $555 million in U.S. imports) accounts for 0.04% (four one-hundredths of one percent) of all U.S. trade. As a trading partner it is also 11th among the 20 MEFTA entities, which together represent 4% of U.S. trade for 2005. The United States, on the other hand, ranks fourth in importance among Oman's trading partners, behind the United Arab Emirates (UAE), Japan, and the United Kingdom for 2004 (most recent data).

In 2005, the most important U.S. imports from Oman (see table 1) were oil and natural gas (75%, constituting 1% of all U.S. oil and gas imports from MEFTA countries), and apparel (10%). The most important U.S. exports to Oman were various types of transport equipment and road vehicles (totaling 56%), and various types of machinery (24%). Since 2001, U.S. exports to Oman have almost doubled to $593 million, for various reasons, while U.S. imports from Oman, at $555 million, have increased by about a third, primarily because of increases in the price of petroleum imports. As a result, for 2005, the United States had a small trade surplus with Oman.

Foreign Direct Investment in Oman

Total U.S. foreign direct investment in Oman was $358 million in 2003, nearly double the $193 million investment in 2002.[7] The Bureau of Economic Analysis does not report on investment by sector for Oman, when investment is highly concentrated in a small number of investors, and such reporting might reveal the identity of individual investors. However, most of it is likely invested in oil and gas-related facilities.

However, the Department of Commerce's *Country Commercial Guide* for Oman reported that the largest investor in Oman is Royal Dutch Shell Oil which holds 34% of Petroleum Development in Oman, the state oil company, and 30% of Oman Liquid Natural Gas. In addition, U.S. firms, Gorman Rupp (water pumps) and FMC (wellhead equipment), have entered into industrial joint ventures with Omani firms, and Dow Chemical announced a joint venture with Oman Oil Company and the government of Oman in July 2004 to develop a large petrochemical plant in Sohar.[8]

The *Country Commercial Guide* for Oman also reported that total investment in listed Omani companies with foreign participation was $2.4 billion in

September 2004, of which 8.94% ($215 million) was (worldwide) foreign investment. Foreign capital also constituted 7.5% of all capital invested in finance, 3% of all capital invested in manufacturing, and 9% of all capital invested in insurances and services.[9]

Table 1. U.S. Imports from and Exports to Oman, 2005

U.S. Imports from Oman			U.S. Exports to Oman		
Import and			Export and		
(SITC number)	$mil	%	(SITC Number)	$mil	%
Petroleum (33)	400	72%	Transport equipment (79)	170	29%
Apparel (84)	53	10%	Road Vehicles (78)	159	27%
Natural Gas (43)	14	3%	Machinery (72,74,71,77)	145	24%
Misc. Manufacturing (89)	57	10%	Scientific instruments (87)	14	2%
Iron and Steel (67)	10	2%	Food/agricultural (1-11)	11	2%
Subtotal	$534	97%	Subtotal	$499	84%
Other	21	3%	Other	94	16%
TOTAL	$555	100%	TOTAL	$593	100%

Source: U.S. International Trade Commission Dataweb; SITC: Standard International Trade Code.

The Proposed U.S.-Oman FTA

The proposed FTA with Oman is similar to other recent FTAs with MEFTA countries (Morocco and Bahrain), with slight variations. The proposed U.S.-Oman FTA has three basic parts: new tariff schedules for each country, broad commitments to open markets and provisions to support these commitments, and protections for labor and the environment.

The USITC argues that the economic effect of the agreement on the U.S. economy is expected to be small but positive, and that the impact on U.S. workers is likely to be minimal because trade with Oman is low. U.S. apparel workers are a group that is potentially adversely affected. Apparel imports from Oman declined by 57% in 2005 over 2004, because the World Trade Organization (WTO) Agreement on Clothing and Textiles (ACT) expired in January of 2005, ending the trade quota system among WTO partner countries. The USITC reports that tariff reductions and elimination under the proposed U.S.-Oman FTA should restore some of the competitiveness of Oman's apparel exports among U.S. purchasers — and estimates that the resulting increase in imports would come at the expense of workers elsewhere in the world, not U.S. workers.[10]

Tariff Provisions

Under the proposed U.S.-Oman FTA, the United States and Oman would provide each other immediate duty-free access for tariff lines covering almost all consumer and industrial goods, with special provisions for agriculture and textiles and apparel. For agricultural products, Oman would provide immediate duty-free access for current U.S. exports in 87% of agricultural tariff lines; and the United States would provide immediate duty-free access for 100% of Oman's current exports of agricultural products to the United States. Both countries would phase out all tariffs on the remaining eligible goods within 10 years.[11]

Textile and apparel products are divided into three categories. Most U.S. imports from Oman are category A (cotton and manmade fibers) for which duties would be eliminated immediately so long as the goods meet the FTA rules of origin requirements. On category B products (home furnishings — mainly bed and kitchen linens) tariffs would be reduced over five years, and for category C products (wool goods), tariffs would be reduced over 10 years. Most apparel must be assembled in an FTA party from inputs (yarn and fabric) made in an FTA party.[12]

At present, virtually all U.S. textile and apparel imports from Oman are dutiable, with an average tariff rate of 15.4% in 2005. At the same time, only 11% of U.S. agricultural imports from Oman are dutiable. These dutiable products carried an average tariff of 10.4% in 2005.[13] Most U.S. exports to Oman incurred the common external Gulf Communications Council (GCC) tariff of 5% to all non-GCC members. The GCC includes, besides Oman, Bahrain, Kuwait, Qatar, Saudi Arabia, and the UAE.

Market Access and Related Provisions[14]

The proposed U.S.-Oman FTA contains broad commitments to open markets in sectors such as banking, insurance, securities, and telecommunications. It also includes protections for U.S. investors, and for holders of copyrights, trademarks, patents, and trade secrets. It includes enforcement measures for intellectual property rights infringement. In addition it contains transparent sanitary and phytosanitary measures, government procurement disciplines, streamlined and transparent customs procedures, commitments to combat bribery, and tools to enforce the trade agreement. More specifically:

Commitments to Open Services Markets. Oman would provide market access across its entire services regime, including audiovisual, express delivery, telecommunications, computer, distribution, and healthcare; and services incidental to mining, construction, architecture and engineering. The agreement would enhance Oman's commitment to the WTO General Agreement on Trade in Services (GATS).[15] Annexes I and II of the agreement indicate the exceptions to the coverage of the agreement that each country has reserved for itself in the case of *services.*

Opportunities for Banks, Insurance, Securities, and Related Services. U.S. financial service suppliers would have the right to establish subsidiaries, branches, and joint ventures in Oman, to expand their operations throughout Oman, and to offer the full range of financial services. Annex III of the agreement lists the exceptions to the coverage of the agreement that each county has reserved for itself in the area of trade in financial services.

New Protections for U.S. Investors. All forms of investment would be protected under the agreement, including enterprises, debt concessions, contracts, and intellectual property. U.S. investors would enjoy in most circumstances, the right to establish, acquire, and operate investments in Oman on an equal footing with Omani investors and with investors of other countries. Annexes I and II of the agreement indicate the exceptions to the coverage of the agreement that each country has reserved for itself in the case of foreign investment.

Open and Competitive Communications Market. U.S. phone companies would have the right to interconnect with a dominant carrier in Oman at nondiscriminatory rates. U.S. firms seeking to build a physical network in Oman would have nondiscriminatory access to key facilities such as telephone switches and submarine cable landing stations.

E-Commerce. Each government would commit to nondiscriminatory treatment of digital products and would agree not to impose customs duties on digital products transmitted electronically.

Copyright Protection in a Digital Economy. Each government would commit to protect copyrighted works, including phonograms, for extended terms consistent with U.S. standards and international trends.

Patents and Trade Secrets. Grounds for revoking a patent would be limited to the same grounds required to originally refuse a patent, thus protecting against arbitrary revocation. Patent terms could be adjusted to compensate for unreasonable delays in granting the original patent, consistent with U.S. practice.

Trademarks. The proposed FTA would apply the principle of "first-in-time, first-in-right" to trademarks and geographical indications, so the first person who acquires a right to a trademark or geographical indication would be the person who has the right to use it. Each government would be required to establish tr*ansparent procedures for the registration of trademarks.*

Intellectual Property Rights (IPR). The proposed FTA would require each government to criminalize end-user piracy, providing a strong deterrence against piracy and counterfeiting. The proposed FTA would mandate both statutory and actual damages under Omani law for IPR violations.

Transparent Sanitary and Phytosanitary Measures and Technical Barriers to Trade. Oman would commit to a science-based regime for sanitary and phytosanitary measures and to transparent procedures for developing and implementing technical regulations.

Government Procurement. U.S. suppliers would be granted nondiscriminatory rights to bid on contracts to supply most Omani government entities; and Omani government purchasers could not discriminate against U.S. firms or in favor of Omani firms when making government purchases above a threshold monetary level.

Customs Procedures. The proposed FTA would require transparency and efficiency in customs administration, including publication of laws and regulations on the Internet and procedural certainty and fairness.

Transparent Rule-Making and Procedural Protections for Traders. Each government would publish its laws and regulations governing trade, and would publish proposed measures in advance, and provide an opportunity for public comment on them. Each government would ensure that a trader from the other country could obtain prompt and fair review of a final administrative decision affecting its interest.

Commitments to Combat Bribery. Each government would be required to prohibit bribery, including bribery of foreign officials, and to establish appropriate criminal penalties to punish violators.

Tools to Enforce the Trade Agreement. All core obligations of the proposed FTA, including enforceable labor and environmental provisions, would be subject to the dispute settlement provisions of the agreement. Dispute panel proceedings would be subject to requirements for openness and transparency.

Protections for Labor and the Environment

Labor Protections

Each government would be required to effectively enforce its own labor laws, as with other FTAs negotiated under the presidential trade promotional authority or "fast track" authority of the Trade Act of 2002 (P.L. 107-210). This would be the only labor provision enforceable through the proposed agreement's dispute resolution process, and the maximum penalty for each violation would be limited to $15 million per violation per year. If the Party complained against fails to pay a monetary assessment, the complaining Party can take other steps to collect the assessment (or otherwise secure compliance), including by the suspension of tariff benefits under the FTA.

However, the labor section of the proposed U.S.-Oman FTA also contains other provisions, which are subject to consultation rather than actual enforcement: Each country would also agree not to weaken or reduce its labor laws to attract trade and investment. Each government would reaffirm its obligations as a member of the International Labor Organization (ILO, which requires it to uphold ILO core labor standards) and commit to "strive to ensure" that its laws provide for labor standards consistent with internationally recognized labor rights (which are defined in the proposed FTA to reflect U.S. trade law, and are slightly different from ILO core labor standards.)[16] Labor ministries together with other appropriate agencies would agree to establish priorities and develop specific cooperative activities. (See section below on "The Labor Debate" for a discussion of most recent labor issues.)

Environmental Protections

Each government would be required to effectively enforce its own environmental laws. This would be the only environmental provision enforceable through the proposed agreement's dispute resolution process, and as with labor provisions, the maximum fine would be limited to $15 million per violation per year.

Each country would also agree not to weaken or reduce its environmental laws to attract trade and investment. As a complement to the proposed agreement, the governments would sign a Memorandum of Understanding on Environmental Cooperation that would establish a Joint Forum on Environmental Cooperation, develop a plan of action, and set priorities for future environment-related projects.

The General Debate over the Proposed Agreement

Arguments in Favor of the Proposed Agreement

Supporters of the Proposed Agreement

Support for the agreement is broad in the business community. Among businesses, support is led by the National Foreign Trade Council and the Business Council for International Understanding which heads up the Middle East Free Trade Coalition (MEFTC), an alliance of about 120 companies and associations including the U.S. Chamber of Commerce, and the National Association of Manufacturers. Support also comes from 24 out of 27 trade advisory committees representing business labor, environment, state and local government, agriculture, various industries, and functional areas (e.g., consumer goods, distribution services, small and minority businesses, customs matters, intellectual property, and standards and technical trade barriers.)[17]

Congressional support on the House side is led by the Congressional Middle East Economic Partnership Caucus (MEEPC), a bipartisan group of lawmakers which began with 16 members and six co-chairs including Representatives Ben Chandler, Phil English, Darrell Issa, William Jefferson, Gregory Meeks, and Paul Ryan.

Congressional support on the Senate side is led by Senator Charles Grassley, Chairman of the Senate Finance Committee, and by Senator Craig Thomas, Chairman of the Subcommittee on International Trade, which held hearings on the proposed U.S.-Oman FTA on March 6, 2006.

Arguments in Favor of the Proposed Agreement

USTR Portman has asserted that the proposed U.S.-Oman FTA would contribute to economic growth and trade between both countries, generate export opportunities for U.S. companies, farmers, and ranchers, help create jobs in both countries, and help American consumers save money while offering them greater choices. He points out that in addition to eliminating tariffs on U.S. exports, Oman would provide substantial market access across the entire services regime, provide a secure, predictable legal framework for U.S. investors operating in Oman, provide for effective enforcement of labor and environmental laws, and protect intellectual property. Furthermore, he argues that this proposed agreement would support and accelerate the market liberalization that Oman started as part of its accession to the WTO in 2000. Portman contends that joint U.S.-Omani efforts would advance economic growth and democracy, raise living standards and promote peace and economic stability in the Middle East — a region of almost 350 million people and a $70 billion trading relationship with the United States.[18]

The overall Advisory Committee for Trade Policy Negotiations (ACTPN) also notes that the proposed agreement, if approved, would strengthen the likelihood of additional agreements in the region and improve and strengthen overall U.S. relations with the countries of the Middle East.[19]

In addition, those in favor of the proposed agreement assert that Oman is one of the most "open" countries in the Middle East. *Economic Freedom of the World, 2005*, published by Canada's Fraser Institute, reports (p. 4) that when measures of economic freedom and democracy are included in a statistical study, economic freedom is about 50 times more effective than democracy in diminishing violent conflict. *Economic Freedom* ranked Oman 17th out of 127 countries in terms of degree of economic freedom afforded in five basic areas.[20] The only MEFTA country it ranked higher was the UAE, which tied for 9th place (with Australia, Luxemburg, and Estonia.) Other MEFTA country rankings were Bahrain (24th), Jordan (25th), Israel (50th), and Egypt, (tied for 78th with Iran and Morocco.)[21]

In 2003, Oman passed a new labor law extending its labor protections for domestic workers to foreign workers (who predominate in the private sector). In response to some calls to strengthen the Omani labor law further, Chuck Ditrich, National Foreign Trade Council vice president, urges patience, acknowledging that Oman still has some areas that may need further legislation, but argues that Omani laws must be viewed in the context of a "very traditional society" that is committed to modernization.[22] For example, the government of Oman reportedly recognizes the need for more explicit provisions for collective bargaining in its laws.[23] Moreover, Oman has reportedly undertaken consultation with the ILO for technical assistance in complying with ILO core labor standards.[24]

Arguments Against the Agreement

Three of the 27 reports by trade advisory committees mandated under the trade promotion authority language of the Trade Act of 2002 have some criticisms of the proposed U.S.-Oman FTA: those committees on the environment, intergovernmental affairs, and labor.

Environment

Most members of the Trade Policy and Environment Committee agreed that the environment and public participation provisions were acceptable; however, they noted that the proposed U.S.-Oman FTA lacks some environmental provisions which have appeared in other agreements and which would have been appropriate. Examples of such provisions are the extensive public participation framework from the Central America Free Trade Agreement (CAFTA) and some basic environmental provisions which appeared in the FTAs with Chile and Singapore.[25]

Intergovernmental Affairs

The Intergovernmental Advisory Policy Committee, in principle, supported the trade liberalization objectives of the proposed agreement. However, the committee stressed the need for trade agreements to continue to respect the authority of state and local governments to regulate in areas under their jurisdiction. They also stressed the need for ongoing consultations with sub-federal governments.[26]

Labor

The labor groups are the most vocal critics. They argue that potential losers from the proposed agreement would be workers in Oman who would miss out on the opportunity to be more fully protected by labor standards. Other implied losers would be U.S. workers for whom the proposed agreement does little to "level the playing field." Main arguments against the proposed FTA offered by labor interests are concentrated primarily on two basic issues: weaknesses in the proposed agreement, and weaknesses in Omani laws and enforcement, for which the proposed agreement does not adequately compensate.

Weaknesses in the Proposed Agreement

Labor critics point out that the *Trade Act of 2002[27]* requires U.S. negotiators to "seek provisions that treat U.S. principal negotiating objectives equally with respect to both: (1) the ability to resort to dispute settlement; and (2) the availability of equivalent dispute settlement procedures and remedies. However, critics argue, the proposed agreement does not do this. Further, they argue, the proposed FTA is a step backward from protections offered Oman under the Generalized System of Preferences:

Not All Labor Provisions Are Treated Equally. The proposed U.S.-Oman FTA identifies three basic labor commitments for partner countries: (1) commitments to comply with ILO standards; (2) commitments to enforce their own labor standards; (3) and commitments to not derogate from those standards in order to attract trade and investment. However, critics argue, only the second of these three commitments is enforceable through the dispute resolution procedures of the proposed U.S.-Oman FTA. This treatment, they argue, contrasts with provisions of the U.S.-Jordan FTA which makes all three commitments enforceable through the dispute resolution process.[28]

Unequal Treatment of Labor Compared to Most Non-Labor Provisions. Second, there are different dispute resolution procedures for labor and non-labor (e.g., intellectual property) violations, For labor (and environmental) violations, the potential penalty for the one labor (and environmental) violation (failure to enforce one's own laws) that is open to the dispute resolution procedures is capped at $15 million per violation per year. For non-labor (and non-environmental) violations, there is no cap on any monetary assessment.

A Step Back from GSP. In addition, the AFL-CIO sees the proposed U.S.-Oman FTA as being a step back from the Generalized System of Preferences (GSP) program. Under GSP, trade preferences for developing countries including Oman are dependent on such countries' taking steps to afford their workers internationally recognized worker rights. A challenge to GSP eligibility for any country begins with a petition to the Office of the USTR documenting that a country is not taking steps to afford its workers such rights. In June of 2005, the AFL-CIO petitioned the USTR to remove Oman from GSP status, arguing that it was not affording its workers internationally recognized worker rights.[29] Oman continues to hold GSP status.

Weaknesses in Omani Law and Enforcement

When there are weaknesses in the proposed agreement, critics argue, if a country's basic laws and enforcement of those laws are strong enough, workers could still be protected. Oman, critics argue, lacks protections in certain areas.

Omani Gaps in Ratification of ILO Core Labor Standards

First, as of the date of this chapter according to the ILO website, Oman has ratified conventions relating to only two of the four basic ILO core labor standards (enumerated in a footnote on p. 7): those protecting against child labor, and those prohibiting forced labor. Oman has not ratified conventions related to the right to organize and bargain collectively and the elimination of employment discrimination.[30]

Lack of Other Omani Laws and/or Enforcement

Furthermore, various sources suggest that Omani labor laws and/or enforcement do not fully cover certain aspects of the following areas relating to core labor standards/internationally recognized worker rights:

Right to Organize and Bargain Collectively. The State Department's *Country Reports on Human Rights Practices, 2004,* finds in the area of "right to organize and bargain collectively," that Omani law does not provide workers with the right to form or join "unions" but does permit them to form representation committees with the goal of taking care of their interests. The LAC reports that where representation committees exist, however, they are by law, not authorized to discuss wages, hours, or conditions of employment.[31] *Country Reports* for 2005 adds an unofficial estimate that 25 representation committees, representing 9.1%

of employees in the private sector, have been registered since 2004 and reports that provisions of the law apply to [Omani] women and foreign workers [as well as Omani men].[32]

Right to Strike. Furthermore, according to *Country Reports* for 2004, the Omani law does not address strikes or explicitly provide for the right to collective bargaining. However, it reports that the 2003 Omani labor law removed a 1973 prohibition on strikes and details procedures for dispute resolution. *Country Reports* for 2005 also indicates that, while labor unrest was rare, there were four reported strikes during the year. The most significant one closed the largest seaport for two days.[33]

Prohibition of Forced or Compulsory Labor. Country Reports for 2004 also finds that the Omani law prohibits forced or compulsory labor, including that of children. *Country Reports* for 2004 further notes that even though the protections of the 2003 Omani labor law apply equally to foreign and domestic workers, at times foreign workers (who account for 80% of private sector workforce and 50% of all workers in Oman) were placed in situations amounting to forced labor.

Country Reports for 2005 echoes the finding that some situations amounted to forced labor and adds that employers sometimes withheld documents that would release workers from employment contracts and allow them to change employers. Without such documents, a foreign worker must continue to work for his current employer or become technically unemployed and consequently a candidate for deportation. *Country Reports* for 2005 further reports that many foreign workers were not aware of their right to take such disputes to the Labor Welfare Board, which "in most cases" released the worker from the service contract without deportation, awarded compensation for time worked under compulsion, reimbursed the worker for back wages, and subjected the guilty employer to fines. However, *Country Reports 2005* states, there were no available statistics on the number of disputes filed or resolutions by the end of 2005.

CONGRESSIONAL ACTIVITY

Before the U.S.-Oman FTA and implementing legislation were formally submitted to Congress, both House and Senate committees held preliminary hearings. The House Ways and Means Committee held full committee hearings on April 5, 2005. The International Trade Subcommittee of the Senate Finance Committee held hearings on March 6, 2006.

Then, on May 10, the House Ways and Means Committee held "mock" markup hearings on the Administration's draft implementing legislation and approved the bill without amendment on a party-line vote of 23-11. On May 18, 2006, the Senate Finance Committee held its "mock" markup, adopting an amendment before passing the bill unanimously. The amendment reflected recent concerns about sweatshop conditions in Jordan (see section below), and implications for production under the U.S.-Oman FTA.

On June 28, the Senate Finance committee approved the draft implementing legislation (S. 3569) for the U.S.-Oman FTA by a vote of 10 to 3. On June 29, the Senate passed the bill by a vote of 60 to 34. On June 29 the House Ways and Means Committee also approved the draft implementing legislation (H.R. 5684) by a vote of 23 to 15. On July 20 the House passed the bill by a vote of 221 to 205.

CURRENT LABOR ISSUES

A report of alleged sweatshop conditions in plants in Jordan producing for export to the United States has been issued by the National Labor Committee (NLC), a nonprofit organization that promotes worker rights around the world. The 161-page report has raised concerns within Congress that similar conditions might exist or occur in other MEFTA countries, including Oman if the U.S.-Oman FTA were to go into effect.

The NLC report entitled *U.S.-Jordan Free Trade Agreement Descends into Human Trafficking and Involuntary Servitude,* released in May of 2006, documents conditions in 28 separate factories in Jordan in foreign trade zones, where clothing is produced by Jordanian and foreign guest workers, mostly for export to the United States. The report estimates that tens of thousands of foreign guest workers who entered employment willingly were subsequently stripped of their passports and trapped in involuntary servitude, sewing clothing in factories for companies including Wal-Mart, K-Mart, Gloria Vanderbilt, Target, Kohl's, J.C. Penney, Victoria's Secret, and L. L. Bean.[34]

The Senate Finance Committee responded to the concerns on May 18, 2006, by unanimously adopting an amendment in its mock markup of the Administration's U.S.-Oman FTA draft implementing legislation. The amendment, offered by Senator Kent Conrad, would prohibit any products made in Oman "with slave labor (including under sweatshop conditions so egregious as to be tantamount to slave labor) or with the benefit of human trafficking," from benefitting from the agreement. Committee Republicans, including Chairman Chuck Grassley, joined Democrats in voting for the conceptual amendment. The committee then unanimously approved the U.S.-Oman draft implementing bill as amended.[35]

Any amendments passed by a committee during the mock markup process are advisory in nature, rather than obligatory. The Administration responded that while they would consider the amendment, they had some concerns. First, they argued, the amendment might fall outside the scope of the provision in the *Trade Act of 2002*, P.L. 107-210, Sec. 2103(b)(3)(ii), requiring that any new statutory language be "necessary or appropriate" to implement the trade agreement.[36]

Second, the Administration argued, Sec. 307 of the Tariff Act of 1930 already prohibits the importation of merchandise produced in whole or in part through prison, forced, or indentured labor, including by those who voluntarily entered into employment but were later subject to *de facto* slave working conditions. In response to the Administration's argument, Senator Conrad pointed out that Sec. 307 of the Tariff Act of 1930 may not be applicable to apparel produced under slave labor conditions in Oman. This, he argued, is because apparel is no longer made in great quantities in the United States; and Sec. 307 does not apply to goods produced under forced or indentured labor if those goods are not domestically produced in quantities that meet the consumption demands of the United States.[37]

Third, the Administration argued that the amendment may be unnecessary because FTA language requiring Oman to enforce its own labor laws, which prohibit forced labor, is strong enough or enforceable enough to discourage or affect its practice. In addition, the Administration pointed out, Oman has approved core labor standards prohibiting forced or compulsory labor and has made commitments to strengthening its labor standards still further. These Omani commitments came from the Omani Minister of Labor as part of an exchange of letters between House Democrats, the Omani Minister, and the USTR. The Omani Minister made eight commitments in March and ten further commitments regarding forced labor and child labor in May. In those commitments Oman promised to issue Royal Decrees and Ministerial Decisions to strengthen the country's labor laws in response to congressional concerns by no later than October 31, 2006.[38]

While some Republicans argued that Oman needs time to craft new laws with technical support from the ILO, some Democrats argued for changes in Omani laws before the U.S.-Oman FTA implementing legislation is considered by Congress.[39]

On July 8, 2006, the Sultan of Oman issued a Royal Decree (74/2006) amending provisions of Omani labor law to provide some labor rights consistent with ILO core labor standards. As amended by the decree, Omani law would permit the right to form unions, the right to bargain collectively, and to engage in other union activities. The law would also prohibit employers and others from imposing any compulsory or forced labor with specific penalties for noncompliance. Penalties are provided for those who would interfere with union activity, or decline to provide the necessary facilitation or information. The Royal Decree delegates promulgation of regulations to the Ministry of Manpower; therefore, specific details regarding its implementation and enforcement are yet to be determined.[40]

Meanwhile, a few days after the Senate Finance Committee markup hearing, Jordan's trade minister Sharif Zu'bi indicated that the NLC report had incorrectly identified three sweatshops that are not even in Jordan, and that three others had been closed before the report was released in May. In addition, he noted that the Jordanian government had formed nine inspections teams to investigate the entire garment trade in the country, and is working with the International Labor Organization, U.S. labor committees, the USTR, the State Department, and U.S. and Jordanian apparel companies to address the challenges and improve their monitoring system.

Current Issues on Port Security

In the Spring of 2006, the U.S. interagency "Committee on Foreign Investment in the United States" raised no objections to the acquisition and continued operation of contracts by the Dubai-owned "Dubai Ports World" company from a British firm that managed port facilities in several cities including New York, New Jersey, Baltimore, New Orleans, Miami, and Philadelphia. After several members of Congress expressed opposition to the $9 billion merger on the grounds that the company might not be as vigilant on port security as required, the company agreed to a 45-day review of its operations at those ports. On March 9, the House Appropriations Committee voted 62-2 on a provision in the FY2006 supplemental funding bill for Iraq and Afghanistan war operations and other costs that would have effectively prevented DP World from operating in the United States.[41] The following day DP World officials announced that they would divest the newly-acquired U.S. port operations to an American owner.[42]

The Oman FTA Provision

Recently, a provision in the Oman FTA has become the focus of increased attention. Some argue that this provision could obligate the United States to open up landside aspects of its port activities to operation by companies such as DP World. Others argue that the provision is not new to bilateral trade agreements, and does not change current U.S. policy.

The provision, contained in Annex II of the U.S.-Oman FTA, addresses cross-border services and investment in the area of transportation. More specifically, the provision sets out two categories of transportation activities: those for which the United States reserves the right to adopt or maintain any measures, and those activities for which the United States does not reserve the right to adopt or maintain any measures — those activities which are exclusions from the above list.

The list for which the United States reserves the right to maintain any measure includes requirements for investment in, ownership and control of, and operation of drill rigs, U.S. flagged vessels, fishing vessels; plus requirements related to documenting a vessel under the U.S. flag, promotional programs, certification licensing, and citizenship requirements, programs, certification licensing and citizenship requirements, manning requirements, and all matters under the jurisdiction of the Federal Maritime Commission.

The excluded list, for which the United States does not reserve the right to adopt or maintain any measure, includes two categories of activities — one unconditional, and one conditional. The first category (a) is vessel construction and repair. On this category the United States reserves no right to adopt or maintain any measure.

The second category (b), for which the United States waives its right to adopt or maintain any of the listed measures on the condition that comparable market access in these sectors is obtained from Oman, includes the following activities:

> landside aspects of port activities including operation and maintenance of docks; loading and unloading vessels directly to or from land; marine cargo handling; operation and maintenance of piers; ship cleaning; stevedoring; transfer of cargo between vessels and trucks, trains, pipelines, and wharves; waterfront terminal operations; boat cleaning; canal operation; dismantling of vessels; operation of marine railways for drydocking; maritime surveyors, except cargo; marine wrecking of vessels for scrap; and shift classification societies.

Some in Congress argue that the provision excluding the above activities from the U.S. government's "right to adopt or maintain any measure" should be removed from the agreement because it poses a potential security risk to the United States. Others are arguing that the provision merely restates what is already the situation in the United States, and is not a problem. The arguments on both sides follow.

Arguments in Favor of the Provision

Those arguing that the provision excluding certain activities from the U.S. "right to adopt or maintain any measure" should remain in the agreement argue that:[43]

It Complies with Most Favored Nation Treatment Obligations

A basic obligation of free trade agreements such as the U.S.-Oman FTA is the obligation (subject to specified exceptions) to treat service suppliers and investors of other parties no less favorably than the United States treats its own service suppliers and investors. This provision meets those requirements.

Provision Exists in Other FTAs

This provision is already included in other agreements, including the North American Free Trade Agreement (NAFTA), the Dominican Republic-Central America Free Trade Agreement, and FTAs with Australia, Bahrain, Chile, and Morocco.

Omani Companies Already Have this Right

Proponents argue that Omani companies are presumably already able to acquire contracts for and perform these services. Currently there are no U.S. laws that prevent either an Omani-owned company or any other foreign-owned company from contracting with port owners to perform "landside aspects of port activities" in the United States.[44]

Coast Guard Protection Exists

The U.S. Coast Guard and Customs and Border Protection play an integral role in ensuring security at U.S. ports; and nothing in the agreement amends or diminishes the authority of these agencies.

No Omani Companies Are Currently Interested in U.S. Port Operations

While Oman already provides market access to U.S. service suppliers and investors, the USTR is not aware of any Omani companies that are currently involved in any U.S. port operations or that might be interested in such operations in the future.

However, If They Were, the "Essential Security" Exception Would "Fully" Protect the United States

According to proponents, if an Omani company were to express such interest in the future, the "essential security" (or "national security") exception (explained below) could arguably be invoked to "fully" protect U.S. national security needs.

The United States Could Deny FTA Benefits to Owners of a "Shell" Operation; to Businesses Whose Owners Were Nationals of Countries Subject to U.S. Sanctions; or to Any Potential Investment Pursuant to the "Essential Security Exception" Described Below

If non-Omani persons set up an enterprise in Oman that was merely a "shell" — i.e., that was engaged in no substantial business activities in Oman — and that enterprise sought to make an investment in the United States, the FTA contains specific language that would arguably permit the United States to deny the FTA's investment-and services-related benefits to that enterprise. Moreover, even if the enterprise set up in Oman had "substantial business activity" in Oman, the United States could deny FTA benefits to it if its owners were nationals of countries subject to U.S. sanctions. Finally, the U.S. government retains the authority to block *any* potential investment pursuant to the "essential security" exception described below.

The "Essential Security" Exception Offers Protection

Chapter 21 of the U.S.-Oman FTA contains several exceptions to the agreement. Article 21.2 addresses "essential security" and provides that:

> Nothing in the agreement shall be construed: (a) to require a Party to furnish or allow access to any information ... which it determines to be contrary to its essential security interests; or (b) to preclude a Party from applying measures it considers necessary for the fulfillment of its obligations [for] the maintenance or restoration of international peace or security or the protection of its own essential security interests.

An "essential security" exception has been included in all U.S. trade agreements dating back to the 1947 General Agreement on Tariffs and Trade (GATT). The United States, among other countries, has consistently interpreted this language (worded similarly to Article 21 of the U.S.-Oman FTA) to be self-judging, and therefore that national security matters are not appropriate for adjudication in a third-party dispute settlement mechanism. In other words, under these provisions it can be argued that nothing in an agreement can prevent the United States from applying measures that it considers necessary for the protection of essential security interests. Moreover, proponents will argue that review of national security claims by international tribunals are without precedent and are highly unlikely because, arguably, no tribunal would accept jurisdiction over the question of what constitutes a country's "national security."[45]

The Exon-Florio Amendment Offers Additional Protection for "National Security" Issues

In addition, U.S. law — in particular the Exon-Florio Amendment to the Defense Production Act of 1950[46] — authorizes the President to block proposed foreign investment in the United States that threatens national security. The President has delegated to the interagency Committee on Foreign Investment in the United States (CFIUS) the responsibility to continuously monitor foreign investment in the United States to ensure against threats to national security; and a CFIUS review could still be performed at the discretion of CFIUS. While it is theoretically possible for Oman to bring a legal challenge to the actions of the United States before a third-party tribunal, proponents argue, the United States would appear to be on solid legal grounds for asserting not only that the panel does not have the legal authority to determine the validity of such a matter, but also that the inconsistent measure is permitted and justifiable given the broad "self-judging" language of the national security exception.[47]

Arguments Against the Provision

Those arguing that the exception provision of Annex II should not be included in the U.S.-Oman FTA argue that such a provision could pose a serious threat to Congress' ability to ensure the security of U.S. port infrastructure. Specific arguments against the provision are as follows:[48]

The Specific Commitments in Annex II Raise Significant National Security Concerns, Opponents Argue

This is because language in Annex II regarding landside port operations would introduce new rights of establishment for foreign companies to own sensitive U.S. infrastructure. These FTA provisions would arguably subject U.S. laws or policies (whether enacted by Congress, the Executive, or the States) that restrict foreign ownership to a challenge in dispute resolution and/or to suit under the investor-state enforcement provisions.

The United States Would Be Required to Offer Oman the Right to Bid to Operate at U.S. Ports — the Very Activities About which Congress Expressed National Security Concerns During the Dubai Ports World Debate

Under the FTA, this right would be conditional upon obtaining comparable market access in this sector from Oman. However, this right covers the very port activities about which Congress expressed national security concerns during the Dubai Ports World debate.

Annex II Language Goes Beyond U.S. Commitments in the WTO

Generally, the service sectors to which the "right to establish" for foreign companies applies in these FTAs is the same as the service sectors that the United States agreed to in the 1994 WTO's General Agreement on Trade in Services (GATS). However, opponents argue, the Oman FTA adds to the U.S. commitments by specifically including (or by not specifically excluding) "landside operations of ports."

Opponents Also Argue that the WTO Text and Practice Says that National Security Claims Are Theoretically Reviewable

The reason for this, they argue, is that neither the GATT agreement nor the FTA expressly exempts these provisions from review by an international tribunal.[49]

Under Annex II, the United States May Not Ban Enterprises of a Party from Owning and Operating Covered Services

Nor can either country limit the number or size of such services, or require specific forms of ownership (i.e., require U.S. partners or require that it be a non-profit organization).

If the United States Took Action to Deny a Company Its New Right to Establish, Opponents Argue, It Would Be a Violation of the FTA, and Subject to Dispute Resolution and Trade Sanctions[50]

Under the FTA, such disputes can be brought in two fora, both of which raise concerns:

In a Government-to-Government Dispute Resolution Fora, Judges with a Narrow Trade Expertise Would Decide between U.S. National Security Needs and Trade Commitments

Government-to-government dispute resolution cases are not heard in U.S. courts, but in three-person trade tribunals under procedures agreed to in Article 20 of the FTA. In these cases, each country in the dispute may select one "judge" from its country and these two tribunalists would choose a third "judge" — from a list of trade experts provided by each country. In such a scenario, "judges" with a narrow trade expertise and perspective including non-U.S. individuals would be empowered to balance competing U.S. interests — national security needs against U.S. trade commitments — to decide which comes first.

In the Investor-State Dispute Resolution Fora, U.N. and World Bank Tribunalists Would Be Empowered to "Second Guess" a U.S. National Security Claim

Investor-state enforcement is enumerated in Chapter 10 of the U.S.-Oman FTA. Under these provisions, even if the Omani government were not to initiate a case, an actual investor/company has the right to privately initiate its own case against the United States. Such a case, if brought, would seek a judgement requiring that the United States pay monetary damages equal to part of the expected future profits it would be denied by an adverse U.S. action. The case would be adjudicated by United Nations or World Bank tribunalists, who would be empowered to "second guess" a national security claim, and possibly order the U.S. government to pay the foreign company for its lost future profits.[51]

If the U.S. Were to Raise an "Essential Security" Exception after a CFIUS Review, an FTA Panel Would Likely Deny the Exception

If the U.S. were to raise the "essential security" exception included in Chapter 21, Article 21.2 as a defense before a trade tribunal and a CFIUS review had been completed without a finding of a security threat (as in the case of Dubai World Ports), opponents argue, there is no doubt that an FTA panel would not permit use of the FTA's "essential security" exception to excuse consequent government action that interfered with the FTA investor right to establish port operations.

If a CFIUS Review Predetermined That an Acquisition Were Not in the National Security Interests of the United States, This Would Not Terminate an FTA Claim

However, the converse is not necessarily true: If a CFIUS review *did* determine that an acquisition were not in the national security interest of the United States, opponents argue, this would not terminate an FTA claim. This is because the FTA sets out procedures for responding to validly raised claims. Thus, even with a CFIUS review, it is argued that the United States would still be required to respond in a United Nations or World Bank tribunal, essentially requiring litigation on the "essential security" defense.

POSSIBLE OUTCOMES OF A CONGRESSIONAL VOTE ON THE FTA AND POTENTIAL CONSEQUENCES

If the proposed FTA is approved, Oman would join four other MEFTA countries with FTAs, and the proposed MEFTA would be one-quarter of the way complete. An agreement with Oman could be a pathway to create private sector jobs for Oman's burgeoning population and a gateway to more openness in the Middle East.

If Congress should not approve the proposed U.S.-Oman FTA, any one of a number of things could happen. On one hand, Oman could just continue trading with the United States as usual. On the other hand, Oman could likely look elsewhere to countries such as China, Russia, or India for support in diversifying beyond the production of oil which could run out in roughly 15-20 years.

In addition, should the proposed U.S.-Oman FTA not be approved, there could be broader implications. For example, Oman has been letting the United States use several military facilities. While many would argue that it would be in Oman's interest to continue to cooperate with the United States military, Oman might be tempted to put further restrictions on the U.S. use of these facilities. Oman might also shrink back from its cooperation on counterterrorism which is said to have included sharing/providing tips on intelligence about possible Al Quaida suspects operating in the Persian Gulf or Oman itself.

References

[1] For MEFTA background in this section see CRS Report RL32638, *Middle East Free Trade Area: Progress Report*, by Mary Jane Bolle. For background on Oman, see CRS Report RS21534, *Oman: Reform, Security, and U.S. Policy*, by Kenneth Katzman; and CRS Report RL31533, *The Persian Gulf States: Issues for U.S. Policy, 2006*, by Kenneth Katzman.

[2] The 16 entities in the Middle East (see map p.2) are Bahrain, Cyprus, Egypt, Gaza Strip and West Bank, Iran, Iraq, Israel, Jordan, Kuwait, Lebanon, Oman, Qatar, Saudi Arabia, Syria, United Arab Emirates, and Yemen; the four in North Africa are Algeria, Libya, Morocco, and Tunisia.

[3] Prenotification was given on October 17, 2005 — three days after negotiations were concluded. Subsequently, the agreement was officially "entered into," or signed, on January 19, 2006.

[4] CRS Report RL32011, Trade Agreements: Procedure for Congressional Approval and Implementation, by Vladimir N. Pregelj.

[5] U.S. Department of State, Bureau of Near Eastern Affairs. Background Note: Oman. February 2006.

[6] *Times of Oman* - Local News, "Oman, U.S. Sign Free-Trade Pact," January 20, 2006; and Gulf Times, "Step Forward in Mideast," January 30, 2006.

[7] Office of the U.S. Trade Representative. 2005 National Trade Estimate Report on Foreign Trade Barriers, p. 458.

[8] U.S. Department of Commerce. *Doing Business in Oman: A Country Commercial Guide for U.S. Companies* (no date). Section on foreign direct investment statistics.

[9] Ibid.

[10] U.S. International Trade Commission (USITC). U.S.-Oman Free Trade Agreement: Potential Economy-Wide and Selected Sectoral Effects, p. 2-4, 2-5.

[11] Office of the USTR, Summary of the U.S.-Oman Free Trade Agreement, Sept. 2005.

[12] USITC, op. cit., p. 2-4, 2-5.

[13] CRS calculations from USITC Dataweb.

[14] This section only, except as otherwise indicated, is from USTR. *Summary of the U.S.-Oman FTA*, op. cit.

[15] USITC op. cit, p. xii (this sentence).

[16] While both ILO core labor standards and U.S. internationally recognized worker rights provisions (defined in the Trade Act of 1972 as amended) refer to similar standards, they differ in one respect. While both lists include

the right to organize and bargain collectively, a prohibition against forced labor, and protections for child labor, the ILO set includes additionally protections against employment discrimination; while the U.S. set includes additionally labor protections relating to minimum wages, maximum hours, and safety and health protections.

[17] Sec. 2104(e) of the Trade Act of 2002 requires that advisory committees provide the President, the U.S. Trade Representative, and Congress with reports required under Section 135(e)(1) of the Trade Act of 1974, as amended, not later than 30 days after the President notifies Congress of his intent to enter into an agreement. Under Section 135(e) of the Trade Act of 1974, as amended, the report must include an advisory opinion as to whether and to what extent the Agreement promotes the economic interests of the United States and achieves the applicable overall and principal negotiating objectives set forth in the *Trade Act of 2002*.

[18] Office of the USTR. United States and Oman Conclude Free Trade Agreement. Oct. 3, 2005.

[19] Letter from William E. Frenzel, former Member of Congress and Chairman of ACTPN, November 15, 2005.

[20] These are: size of government expenditures and taxes, legal structures and security, access to sound money, freedom to trade internationally, and regulation of credit, labor, and business.

[21] The Fraser Institute. *Economic Freedom of the World, 2005 Annual Report*, by James Gwartney, Florida State University, Robert Lawson, Capital University, with Erik Gartzke, Columbia University. 188 p. The five areas are: (1) size of government; (2) legal structure and protection of property rights; (3) access to sound money; (4) international exchange; and (5) regulation.

[22] Labor Promising Battle Over Bush's Mideast Trade Agenda. *Congress Daily*. March 2, 2006.

[23] Response from the Sultanate of Oman to the House Ways and Means Trade Subcommittee Minority Staff, January 4, 2006.

[24] Letter from Ambassador Hunaina Al-Mughairy, Omani Ambassador to the United States, to the Minority Chief Counsel of the Trade Subcommittee, House Ways and Means Committee accompanying *Response from the Sultanate of Oman to the House Ways and Means Trade Subcommittee Minority Staff*, January 4, 2006.

[25] Trade and Environment Policy Advisory Committee. *The U.S.-Oman Free Trade Agreement*. November 15, 2005. 30 p.

[26] Office of the USTR, *Trade Advisory Committees Support U.S.-Oman FTA*. Nov. 18, 2005. See also Intergovernmental Policy Advisory Committee, *The U.S.-Oman Free Trade Agreement (FTA)*. November 15, 2005.

[27] P.L. 107-210, Sec. 2102(b)(12)(G). This law gives the President authority to negotiate trade agreements that will then be considered by Congress on an expedited basis.

[28] Even though both parties committed to this enforcement pattern in the U.S.-Jordan FTA, the countries exchanged letters just before Congress debated the agreement, promising to "make every effort to resolve [any differences] without recourse to formal dispute settlement procedures."

[29] Before the United States Trade Representative: Petition to Remove Oman From the List of Beneficiary Developing Countries Under the Generalized System of Preferences ("GSP"), June 15, 2005. Source: USTR website at [http://www.USTR.gov].

[30] ILO Database of International Standards.

[31] Labor Advisory Committee for Trade Negotiations and Trade Policy (LAC), "The U.S.-Oman Free Trade Agreement," November 15, 2005, p. 5. *Country Reports* for 2005 indicates that the minimum wage is insufficient to provide a decent standard of living for a worker and family.

[32] *Country Reports* for 2005 was released March 8, 2006.

[33] Materials received by CRS on April 4, 2006 from the firm of Baker Donelson Bearman Caldwell and Berkowitz representing the Omani government also report that there were 33 strikes in 2004 in Oman, representing almost 6,000 workers in 17 industries.

[34] The report is available at [http://www.nclnet.org].

[35] *Washington Trade Daily*, "Finance Approves Oman FTA Bill," May 19, 2006.

[36] World Trade Online, *Inside U.S. Trade*, "USTR Cool to Finance Labor Amendment To Oman Draft FTA Bill," May 19, 2006.

[37] Ibid.

[38] Ibid; a letter from Rep. Charles B. Rangel and Benjamin L. Cardin to Her Excellency Hunaina Sultan Ahmed Al-Mughairy, Ambassador of the Sultanate of Oman on April 6, 2005; and a letter from Maqbool Ali Sultan, Minister of Commerce and Industry of the Sultanate of Oman to USTR Robert Portman on May 8, 2006.

[39] *International Trade Daily*, "Bilateral Agreements: House Democrats Again Press Oman on Labor Laws Ahead of Free Trade Vote," April 12, 2006; *Washington Trade Daily*, "Ways and Means Approves Oman FTA," May 11, 2006; *Congress Daily AM*, "Dems Urge Slowdown On Trade Deals to

Stress Labor Rights," June 6, 2006; and news release from Representative Charles B. Rangel on May 19, 2006.

[40] Qaboos bin Sa'id, Sultan of Oman. Royal Decree 74/2006. Amending Some Provisions of the Labor Law. See also July 12, 2006 Letter of Omani Ambassador Humaina Al-Mughairy to USTR Susan Schwab summarizing its provisions, [http://www.nftc.org/default/trade/mefta/oman/071206%20 Oman%20ltr%20to%20UST R%20re%20labor.pdf].

[41] CRS Report RS21852, The United Arab Emirates (UAE): Issues for U.S. Policy, by Kenneth Katzman.

[42] CRS Report RL33388, *The Committee on Foreign Investment in the United States (CFIUS)*, by James K. Jackson; and Weisman, Jonathan, and Bradley Graham, "Dubai Firm to Sell U.S. Port Operations," *The Washington Post*, March 10, 2006, p. A1.

[43] Except as otherwise noted, these arguments are taken from Office of the USTR. Trade Facts. Free Trade Agreements and the Supply of Services at U.S. Ports, June 2006.

[44] CRS general distribution memorandum, Legal Issues Related to the Proposed Oman Free Trade Agreement and Port Security, by Todd Tatelman, July 18, 2006, p. 2.

[45] CRS general distribution memorandum, *National Security Issues and the Proposed U.S.-Oman Free Trade Agreement*, by Todd B. Tatelman, July 19, 2006.

[46] P.L. 100-418, Title V, Subtitle A, Part II (50 USC appl 2170). See CRS Report RL33312, *The Exon-Florio Test for National Security*, by James K, Jackson.

[47] Tatelman, July 18 and 19, 2006, op. cit, and USTR, Trade Facts, op. cit.

[48] Except as otherwise footnoted, these arguments are from Public Citizen, Oman FTA provisions that grant foreign investors the right to own or operate sensitive infrastructure within the U.S. Memorandum from Lori Wallach, May 11, 2006.

[49] House Ways and Means Democrats. "New CRS Report Raises New Nat'l Security Problems ... Potential New Opportunities for Dubai Ports World."

[50] Public Citizen, Oman FTA provisions that grant foreign investors the right to own or operate sensitive infrastructure within the U.S., by Lori Wallach, May 11, 2006; House Ways and Means Democrats, "New CRS Report Raises New Nat'l Security Problems... Potential New Opportunities for Dubai Ports World"; and the Honorable Byron Dorgan, "Talking Points on Oman Free Trade Agreement."

[51] See also, House Ways and Means Democrats, op. cit.

In: Politics and Economics of the Middle East ISBN: 978-1-60456-719-9
Editors: W. Evans & D.J. Harris

Chapter 6

MIDDLE EAST FREE TRADE AREA: PROGRESS REPORT*

Mary Jane Bolle

ABSTRACT

On May 9, 2003, the Bush Administration proposed the establishment of a U.S. Middle East Free Trade Area (MEFTA) within a decade (by about 2013). This proposal came a year and a half after the September 11, 2001 terrorist attacks on the U.S. World Trade Center and the Pentagon. The MEFTA was billed as part of a plan to fight terrorism — in this case, by supporting the growth of Middle East prosperity and democracy — through trade. On June 23, 2003 the Bush Administration described a six-step process for Middle East entities to become part of that MEFTA: (1) joining the World Trade Organization (WTO); (2) possibly participating in the Generalized System of Preferences; successively entering into (3) trade investment framework agreements (TIFAs), (4) bilateral investment treaties (BITs), and (5) free trade agreements (FTA) with the United States; and (6) participating in trade capacity building.

The MEFTA would cover 20 entities in what many refer to as the Middle East/North Africa — 16 in the Middle East: Bahrain, Cyprus, Egypt, the Gaza Strip/West Bank, Iran, Iraq, Israel, Jordan, Kuwait, Lebanon, Oman, Qatar, Saudi Arabia, Syria, the United Arab Emirates and Yemen; and four in North Africa: Algeria, Libya, Morocco, and Tunisia.

---

* Excerpted from CRS Report RL32638, dated January 27, 2006.

Although U.S.-Middle East trade is small (4-5% of total U.S. trade), oil and gas are key imports, accounting for roughly one-tenth of all oil and gas consumed in the United States each year. Textiles and apparel are the second most important imports from these entities. The most important U.S. exports to these entities are machinery and transportation equipment.

The Bush Administration's initiative aims to help diversify and improve the economies of the Middle East, provide jobs for the rapidly growing population, stimulate U.S. exports, and help Middle East countries make economic reforms —values echoed by *The 9-11 Commission Report* as part of a comprehensive strategy to countering terrorism.

Since the Bush Administration first announced its trade initiative, it has made substantial progress in working with MEFTA entities to support WTO membership, and to develop TIFAs, BITs, and FTAs and progress along the steps outlined above. Since the beginning of 2003: Saudi Arabia has joined the WTO, and Iraq, Iran, Lebanon, Yemen, and Algeria are negotiating accession. In addition, TIFAS have been completed with seven countries: Kuwait, Oman, Saudi Arabia, the United Arab Emirates, Yemen, Qatar, and Iraq, bringing the total to 12. Other TIFA partners are Bahrain, Egypt, Jordan, Algeria, Morocco, and Tunisia. BITs have been completed with one country, Jordan, bringing the total to five. Other BIT partners are Bahrain, Egypt, Morocco, and Tunisia. Finally, a bilateral free trade agreement has been implemented with Jordan, Israel, Morocco, and Bahrain; signed with Oman (January 19, 2006); and is under negotiation with the United Arab Emirates. This brings the number of MEFTA FTAs to four implemented, one awaiting congressional action, and one under negotiation. FTA negotiations underway with Egypt have been suspended over human rights issues.

INTRODUCTION

After the terrorist attacks against the New York World Trade Center and the Pentagon on September 11, 2001, a U.S. objective became, in the words of U.S. Trade Representative Robert B. Zoellick, to fight terrorism by "spreading the message of prosperity and democracy throughout the world."[1] One way the Bush Administration chose to spread that message was through a proposed Middle East Free Trade Agreement (MEFTA).

The MEFTA Initiative was proposed by President Bush on May 9, 2003, and was slated for completion within a decade (i.e., by around 2013). More detail on the Bush Administration's plan was revealed on June 23, 2003 at the World Economic Forum in Jordan, when U.S. Trade Representative Zoellick spoke on the conceptual details. USTR Zoellick outlined six-steps for Middle East entities wishing to enter into a free trade agreement with the United States.

The purpose of this chapter is to describe MEFTA in terms of: (1) its impetus, (2) its major elements; (3) background trade data, (4) details; and (5) arguments for each.

At the back of this chapter are five tables. Table 1 outlines the basic elements of MEFTA. Table 2 tracks the steps each entity has taken toward a free trade agreement with the United States: WTO membership, eligibility for the Generalized System of Preferences, and achievement of three types of agreements — trade investment framework agreements, bilateral investment treaties, and free trade agreements. Tables 3 and 4 list for each entity, U.S. import and export totals and shares of key commodities traded. Table 5 shows the current value and share of world and U.S. foreign direct investment, respectively, in various entities.

Table 1. Brief Summary of the MEFTA Initiative

MEFTA Entities	Middle East: Bahrain, Cyprus, Egypt, Gaza Strip/West Bank, Iran, Iraq, Israel, Jordan, Kuwait, Lebanon, Oman, Qatar, Saudi Arabia, Syria, United Arab Emirates, Yemen North Africa: Algeria, Libya, Morocco, Tunisia,
Efforts Toward a Middle East Free Trade Agreement or Area	Steps for each entity:* 1. World Trade Organization Membership; 2. GSP; 3. Trade Investment Framework Agreement (TIFA); 4. Bilateral Investment Treaty (BIT); 5. Free Trade Agreement (FTA) to which other eligible countries may "dock"; and 6. Trade capacity building (through various U.S. assistance efforts.)
Time line of the initiative	Aim for MEFTA "within 10 years" (i.e., by 2013.)
Requirements for eligibility	The Bush Administration has indicated that the entities need: • to be "peaceful"; • to be prepared to undertake economic reform and liberalization; • to not participate in a primary, secondary, or tertiary boycott of Israel.

* See Table 2 for the status of various entities.

Impetus for the Initiative

MEFTA captured an idea that was already being debated in Washington — using trade as a tool to fight terrorism. For example, in February 2003, a report by policy analyst Edward Gresser argued that the Muslim world had been the "blank spot" on the U.S. trade agenda, a fact that risked "undermining rather than supporting the war on terrorism." Gresser pointed to an economic crisis affecting almost all of the western Muslim states, which have "seen their share of world trade and investment collapse since 1980," resulting in "stagnant growth, [and] falling income," with social consequences of "unemployment, political tension, and rising appeal for religious extremists."[2]

Gresser argued that, "A strategic initiative for the Muslim[3] world could end —or at least ease — the tilt." Gresser called for an initiative "analogous to the programs now available for Central America, the Andean Nations, and Africa" in order to possibly spark "growth and creation, and so reduce the attraction of radicalism and religious fundamentalism."

Another article written by policy analyst Brink Lindsey of the CATO Institute argued for two concepts. The first was an additional shorter-term program to include "temporary duty-free, quota-free access to the U.S. market for exports of selected Muslim countries." The shorter term program, he declared, would give tangible, dramatic proof of U.S. commitment to the region, thereby providing an impetus for the longer, arduous process of negotiating free trade agreements. The second concept Lindsey called for was the expansion of the definition of "Middle East" beyond the traditional geographic area to include other countries with "geopolitical significance."[4]

More recently, *The 9-11 Commission Report* affirmed these ideas. It included a recommendation which reads, "A comprehensive U.S. strategy to counter terrorism should include economic policies that encourage development, more open societies, and opportunities for people to improve the lives of their families and to enhance prospects for their children's future."[5]

Major Elements

The Bush Administration's MEFTA plan, in aiming to support economic development, job creation, and political, and humanitarian changes, reflects elements of the two articles referred to above:

- Primary Focus. The primary focus of the Bush Administration's plan would be on the long-term establishment of a Middle East Free Trade Area by around 2013.
- Short-Run Trade Preference Program. The Bush Administration's short-run trade preference component would be to continue the Generalized System of Preferences (GSP) currently available to some Middle East

countries. The Bush Administration is also considering offering sub-regional groups within the Middle East some eligibility to export goods to the United States tariff free or at reduced tariffs.

- Long-Term Plan. The Bush Administration's long-term plan would be for eligible countries to: (1) join the World Trade Organization and then sequentially enter into (2) trade investment framework agreements (TIFAs), (3) bilateral investment treaties (BITs), and (4) free trade agreements (FTAs) with the United States. Once a country has entered into an FTA with the United States, other neighboring countries could achieve some FTA tariff benefits by "cooperatively producing" (with two or more countries contributing to the same product) with that country.
- Definition of "Middle East." The Bush Administration's plan uses the Office of the U.S. Trade Representative definition of "Middle East" and includes countries traditionally identified as in the Middle East or North Africa.[6] (See figure 1.)
- Eligibility Requirements The Bush Administration's plan specifies very few eligibility requirements for countries wishing to join the MEFTA.

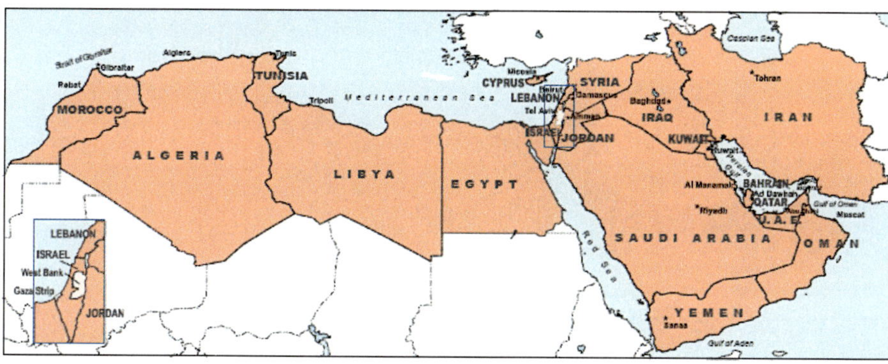

Source: Map Resources. Adapted by CRS. (K.Yancey 10/4/04)

Figure 1. Entities Included in the Bush Administration's Definition of "Middle East / North Africa".

SOME KEY INDICATORS OF U.S. ECONOMIC TIES TO THE MIDDLE EAST

U.S. trade with the Middle East is small. U.S. trade with the 20 Middle East entities covered in this chapter accounted for less than 4% of all U.S. exports and less than 5% of all U.S. imports in 2003. An important U.S. economic interest in the Middle East, however, is oil and gas.

U.S. Imports

More than 56% of all oil and gas *consumed* in the United States each year is imported: 10% is imported from the Middle East, 46 % is imported from other countries, and 44% is produced domestically.

Figure 2 below looks at just the *imported* oil and gas and shows where it comes from. Of all imported oil and gas, close to one-fifth (19%) comes from Middle East countries. Of that, nearly half (11%) comes from Saudi Arabia, and the following countries contribute lesser amounts: Iraq (3%), Algeria (3%), Kuwait (1%), and all others (1%). (See figure 2 below.)[7]

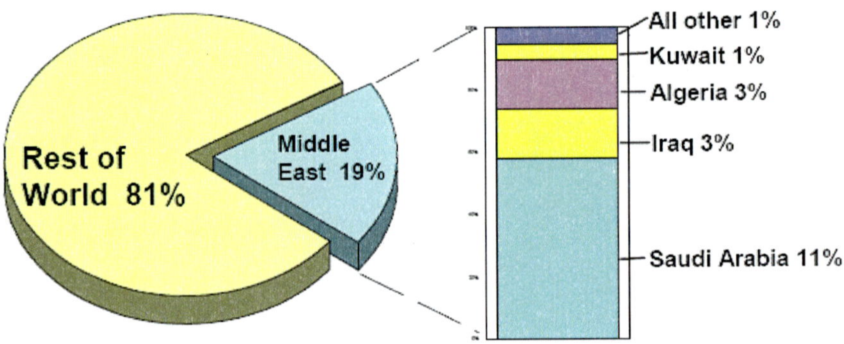

Data Source: USITC Dataweb.

Figure 2. Sources of Total U.S. Oil and Gas Imports, 2003.

Imports of oil and gas from the Middle East constitute a little more than half (53%) of *total* U.S. imports from that region. (See figure 3.) After gas and oil, the next most important imports from Middle East countries are textiles and apparel, which together account for another 15% of U.S. imports from the Middle East. Other key import categories are diverse — nonmetallic minerals (3%), electronics (2%), organic chemicals (2%), pharmaceuticals (1%), telecommunications equipment (1%), and scientific instruments (1%).

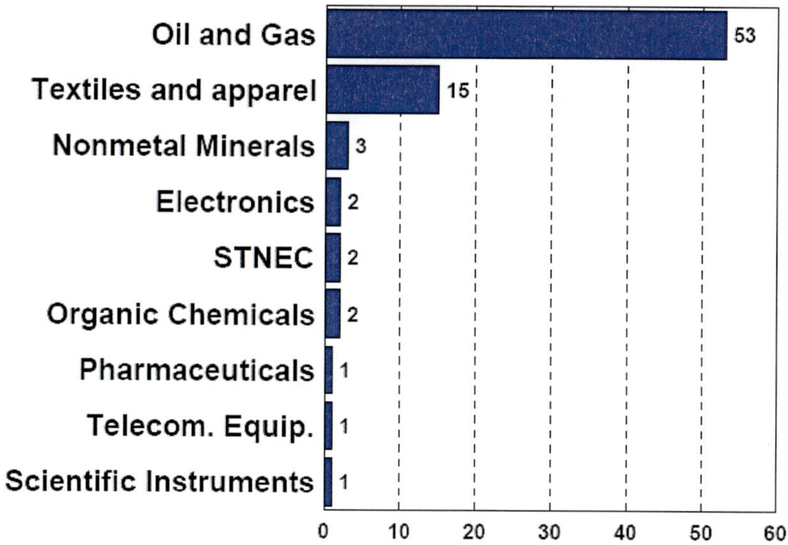

Data source: USITC Dataweb; STNEC: military items returned to U.S.

Figure 3. Key U.S. Imports from the Middle East, 2003 (as a % of all imports from the Middle East).

U.S. Exports

U.S. *exports* to Middle East countries are also heavily concentrated in two industries: machinery and transportation equipment.[8] One quarter (24%) of U.S. exports to Middle East countries is machinery of various types: general industrial machinery, machinery specialized for particular industries, power generating machinery, electrical machinery, and office machinery. An additional one-fifth (21%) of U.S. exports to Middle East countries is transportation equipment including various types of road vehicles. Other key exports include nonmetallic minerals (8%), cereals (6%), scientific instruments (4%), telecommunications equipment (3%) and textile fibers (3%). (See figure 4.)

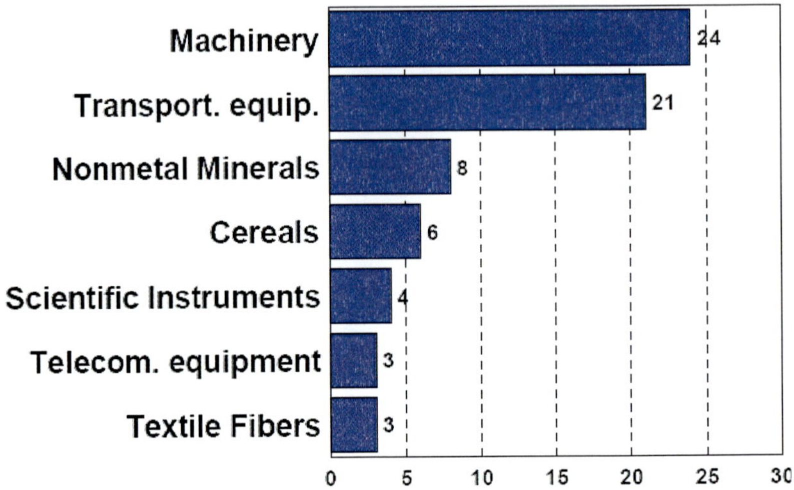

Data source: USITC Dataweb.

Figure 4. Top U.S. Exports to the Middle East, 2003 (as a % of all U.S. Exports to the Middle East).

Appendix tables 3 and 4 detail U.S. imports from and exports to each of the 20 Middle East entities covered by this chapter. Those tables include, for each country: (a) the total value of U.S. imports or exports, (b) the main items imported or exported, and (c) the percent of total imports/exports represented by each key commodity.

U.S. Investment

U.S. investment in the Middle East is limited. The stock of U.S. foreign direct investment (FDI) in Middle East countries in 2002 totaled $17.1 billion, or 1.1% of total U.S. FDI. However, U.S. FDI represents nearly one-quarter of world FDI in the Middle East. (See Table 5 for world and U.S. FDI totals in the various entities.) Half of the U.S. total is in two key sectors: mining 26% (primarily oil and gas), and manufacturing (25%). The remaining 49% of U.S. foreign direct investment in the Middle East is distributed throughout the service sector — especially the information sector (13%), and professional, scientific and technical services (7%).[9] In addition, Americans may have considerable portfolio investment in Israel including Israeli bonds.

Recent Growth in Trade with MEFTA Entities

Between the end of 2002 and the end of 2003 (most recent data available), U.S. exports to Middle East/North African countries declined by 1% while U.S. imports from these entities increased 24%. The greatest growth in imports was in petroleum and natural gas. Petroleum imports increased 38% while natural gas imports increased 118%. Other major sectors which showed increases in imports include apparel (9%), textiles (8%), and medicinal and pharmaceutical products (32%).

DETAILS OF THE MEFTA PROGRAM

MEFTA can be examined in terms of four basic components: (a) trade preferences, (b) steps or activities leading toward free trade agreements, (c) requirements for country eligibility, and (d) time lines for each initiative. An overview chart outlining these components is included as table 1.

Trade Preference Components

In the short run, the Bush Administration would continue the Generalized System of Preferences (GSP) which includes duty-free entry to the U.S. market for at least 3,500 products from 140 developing countries. The following Middle East countries are currently eligible for GSP benefits: Bahrain, Egypt, Jordan, Lebanon, Oman, Yemen, Algeria, Morocco, and Tunisia. Remaining countries covered by this chapter are not eligible for GSP benefits. Of those not eligible, some are no longer considered "developing."[10] Others do not meet the Bush Administration's eligibility requirements. GSP limits country participation on the basis of: (a) per-capita income, and (b) participation in the Organization of Petroleum Exporting Countries (OPEC). It also limits product preferences on the basis of import sensitivity.[11]

Steps or Activities Leading Toward Free Trade Agreements[12]

The Bush Administration's proposed program consists of six steps which each country may take, culminating in a free trade agreement with the United States. The second step, GSP participation, was discussed above as the trade preference component. Table 1 lists each country included in the USTR definition of Middle East / North Africa, and for each country indicates which steps it has already fulfilled. The other five steps are:

First

World Trade Organization (WTO) membership to promote integration into the world trading system. Nine Middle East entities are not yet members of the WTO: the Gaza Strip and the West Bank, Iran, Iraq, Lebanon, Saudi Arabia, Syria, Yemen, Algeria, and Libya.

Second

The continuation of GSP, discussed above.

Third

Trade and investment framework agreements (TIFAs) to establish a framework for expanding trade and for resolving outstanding disputes. Eight Middle East entities do not have TIFAs with the United States: Cyprus, the Gaza Strip and the West Bank, Iran, Iraq, Lebanon, Oman, Syria, and Libya,

Fourth

Bilateral investment treaties (BITs) oblige governments to treat foreign investors fairly and to offer them legal protections equal to those afforded domestic investors. BITs make the business climate more attractive to U.S. companies. The following 14 Middle East entities do not have BITs with the United States: Cyprus, the Gaza Strip and the West Bank, Iran, Iraq, Kuwait, Lebanon, Oman, Qatar, Saudi Arabia, Syria, the United Arab Emirates, Yemen, Algeria, and Libya.

Fifth

Free trade agreements (FTAs), typically to remove tariff and non-tariff barriers to trade across all sectors. Currently three countries in the Middle East — Israel, Jordan, and Morocco — have congressionally-approved free trade agreements with the United States. In addition, the United States completed negotiations on a free trade agreement with Bahrain on September 14, 2004; it awaits consideration by Congress.

The Bush Administration is considering including "cumulation clauses" which would afford sub-regional groups within the Middle East some eligibility to export goods to the United States tariff-free or at reduced tariffs. Stipulations would likely require that (1) those goods be produced in concert with a neighboring country which already has a free trade agreement, and that (2) the exported products meet rules of origin requirements.[13] Under the Bush Administration's initiative, now that the FTA is implemented with Morocco, and once it is implemented with Bahrain (should Congress approve the FTA with Bahrain), for example, other North African countries might be able to "dock" with and co-produce with Morocco; and other Gulf countries could "dock" with and co-produce with Bahrain. So, for example, to qualify for tariff benefits under a U.S.-Bahrain FTA, products could be jointly produced by Bahrain and Qatar or Oman or the United Arab Emirates, or a combination of the named countries.[14] The program whereby Jordan, Egypt, the Gaza Strip and the West Bank were authorized gain tariff relief by co-producing with Israel under the U.S.-Israel free trade agreement is an example of this concept.[15]

In addition, on September 8, 2004, U.S. Trade Representative Robert B. Zoellick reportedly said that the Bush Administration is considering initiating free trade agreement negotiations with the United Arab Emirates and Oman. The 9/11 Commission study endorsed "economic policies that encourage development, more open societies, and opportunities" in the Middle East.[16]

Sixth

The final step in the Bush Administration's plan is trade-capacity building to help countries realize more fully the benefits of open markets (e.g., build the "legal entrepreneurial infrastructure"). The Middle East Partnership Initiative would help allocate structural adjustment funding to partner countries to help ease the burden of free trade's impact on local industries. The initiative would also be aimed at increasing educational opportunities, strengthening civil society and rule of law, and supporting small business.[17] The Middle East Partnership Initiative would help target more than $1 billion of annual funding from various Government agencies and spur partnerships with private organizations and businesses that support trade and development. For 2003, funding for U.S. Trade Capacity Building totaled $752 million, of which $174 million, or 23% went to Middle East countries.[18]

Requirements for Eligibility

The Bush Administration's plan is open to: a) those "peaceful" countries that seek an increased trade relationship with the United States and b) "all those countries that are prepared to participate in economic reform and liberalization." Eligible countries must among other things: (1) "be prepared to participate in economic reform and liberalization," and (2) not participate in a primary, secondary, or tertiary boycott of Israel.[19]

Time Line

The Bush Administration aims for a Middle East Free Trade Area within 10 years (by about 2013). Cathi Novelli, USTR's chief negotiator on FTAs with countries in the Middle East until the fall of 2005, has indicated that the overall objective of the MEFTA exercise is not to meet the deadline, which she calls "ambitious," but to push the reform process in the region along.[20]

PROGRESS SO FAR

According to the Bush Administration, each of the steps listed above would aim to address political, economic, and humanitarian objectives in order to help Middle East countries to become "sustainable trading partners."[21] The hope is that each of the successive steps involved in negotiating TIFAs, BITs, and FTAs might help induce internal changes in the laws and regulations of the various countries.

Since the MEFTA program was announced in 2003, Saudi Arabia has joined the WTO, and the United States has negotiated new TIFAS with seven countries (Kuwait, Oman, Saudi Arabia, the United Arab Emirates, Yemen, Qatar, and Iraq). (See table 2.) Thus, almost three-quarters of the MEFTA entities (14) now have TIFAs with the United States. Other countries with which it already has TIFAS are Bahrain, Egypt, Jordan, Israel, Algeria, Morocco, and Tunisia.

In addition, since the MEFTA program was announced, a BIT between the United States and Jordan has been fully approved. As a result, the United States currently has BITs with more than one-quarter (6) out of 20 of the MEFTA entities. Other countries with which the United States already had BITS were Bahrain, Egypt, Jordan, Morocco, and Tunisia.

Finally, since the MEFTA program was announced, the United States has completed bilateral trade agreements with three countries: Morocco, Bahrain, and Oman. The President signed implementing legislation for the Morocco FTA in August, 2004 (P.L. 108-302); and for the Bahrain FTA on January 11, 2006 (P.L. 109-169). An FTA with Oman was signed by the two countries on January 19, 2006, and awaits congressional action. FTAs were already in effect for Israel and Jordan. In addition, an FTA with the United Arab Emirates is under negotiation.

Thus, currently one-quarter (five) MEFTA entities have signed trade agreements with the United States; one of those awaits final consideration by Congress; and a sixth awaits completion by the negotiators. A seventh FTA under negotiation with Egypt has been suspended over human rights issues in Egypt.[22]

CONCLUSION

The MEFTA would aim to help stimulate greater economic development in the Middle East. Shorter term goals from these stimuli would be: (a) for the region to grow enough to begin absorbing some of the unemployment (which averages around 22%)[23] — arguably the region's most pressing economic problem; and (b) for the region to begin attracting more foreign investment to help diversify output beyond oil and gas, textiles and apparel, and a few other commodities. As the shorter term stretches into the longer term, goals would be for the Middle East to develop alternative economic resources and industries that could help ease and even reverse its declining share of world economic growth and investment, its unemployment, and perhaps some of the conditions in the Middle East that support terrorism.

Table 2. Entities Covered by the MEFTA: Progress toward a Bilateral Free Trade Agreement with the U.S.

MEFTA Entity	Steps Toward an FTA with the United States				
	WTO Membership and year of joining	GSP eligibility[c]	TIFA with the U.S. and Year TIFA was signed	BIT with the U.S. and year BIT was signed	Bilateral Trade Agreement with the U.S.
Middle East					
Bahrain	+1995	ineligible	+2002	+ 2001	+ Approved 1/11/2006
Cyprus	+1995				
Egypt	+1995	+	+ 1999	+ 1992	See table note b
Gaza Strip and West					
Bank					See table note b
Iran	Negotiating accession	ineligible			
Iraq	negotiating accession	ineligible	+ 2005		
Israel	+1995	ineligible	+ b	+ b	+ 1985
Jordan	+2000	+	+ b	+ 2003	+ 2001
Kuwait	+1995	ineligible	+ 2004		
	negotiating				
Lebanon	accession	+			
Oman	+2000	+	+ 2004		+ Signed 1/19/2006
Qatar	+1996	ineligible	+ 2004		
Saudi Arabia	+2005	ineligible	+ 2003		
Syria		ineligible			
United Arab Emirates	+1996	ineligible	+ 2004		Under negotiation
Yemen	negotiating accession	+	+ 2004		

Table 2. (Continued).

MEFTA Entity	Steps Toward an FTA with the United States				
	WTO Membership and year of joining	GSP eligibility[c]	TIFA with the U.S. and Year TIFA was signed	BIT with the U.S. and year BIT was signed	Bilateral Trade Agreement with the U.S.
North Africa					
	negotiating				
Algeria	accession	+	+ 2001		
Libya	observer	ineligible			
Morocco	+ 1995	+	+ b	+ 1991	+ Effective 1/1/2006
Tunisia	+ 1995	+	+ 2002	+ 1993	

Source of data: World Trade Organization, USTR. [Step is currently in effect.

[a]. USTR materials indicate that these TIFAS or BITs are in existence, but do not specify the dates.

[b]. Goods are eligible for U.S. free trade benefits under a1996 amendment to the United States-Israel Free Trade Area Implementation Act of 1985, P.L. 104-234 if co-produced with Israel, Jordan, or Egypt in a Qualifying Industrial Zone (QIZ) in compliance with rules of origin requirements, or wholly produced in the Gaza Strip/West Bank.

[c]. Ineligibility may reflect a high income level or a country viewed as a state sponsor of terrorism.

Table 3. Top U.S. Imports (and % of total that they represent) from 20 Middle East Entities (2003)

c	Value of U.S. Imports ($million)	Main U.S. imports and % of all U.S. imports from these that they represent	
Saudi Arabia	18,047	petroleum (96%), chemicals (3%)	= 99%
Israel	11,823	apparel (86%), misc. mfg.(8%) STNC* (4%)	= 98%
Iraq	4,574	petroleum (100%)	= 100%
Algeria	4,753	petroleum (86%), natural gas (13%)	= 99%
Kuwait	2,276	petroleum (93 %) , STNC* (2%), apparel (2%)	= 97%
United Arab Emirates	1,102	apparel (23%), petroleum (21%), STNC* (13%)	= 63%
Egypt	1,096	apparel (34%), petroleum (15%), textiles (13%)	= 62%
Oman	695	petroleum (57%), apparel (19%), STNC* (10)	= 86%
Jordan	670	apparel (86%), misc. (8%), STNC*(4%)	= 98%
Bahrain	378	apparel (43%), STNC* (22%), non-ferrous metals (10%)	= 75%
Morocco	369	electronics (23%),apparel (20%), fertilizer (18%), petrol. (15%)**	= 61%
Qatar	331	apparel (26%), gas (18%), fertilizer (17%)	= 61%
Syria	258	petroleum (77%), apparel (12%), misc. mfg. (4%)	= 93%
Iran	161	textiles (80%), Misc. mfg. (12%), fish (5%)	= 92%
Tunisia	96	apparel (34%),petroleum (24%), iron and steel (9%)	= 67%
Lebanon	88	misc manufacturing (22%), tobacco (22), furniture (12%)	= 56%
Yemen	66	petroleum (90%), coffee, tea (7%)	= 97%
Cyprus	24	STNC* (42%), apparel (14%),dairy (6%)	= 62%
Libya	0		

Table 3. (Continued).

Entity	Value of U.S. Imports ($million)	Main U.S. imports and % of all U.S. imports from these that they represent	
Gaza Strip/the West Bank	0		
TOTAL	48,650		

Source: U.S. International Trade Commission (USITC) Dataweb, based on the Standard Industrial Trade Classification (SITC).

Note: No data are available for the West Bank/Gaza Strip, or Libya.

* "STNC" refers to "special transactions not classified" According to the Department of Commerce, these exports are typically military items that are returned to the United States.

** petroleum is not counted in the top three exports.

Table 4. Top U.S. Exports (and % of total that they represent) from 20 Middle East Entities (2003)

Entity	Value of U.S. exports ($million)	Main U.S. Exports and % of all U.S. exports to these entities that they represent	
Israel	6,878	nonmetals (30%), transport equip (11%), electronics (8%)	= 49%
Saudi Arabia	4,596	machinery (28%), transport equip. (25%)	= 53%
United Arab Emirates	3,510	transport equip. (30%), machinery (29%)	= 59%
Egypt	2,660	cereals (29%), transport equip. (14%), machinery (16%)	= 59%
Kuwait	1,509	transport equip. (38%), machinery (21%), telecom.	= 44%
		equip. (4%)	
Bahrain	509	transport vehicles (55%), machinery (11%)	= 66%
Jordan	492	transport equip. (32%), cereals (9%), telecom. equip. (7%)	= 48%
Algeria	487	cereals (29%), machinery (26%), animal food (8%)	= 63%
Morocco	465	Transport equip. (28%), cereals and seeds (28%), machinery (7%)	= 63%
Qatar	408	Machinery (50%), transport. equip. (17%), scientific inst. (7%)	= 74%
Cyprus	327	transport equip. (74%), cereals (3%), tobacco (3%)	= 80%
Iraq	316	machinery (57%), food (25%)	= 82%
Oman	323	machinery (34%),Transport. equip (29%)	= 63%
Lebanon	314	transport equip. (14%), tobacco (13%), cereal % seeds (15%)	= 42%

Table 4. (Continued).

Entity	Value of U.S. exports ($million)	Main U.S. Exports and % of all U.S. exports to these entities that they represent	
Syria	214	cereals (32%), machinery (22%), tobacco (7%)	= 61%
Yemen	195	cereals (36%), machinery (35%)	= 71%
Tunisia	171	cereals (24%), veg. oils (19%), transport. equip. (6%)	= 49%
Iran	99	oil seeds (44%), tobacco (34%), pharmaceuticals (6%)	= 84%
Gaza Strip / the West Bank	0		
Libya	0	cereals (92%), electronics (6%)	= 98%
TOTAL	23,474		

Source: USITC Dataweb, based on the Standard Industrial Trade Classification (SITC).
Note: No data are available for the West Bank/Gaza Strip, or Libya.

Table 5. Foreign Direct Investment in Middle East Entities: Stock of Investment by the World, 2000 and by the United States, 2002 ($ Millions)

	Stock of World Foreign Direct Investment, 2000		Stock of U.S. Foreign Direct Investment, 2002	
Entity	Value in $ millions	% of world total	Value in $ millions	% of U.S. total
World	6,314,271	100	1,520,965	100
Total Middle East	96,700	1.38	17,113	1.11
Algeria	1,407	0.02		
Bahrain	5,908	0.09		
Egypt	19,005	0.30	2,959	0.19
Iran	2,115	0.02		
Israel	NA		5,207	0.34
Jordan	1,771	0.02		
Kuwait	527	0.01		
Lebanon	998	0.02		
Morocco	5,848	0.02		
Oman	2,517	0.01		
Qatar	1,987	0.03		
Saudi Arabia	28,845	0.46	3,687	0.24
Syria	1,338	0.02		
Tunisia	11,566	0.18		

Table 5. (Continued).

	Stock of World Foreign Direct Investment, 2000		Stock of U.S. Foreign Direct Investment, 2002	
Entity	Value in $ millions	% of world total	Value in $ millions	% of U.S. total
United Arab Emirates	2,645	0.04	1,398	0.09
Yemen	888	0.01		
Other Middle East (non- identified)			3,862	0.25

NA: Not available

Source: For World: Economic Research Forum. *Economic Trends in the MENA Region, 2002* p. 52; for the United States: *Survey of Current Business*, September, 2003, p. 121.

REFERENCES

[1] "A Man of Many Missions." *Business Week.* March 31, 2003, p. 94-95.

[2] Gresser, Edward. *Blank Spot on the Map: How Trade Policy is Working Against the War on Terror.* Public Policy Institute. February 2003. Unemployment in the Middle East in 1999 averaged roughly 25%. Source: The Economic Research Forum for the Arab Countries, Iran and Turkey. *Economic Trends in the MENA Region*, 2002.

[3] All but two of the entities that would be covered by the initiatives (Israel and Cyprus) are at least two-thirds Muslim.

[4] Lindsey, Brink. The Trade Front: Combating Terrorism with Open Markets. CATO Institute. August 5, 2003.

[5] National Commission on Terrorist Attacks Upon the United States. *The 9-11 Commission Report,* released on August 29, 2004.

[6] Iran, Libya, and Syria are countries the United States has considered as state sponsors of terrorism. *Inside U.S. Trade.* May 30, 2003; and Office of the U.S. Trade Representative. *Transcript of Background Press Conference Call to Discuss Proposed Mideast Free Trade Area Announced by President Bush*, May 9, 2003.

[7] U.S. Energy Information Administration, U.S. Department of Energy. *Monthly Energy Review*, February, 2004.

[8] The Middle East, in general, has high barriers to trade. While the "weighted mean tariffs" (the mean tariffs after the proportion of goods imported for each category is factored in) of some countries are under 10%, they average

more than 20% for many other countries, including Egypt (21%), Algeria (22%), Morocco (32%), and Tunisia (31%) Source: The World Bank. *World Development Indicators '03*, p. 327.

[9] Data source: U.S. Bureau of Economic Analysis. Economics and Statistics Administration. U.S. Department of Commerce. *Survey of Current Business*, September, 2003, p. 121.

[10] For example, Bahrain is scheduled to "graduate" from the GSP program on January 1, 2006.

[11] Only nine out of the 20 entities covered by the two Middle East Trade Initiatives are already eligible for GSP (as indicated in table 2.) GSP provisions [U.S. Trade Act of 1974 as amended (19U.S.C. 2461)] specifically exclude from tariff preferences certain textiles and apparel (the second most important export category from these Middle East entities), watches, footwear, handbags, luggage, flat goods (e.g. wallets and briefcases), work gloves, and other leather wearing apparel, steel, glass, and electronics. As a result, for the 20 Middle East entities covered by this report, imports under GSP represent only a fraction (2% for 2003) of all imports from these entities.

[12] These steps are taken from Office of the U.S. Trade Representative (USTR). *Trade Facts*, June 23, 2003. Additional explanatory material is taken from Office of the USTR. *Transcript of Background Press Conference Call to Discuss Proposed Mideast Free Trade Area Announced by President Bush*, May 9, 2003 (hereafter referred to as "Transcript of May 9, 2003.") This transcript specifies that the USTR official holding the press briefing be identified only as a "senior administration official."

[13] U.S. Department of State. *Middle East Trade Initiative*. Office of the USTR, February 27, 2003.

[14] Office of the USTR. Transcript of Joint Press Conference: Secretary of State Colin L. Powell, Jordanian Foreign Minister Marqan Muasher, Robert B. Zoellick, U.S. Trade Representative, Jordanian Minister of Trade Salah Bashir, Movenpick Hotel, Dead Sea, June 23, 2003.

[15] Under this legislation, goods wholly produced by the Gaza Strip or the West Bank could also enter the United States duty-free under the terms of the U.S.-Israel free trade agreement.

[16] This speech is not listed on the USTR Website. However, it is referenced in the Bureau of National Affairs, *International Trade Reporter,* September 16, 2004.

[17] CRS Report RS21457, The Middle East Partnership Initiative: An Overview, by Jeremy M. Sharp.

[18] U.S. Agency for International Development. *U.S. Contributions to Trade Capacity Building*, September, 2003, p. 2.

[19] Office of the USTR. Transcript of May 9, 2003; and Global Trade and the Middle East: Reawakening a Vibrant Past, Robert B. Zoellick, USTR, Remarks at the World Economic Forum, Dead Sea, Jordan, June 23, 2003. The primary boycott of Israel banned all trade relationships with Israeli companies; the secondary boycott prohibited any entity in the League of Arab States* from doing business with other firms that contribute to Israel's military or economic development; the tertiary boycott was the injunction on Arab countries from doing business with foreign companies that had been blacklisted because of their ties with Israel. Source: "U.S. Government to Enforce Laws in Face of Arab League Threat to Israeli Trade," Global Business Magazine. Oct 10, 2002. * The 22 members of the League of Arab States are Bahrain, Egypt, Iraq, Jordan, Kuwait, Lebanon, Oman, Qatar, Saudi Arabia, Syria, the United Arab Emirates, Yemen, Algeria, Libya, Morocco, Tunisia, Comoros, Djibouti, Mauritania, Palestine, Somalia, and Sudan.

[20] Bush's Plan to Create Mideast Free Trade Area by 2013 Could Take Off This Year. *International Trade Reporter*, 2006 Outlook, Jan. 19, 2006, p. 103.

[21] Transcript of Background Press Conference Call to Discuss Proposed Mideast Free Trade Area Announced by President Bush, May 9, 2003.

[22] The Realities of Exporting Democracy. *The Washington Post,* January 25, 2006, p. A-1.

[23] Galal, Ahmed and Bernard Hoekman, editors. *Arab Economic Integration: Between Hope and Reality.* Egyptian Center for Economic Studies*, 2003*. p. 29. (The data were based on The World Bank. *World Development Indicators '01* CD-ROM. This unemployment estimate is slightly smaller than that included in footnote 2. This different estimate is included here to show a range of estimates on a subject (a) that is difficult to quantify, (b) that suffers from statistical problems, and (c) whose numbers may vary from year to year and may also depend on the countries included in the various estimates.)

In: Politics and Economics of the Middle East ISBN: 978-1-60456-719-9
Editors: W. Evans & D.J. Harris

Chapter 7

PALESTINIAN ELECTIONS*

Aaron D. Pina

ABSTRACT

Fair and transparent elections are seen by experts and policymakers as a necessary step in Palestinian democratization and for the peace process. In 2002, the Palestinian Authority (PA), under increasing internal and external pressure, announced a so-called "100-Day Reform Plan" for institutional reform and elections in order to rejuvenate PA leadership. The 2006 legislative elections were the final and perhaps most critical test for Palestinian democratic institutions. On the one hand, the Palestinian Legislative Council elections may improve the day-to-day lives of Palestinians, renew public confidence in the PA, and bolster the peace process. On the other hand, the clear-cut legislative victory of Hamas, which does not recognize the state of Israel and calls for an Islamized Palestinian state, may increase the possibility that Palestinians will find themselves isolated.

Palestinian political reform is an important element in the U.S. policy of promoting democracy, civil society, and good governance in the Middle East. Still, a PA that is dominated by a democratically elected Hamas is uncharted diplomatic territory for the United States government and international community. It remains unclear how U.S. policy toward the Palestinians will change now that a designated terrorist organization is set to head the government. Additionally, as Israel holds its own parliamentary election this

---

* Excerpted from CRS Report RL33269, dated Feb 9, 2006.

spring, any new government will face decisions whether to curb economic and diplomatic relations with the Palestinians.

The Palestinian political landscape has changed dramatically since the death of Yasir Arafat in 2004. Violence between Palestinians and Israelis, ineffective PA government, and an elusive political solution to the Israeli-Palestinian conflict prompted Palestinians to opt for change. The shift from a secular Fatah government toward a militant, Islamist government, however, does not necessarily mean all Palestinians accept the ideology of Hamas. The public's support for Hamas is conditional and may erode if Hamas does not improve the lives of Palestinians in demonstrable ways.

President Bush expressed support for the conduct of the Palestinian elections, but he and other Administration officials contend that there should be no place in the political process for groups and individuals who refuse to denounce terror and violence, recognize Israel's right to exist, or disarm. Since 1993, Congress has authorized over $1.5 billion in assistance to the Palestinians, and U.S. assistance to the Palestinians has increased over the past few years. Some in Congress support restricting or ending economic assistance to the Palestinians so that U.S. aid does not benefit a foreign terrorist organization. Others are wary of initiatives that may weaken Palestinian President Abbas.

The report will be updated periodically as events warrant. For discussion of the Palestinian-Israeli conflict, see CRS Report RS21235, *Palestinian Factions*, by Aaron Pina and CRS Issue Brief IB91137, *The Middle East Peace Talks*, by Carol Migdalovitz, and CRS Report RS22370, *U.S. Foreign Aid to the Palestinians*, by Jeremy M. Sharp.

OVERVIEW

Political reform within the Palestinian Authority (PA) is seen by experts and policymakers as a necessary step in Palestinian democratization and the Israeli-Palestinian peace process. The PA continues to underperform: its security services are ineffective, the national economy is nearly bankrupt, and post-withdrawal Gaza is devolving further into ungoverned space. These factors, combined with the public's dissatisfaction with institutional corruption, contributed to a convincing win by Hamas in the January 2006 parliamentary election. With Hamas poised to lead the next Palestinian legislative session and form a new cabinet, policymakers face a situation wherein the PA is to be led by a designated terrorist organization whose Covenant states the group's commitment to the destruction of the state of Israel.[1] This development, combined with Israeli Prime Minister Sharon's incapacity and Israeli elections in March, will continue to fuel speculation on the future of a viable and comprehensive settlement to the

Israeli-Palestinian conflict and the Bush Administration's wider goal of democratic reform in the Middle East.

In 2002, President Bush declared support for a democratic Palestinian state existing alongside a secure Israel to result from the "road map," the only internationally accepted political framework for achieving a peaceful solution to the Israeli-Palestinian conflict. Though supportive of Palestinian democracy, President Bush and much of the international community appear gravely concerned that Hamas, despite its democratic victory, will not cease its terror campaign against Israel in favor of a non-violent negotiated settlement. After encouraging Mahmoud Abbas to remain President of the PA in the wake of the Hamas parliamentary victory, President Bush remarked "I have made it very clear that a political party that articulates the destruction of Israel as part of its platform is a party with which we will not deal."[2] The manner in which the Bush Administration addresses the Hamas question may resonate throughout a region where Islamic participation in government is trending upward.

Many in Congress are also concerned that Hamas may enter government without first renouncing violence and accepting the state of Israel. After witnessing Hamas' gains in municipal polls, the House of Representatives passed H.Res. 575 (December 16, 2005), asserting that terrorist groups, like Hamas, should not be permitted to participate in Palestinian elections until such organizations "recognize Israel's right to exist as a Jewish state, cease incitement, condemn terrorism, and permanently disarm and dismantle their terrorist infrastructure."

Current Political Issues

Recent party, local, and parliamentary elections were carried out by Palestinians in an uncertain political environment. Several issues dominated the various election campaigns in 2005 and 2006. The manner in which a Hamas-led government addresses these concerns may go a long way in determining its political future and the likelihood of re-starting the peace process.

Security

Those who seek to advance the peace process have repeatedly called for the Palestinian police to disarm militants and to re-organize themselves into a coherent security force. In June 2003, Abbas stated "there will be no military solution for this conflict, so we repeat our renunciation of terrorism against the Israelis wherever they might be."[3] Since then, Abbas has continually denounced violence as a means to achieve independence. Though Secretary of State Condoleezza Rice credits Abbas with taking "some good, concrete steps toward security reform," the Palestinian leadership still faces technical obstacles to security reform (recruitment, training, equipment, and funding sources) and political challenges (reining in militant Palestinians and stabilizing Gaza).

By most accounts, Abbas inherited a "Balkanized" security apparatus weakened by the current *intifada*, a debilitated infrastructure, and the re-appearance of local gangs and warlordism.[4] The degree to which President Abbas is able to reform Palestinian security institutions may also impact the outcome of final status issues like the status of refugees, Jerusalem, and political borders between Israel and any future Palestinian state. Abbas recently signaled he may resign if his political program is not followed and has repeated this threat several times in the past.[5] A growing area of concern for policymakers is whether a Hamas-led PA will strengthen security and halt terror. Though its policy on PA security institutions is not clear, Hamas embraces violence against Israel and may hamper any attempt to reform PA security institutions.

Corruption

Charges of widespread corruption have plagued the Palestinian party of Fatah. Its leaders have oftentimes been accused of siphoning funds from ministry budgets, passing out patronage jobs, accepting favors and gifts from suppliers and contractors, and soliciting bribes. Appointing former World Bank official Salam Fayad as head of finance may have reduced the level of corruption, but with Fayad's departure in 2005 to enter politics, many doubt the financial reforms he began will embed themselves within the PA. Perhaps the biggest challenge for Fatah candidates has been how to convince Palestinians of their commitment to anti-corruption efforts. In contrast, Hamas is seen as largely untouched by corruption and exploited this image during the campaigns. Hamas' anti-corruption message during the parliamentary election was apparently successful and many reports and exit polls cited anti-corruption as a motivation to vote for Hamas. Ahmed al-Meghani Meghani, the Palestinian Attorney General, recently announced that a recent investigation into the PA's finances showed that $700 million was missing from PA coffers.[6]

Economy

Economic stagnation has been another pressing domestic concern. Prior to the Palestine Legislative Council (PLC) elections, the consensus was that openly contested, free elections, and ongoing reforms would have increased the likelihood of international aid to Palestinians, particularly from the United States. Instead, the Hamas victory in the PLC election places all international assistance in jeopardy, as most donors have refused to lend financial assistance to a terrorist group. Furthermore, efforts by international organizations like the World Bank to improve the Palestinian economy may also be hampered by the Hamas victory.

James Wolfensohn, former head of the World Bank, was appointed special U.N. representative to Gaza to coordinate reconstruction efforts after Israel's withdrawal from Gaza. In his official capacity, Wolfensohn has advocated more freedom of movement, facilitated border crossing, and changing the overall economic dynamic within the West Bank and Gaza. The World Bank estimates that real GDP growth in the West Bank and Gaza may have reached 8-9 percent in 2005, continuing the modest recovery that began two years ago, but the Palestinian economy still operates at well below its potential, with real GDP per capita almost 30 percent lower than in 1999.[7] The World Bank report concludes that the lackluster Palestinian economy is the result of restrictions on the movement of people and goods, high unemployment (20% in the West Bank and 29% in Gaza), leading to 43% of the Palestinians living below the poverty line.[8]

In reaction to the Hamas victory, Israeli spokespersons announced that Israel would withhold tax revenues it collects on behalf of the Palestinians (roughly $50 million per month). Recently, the government of Israel released this month's revenues to the PA, but all future allocations are subject to review and may not go through as long as Hamas refuses to recognize Israel and renounce violence. Reports claim that Saudi Arabia promised $20 million and Qatar pledged $13 million in aid to help the PA pay January salaries to 137,000 employees.[9] International assistance, which comprises a significant portion of the PLC budget, is also at risk. For example, on March 31, 2005, the PLC approved a $2.2 billion budget that assumed that pledges of $1.2 billion in international aid, made at the March 1, 2005, London Conference, will be forthcoming. Since last spring however, the Palestinian economy worsened and the E.U. reportedly announced on January 17, 2006 that it will suspend $42 million in aid to the Palestinians, citing their lack of budgetary discipline.[10] In a government statement, Japan, the largest source of Palestinian economic assistance outside of the E.U. and U.S., stated that it hopes Hamas will move on the track of coexistence and co-prosperity with Israel after leading a new government.[11]

Disengagement

Israel's unilateral decision to disengage from Gaza and portions of the West Bank was another domestic concern for Palestinians. The apparent inability of the PA to effectively govern Gaza, end warlordism, and begin to improve the day-to-day lives of Palestinians increased the popularity of Hamas in the run-up to municipal and parliamentary elections. It is unclear whether a politically empowered Hamas will follow the mainstream Palestinian acceptance of withdrawal or act as spoiler. The failing health of Sharon and upcoming Israeli elections also complicate the future of disengagement and the larger peace process.

In April 2002, in reaction to Palestinian suicide-bombings, Israel approved the construction of a barrier between Israeli and Palestinian-held territory, largely built inside the Palestinian side of the "Green Line" (the 1967 cease-fire line separating the West Bank from Israel). Some Israelis contend their security depends on the construction of the barrier, noting decreased suicide bombings in Israel since the barrier's partial construction. Critics of the barrier see it as *de facto* Israeli annexation of portions of the occupied West Bank. In another move to disengage from Palestinians, Prime Minister Sharon announced on December 2003 that Israel would unilaterally withdraw from Gaza and portions of the West Bank. The withdrawal began on August 17, 2005, and was completed on August 23. Some claim that Israel's disengagement masks unilateral action designed to freeze the peace process. Others assert that disengagement demonstrates Israel's commitment to peace and the two-state solution.

Leading Palestinian Factions

Many observers claim that factions, and the contentious political environment they often inhabit, may harm democratic reforms in the West Bank and Gaza by reserving power for themselves and maintaining systems of patronage, cronyism, and nepotism. Others assert, however, that factions may help cobble together a loose national consensus as power-sharing, political compromise, and the rule of law become a reality. While Hamas and Fatah have vastly outperformed all other challengers in elections, political alternatives like Mustafa Barghouti's Independent Palestine Party and former PA Finance Minister Salam Fayad's Third Way Party are proposing a democratic vision that is primarily based on transparency, accountability, security, and non-violence. The "middle" way political parties secured six out of 132 parliamentary seats.

In the absence of a political alternative, Hamas and Fatah continue to monopolize the political landscape in the West Bank and Gaza. The Palestinian extreme "Left," once key players in Palestinian politics, lost political influence with the collapse of their Soviet patron. The left's initial rejection of the Israeli-Palestinian peace process and the rise of Hamas sidelined Leftists like the Popular Front for the Liberation of Palestine (PFLP), PFLP-General Command, and the Democratic Front for the Liberation of Palestine (DFLP).[12]

Fatah

Fatah is a "big-tent" party that includes nationalists, Islamists, secularists, and leftists and served as Yasir Arafat's power base within the PLO for four decades. Until the 2006 PLC election, Hamas dominated much of the political scene in the West Bank and Gaza and has never been outside of power. Since the death of Arafat in 2004, Fatah has been plagued by allegations of corruption and cronyism, a weak economy and astronomical unemployment, ineffective preventive security forces, and rising crime. Post-withdrawal Gaza, once hailed by Palestinians as a burgeoning success story for the PA, now resembles ungoverned space and exacerbates anti-Fatah sentiment.

From the standpoint of Fatah, and by extension the PA, the lack of political cohesion and decisiveness over the past year was a boon for Hamas. Unable to agree on the composition of its national list, Fatah registered multiple lists just before the December 14, 2005 deadline. The main Fatah list was topped by the jailed militant activist Marwan Barghouti. *Al-Mustaqbal* (the Future), a Fatah breakaway, was headed by former Civil Affairs Minister Mohammad Dahlan and former PA preventive security chief Jibril Rajoub. A second breakaway party, Independent Palestine, was headed by Mustafa Barghouti (former presidential candidate and a distant cousin of Marwan Barghouti). A third breakaway party, The Third Way, was headed by Former PA Finance Minister Salam Fayad and former PLC Member Hanan Ashrawi. In addition to the public's dissatisfaction with Fatah, the multiplicity of Fatah candidates probably contributed to electoral losses in Fatah strongholds like Nablus, Tubas, and Tulkaram. Unlike Hamas, which offered one candidate in each race, Fatah often ran several candidates in each race. As a result, support for Fatah candidates was often divided, while all support for Hamas typically went to one candidate in any given race.

In the wake of an unprecedented rejection of its leadership and vision, Fatah no longer controls the levers of Palestinian political authority. Fatah seems to have underestimated the popularity of Hamas and the seriousness of its political challenge. Fatah's lack of electoral success also was due to the inability to speak with one voice after the death of Arafat, develop a coherent political strategy, or effectively extend the rule of law to all Palestinians. Public confidence in PA institutions, which are also identified with Fatah, is at an all time low and many Palestinians see Fatah and the PA as ineffectual and overly corrupt. Still, regardless of their current political circumstance in Palestinian society, Fatah is widely regarded as the face of Palestinian nationalism even among Hamas supporters.

Hamas

Hamas is a Palestinian offshoot of the Muslim Brotherhood Society in Palestine, established by the late Sheik Ahmad Yasin in 1988.[13] Hamas belongs to a constellation of Palestinian groups which, after the Arab-Israeli war of 1967, were dismayed that Arab secular governments failed to secure a Palestinian state. Allegedly, Israel lent support for Hamas in its early stages, as a counterweight to Fatah and Palestinian secular nationalism. Over the past three decades, Hamas has risen to prominence, in part due to a well-organized social service network that provides services and charitable programs to Palestinians. The appearance of Fatah corruptibility also aided the popularity of Hamas. Through its military wing, the Izz Eddine al-Qassam Brigades, Hamas has frequently claimed responsibility for attacking and killing scores of Israeli civilians and soldiers. The State Department designated Hamas as a Foreign Terrorist Organization in 1997 and re-designated the organization on October 25, 2005.

The decision of Hamas to participate in the PLC election and commit to a truce (or *hudna*) may have intensified internal strife and threatened the vaunted unity of Hamas. As a result, there is increasing speculation that Khaled Meshaal, Hamas' Political Bureau Chief, based in Damascus, Syria, may formally divide Hamas into military and political organs. The purported split between the Damascus-based Hamas political leadership who appear to oppose non-violent engagement and the West Bank/Gaza leadership who support a cease-fire and political participation may affect Hamas' post-election strategy. The overall approach Hamas took toward the PLC election was disciplined and coherent. Yet, most analysts question whether Hamas will sustain a pragmatic approach, or continue with a violent, anti-Israeli agenda.

2005-2006 ELECTIONS

Background on Electoral Reform

Demands for electoral reform picked up in 2002 with the resurgence of Palestinian reformers who felt that elections might renew institutions that had lagged during the anti-occupation *intifada* (uprising). The call for elections accompanied widely circulated reports that many Palestinian politicians view civil society and political party development increasingly as a prerequisite for systemic reform. Increased pressure from the Bush Administration and Israel on the PA to reform political institutions, as a precursor to re-igniting the peace process, is often cited as an external factor in nudging the PA toward government reform. The Bush Administration, possibly hoping to decentralize Palestinian political authority, also insisted that the late PA President Yasir Arafat name a Prime Minister, which he did in 2003.

The September 1995 Israeli-Palestinian Interim Agreement on the West Bank and Gaza (known as Oslo II) created the Palestinian National Authority (PNA or PA), a transitional executive body with a mandate over political, civil, and security matters for Palestinians. Palestinian elections and procedures are governed by the 1995 Election Law (amended in 2005), and the PA generally supports the concept of representational government[14] (See Appendix A for a recent history of Palestinian elections). Due to the patronage and corruption of the Arafat regime, however, true representational government did not materialize. The lack of electoral consistency fostered "Arafatism," whereby autocracy, weak institutions, corruption, and haphazard voting procedures often circumvented good governance. Conversely, some describe the PLC as one of the most vibrant political institutions in the Middle East.[15]

The PA often combined autocratic practices with a strong, growing, and detailed verbal commitment to liberal democratic politics. It passed laws, wrote a constitution, formed committees, issued proclamations, and occasioned speeches all promising a democratic Palestinian government. The PLC succeeded in laying down some of the foundations for governing institutions (a constitution, judiciary, elections commission). Although the Palestinian parliament established a working legislature, Yasir Arafat's presidency dominated Palestinian institutions. Hence, the legislative branch is not fully autonomous and continues to remain within the President's orbit.

Perhaps the most important electoral institution within the PA is the Central Elections Commission (CEC). Under the Election Law, the nine member CEC supervises elections. The stated aims of the CEC are to adhere to Election Law provisions, adopt procedures that permit impartial and transparent elections, monitor and report electoral processes, and validate the results of elections. The CEC is composed of three university presidents, five judges, and one United Nations Relief and Works Agency (UNRWA) official. Together the Commission supervises an elections director, a staff of about 3,000 workers, and another 15,000 workers who staff the polls and coordinate foreign and domestic elections observers.

Presidential Elections

Yasir Arafat died on November 11, 2004 and Palestinian presidential elections were held soon thereafter. Under the Basic Law and the Election Law, Arafat was succeeded by the Speaker of the PLC, Rawhi Fatuh, who decreed immediately that presidential elections would be held January 9, 2005. Seven candidates competed in the poll. Mahmoud Abbas (a.k.a. Abu Mazen) won 67% of the vote and was appointed to a four-year term, Mustafa Barghouti received 21%, and five candidates split the remaining 12%. High voter turnout (around 65% despite a Hamas boycott), the presence of international and domestic observers, and a relative absence of violence contributed to a successful election. However, the presidential poll was not without incident, with widespread observer reports claiming the election was plagued by inconsistent voter lists, limited media access, and curbs on freedom of movement.

Table 1. January 9, 2005, Palestinian Presidential Election Results

Candidates	Votes (%)	Votes (total)
Mahmoud Abbas (Fatah)	65.52	501,448
Mustufa Barghouti (Independent)	19.48	156,227
Tayseer Khaled (DFLP)	3.35	26,848
Abd Alhalim Ashqar (Independent)	2.76	22,171
Basam Al Salhi (Palestine People's Party)	2.67	21,429
Assayed Barakeh (Independent)	1.30	10,406
Abd Al-Karim Shbair (Independent)	0.71	5,717

Source: Palestinian Central Elections Commission.

Municipal Elections

Between 2004 and 2006 Palestinians voted in multiple municipal elections to fill 900 local council seats that are attached to the Palestinian Ministry of Government Affairs. Municipal councils are tasked with developing infrastructure (water, sewage, construction, roads), city planning, and bridging the rural-urban development gap. The series of elections were the first Palestinian municipal elections since 1976 and are generally regarded as a barometer for public opinion and a precursor to PLC elections (See Appendix B for election results). It appears that Hamas' showing in the municipal elections was a precursor to its victory in the parliamentary round. Hamas managed to out-mobilize Fatah at the local municipal level by harnessing its tradition of delivering social services to Palestinians. Furthermore, some maintain that although Hamas lacks the governing experience of Fatah, its local activities and grassroots approach may be successfully applied in larger governing institutions such as the parliament. Others doubt whether Hamas can effectively move beyond local social needs toward larger national governing strategies.

Palestinian Legislative Council Elections

Composition

The Palestinian Legislative Council (PLC) is the legislative arm of the PA and confirms the Prime Minister and approves all government cabinet positions. The 2006 legislative elections were the first to be held since 1996. In the 1996 poll, Fatah won 49 seats, affiliated "independents" won 15 seats, and the bulk of the remaining 24 seats went to nominally independent candidates. Hamas boycotted the 1996 poll in rejection of the Oslo accords that had established the legislature, but Islamists did win a handful of seats. Subsequent polls were slated for 2000 and 2003, but the outbreak of the *intifada* (uprising) and internal wrangling over the composition of the PLC led to two postponements.

In June 2005, the PLC amended the 1995 election law to respond to internal criticism over proportionality and replaced a majority model with a mixed electoral system. The PLC also increased from 88 members to 132, one-third of which would be elected in the single list national system, and two-thirds under a regional district system. Under the new system, each voter receives two ballots. The first ballot contains the names of candidates competing for the seats of the electoral district from which the voter selects a number of candidates not to exceed the number of seats assigned for each district. The second paper contains competing national lists from which the voter chooses one slate. Thus, voters may cast "split-ticket" votes. Six out of the 66 seats allocated to the national list are reserved for Christians.[16] Both lists must include at least one woman in the first three names, at least one woman in the next four names, and at least one woman in each group of five names that follow.

Results

The CEC reported that over 77% of eligible voters (980,000 out of 1.273 million) took part in the January 25, 2006 PLC election. The election was overseen by 17,268 domestic observers, complimented by 900 credentialed international monitors. The conduct of the election was widely considered to be free and fair. Palestinians voted in one of 1,008 polling stations (754 in the West Bank and 254 in Gaza) and 132 seats were contested by 728 candidates (414 in districts and 314 on party slates).[17]

Initial observer reports stated that nearly all polls opened on time and the election was carried out in an efficient and orderly manner. No serious incidents of violence were reported and over 13,000 PA preventive security personnel provided security for the election. Likewise, in East Jerusalem, Israeli Defense Forces provided security and generally unfettered access for voters and observers. Some observer organizations reported limited voter access in Hebron and East Jerusalem, the presence of some guns at polling sites, and factional clashes at some polls.[18]

Table 2. January 25, 2006, Palestinian Legislative Council Election Results

Candidates	Seats Won
Change and Reform (Hamas)	74
Fatah Party	45
Palestinian Front for the Liberation of Palestine	3
The Third Way Party	2
The Alternative Party	2
The Independent Palestine Party	2
Independents	4
Total	132

Source: Palestinian Central Elections Commission.

INTERNATIONAL REACTIONS

United States

The Bush Administration accepted the outcome of the Palestinian legislative elections and praised the PA for holding free and fair elections. Following the election, President Bush held a news conference wherein he expressed his support for the democratic election and said that the results had "given a wake-up call to the leadership."[19] However, President Bush reiterated the Administration's stance toward Hamas, saying that "a party that articulates the destruction of Israel is a party with which we will not deal. I don't see how you can be a partner in peace if you advocate the destruction of a country."[20] Observers speculate that the Hamas electoral victory may complicate U.S. policy toward the Palestinians and democracy promotion in the Middle East.

On January 30, 2006, the Quartet (U.S., E.U., Russia, and the U.N) discussed the Palestinian elections. In a released statement the Quartet stated that all future assistance to the PA will be reviewed by donors against the Palestinian government's commitment to non-violence, recognition of Israel, and acceptance of previous agreements and obligations, including the roadmap. Secretary of Rice commented that "The U.S. can't fund a government that is run by an organization that it lists as a terrorist organization. It's just a practical matter." Many experts predict that any possible curtailment of U.S. assistance may not include humanitarian aid.

Israel

Ehud Olmert, the acting Israeli Prime Minister, announced that "a Hamas-led Palestinian Authority is not a partner."[21] Under Olmert and the Kadima Party, the government of Israel may quicken the pace of disengagement and the completion of the separation barrier and many analysts doubt that any Israeli government will engage Hamas on the substantive issues of the road map. Additionally, the Hamas victory may also influence Israel's current electoral campaign. Yuval Steinitz, Chairman of Israel's Foreign Affairs and Defense Committee stated that "these elections contradict the Oslo Agreement and contradict democracy."[22] Benjamin Netanyahu, the former Israeli Prime Minister, commented that "Hamastan has been formed, a proxy of Iran in the image of the Taliban."[23] Some in Israel suggested that the election of Hamas to head the PA demonstrates the failure of recent negotiations and the peace process.

Middle East, European, and Other International Reactions

Egypt's Foreign Minister, Ahmed Abu Gheit, reportedly stated that "negotiations cannot take place under violence and fire. Therefore, violence must be renounced," adding that Hamas "must recognize Israel and honor previous diplomatic agreements made by the Palestinian Authority."[24] Muhammad Mahdi Akif, the head of Egypt's Muslim Brotherhood, the oldest Islamic political organization in the Middle East, declared that "the success attained by Hamas is tantamount to a vote by the Palestinian people in favor of the Islamic line for the solution of the Palestinian issue."[25]

In Jordan, Nasir Judah, government spokesman asserted that "Jordan respects the Palestinian people's choices in the elections and the outcome of the legislative elections reflects the democratic process and the Palestinian people's choices, and we respect that."[26] During a live broadcast of Friday prayers, Ayatollah Mohammad Emami-Kashani, a member of Iran's Guardian Council claimed, "Hamas and Fatah must follow a pious path and maintain unity. The West is unhappy about the victory of Hamas and they must realize that it was the people who voted for Hamas."[27] Pakistani President General Pervez Musharraf, a key U.S. ally in the global war on terror, issued a statement that the "international community should accept the reality and verdict in the Palestinian elections and not shut its door on the newly elected Hamas authority."[28]

French Prime Minister Dominique de Villepin stated that any prerequisite to working with the Palestinian government included "the renunciation of violence and the recognition of Israel."[29] British Prime Minister Tony Blair said Hamas must now choose between "a path of democracy or a path of violence."[30] The U.N. Security Council stated that any future Palestinian government must recognize Israel and commit itself to a negotiated settlement of the Mideast conflict culminating in two independent states living in peace. Arab League Secretary General Amr Moussa claimed that "Hamas will have to accept the Beirut initiative, which calls for full Arab recognition of Israel, despite its declared stands."[31] The European Union (EU), the Palestinians largest source of aid, has demanded that Hamas renounce terror, but has not formally pledged to cut aid.[32]

PALESTINIAN REACTION

Fatah

Fatah leaders, if not their supporters, have accepted the outcome of the election and will not challenge the results. While Fatah leadership appeared to support the outcome, young Fatah supporters demonstrated and clashed with Palestinian security services. Generally, the protesters displayed a lack of confidence in Fatah and have called for the resignations of the Fatah Central Committee. Ahmad Qureia, Prime Minister and Fatah member, resigned his post and expressed a willingness to see Hamas form a new government. Though it is unclear whether Fatah will join a Hamas-led government, reports claim Fatah will be a loyal opposition while it attempts to revive its party and public appeal. President Abbas may resuscitate the Palestinian Liberation Organization (PLO) and negotiate with Israel through its good offices. Many felt that President Abbas's speech to the parliament on February 18 will outline the future of Hamas-Fatah relations.

Hamas

The leadership of Hamas contends that the outcome of the parliamentary election demonstrated that Palestinian people aspired to new leadership and a new program based on comprehensive reform. Following the election, Khaled Meshaal, the head of Hamas, immediately called for a Hamas-Fatah coalition government. For its part, Fatah generally rejects the Hamas call for a unity government, yet Abbas has meet with Hamas leaders to discuss such a proposal. Many feel that Hamas may not have anticipated such a resounding victory and is not prepared to lead the next Palestinian government. While Hamas has issued politically pragmatic statements in the days following the election, some Hamas leaders such as Mahmoud Al-Zahhar also suggest that Hamas may try to eliminate the peace process and "kill any trace of the Oslo peace process."[33] There were also reports that Hamas may offer to extend the cease-fire (*hudna*) for an undetermined time.

OUTLOOK

A New Palestinian Government

By most accounts, Abbas and Fatah apparently gambled that once in the PLC Hamas would no longer ignore the rule of law and would choose a path toward political normalization. Still, the Abbas camp in all likelihood did not foresee Fatah losing total political authority as a result of Hamas' participation. Though Ahmed Qureia, Prime Minister of the PA, tendered his resignation in reaction to the Hamas victory, President Bush urged President Abbas to remain in office to continue guiding the peace process with Israel.[34] Given Hamas' total victory, Abbas is meeting with Hamas officials to discuss the formation of the next government in the coming weeks. He will ask the next government to respect his political platform, which calls for renouncing violence, commitment to peace negotiations, and the two-state solution. Though Hamas appears to want to lead a coalition government, some suggest that Fatah may resist national political unity and attempt to isolate Hamas. The result of Fatah's go-it-alone strategy may produce a political deadlock that many fear will lead to internecine violence and civil war.[35] Others contend that Abbas may re-tool the PLO, which does not currently include Hamas, as the primary Palestinian representative in future negotiations.

Hamas Governance

The death of Arafat, and resulting fracturing of Fatah unity, provided Hamas with an opportunity to participate in the political realm. Hamas' PLC candidates are generally well-respected, educated, and many have a reputation for probity and high-minded public service.[36] Therefore, it is possible that Hamas will continue to express a willingness to include Fatah or Fatah "independents" in a governing coalition. Still, whether internal debate within Hamas will produce clear divisions between political and military "wings" remains in doubt.

Despite a clear victory in the Palestinian parliamentary election, Hamas offered scant details on its intended political program beyond anti-corruption measures. While Hamas clearly profited from the untainted image enjoyed by all opposition parties, it may not possess the technocratic, political, and bureaucratic savvy to administer Palestinian affairs. Hamas' stance on the possible implementation of Islamic law (or *sha'ria*) is also difficult to ascertain. Some reports of "morality police" have surfaced, although Hamas officials claim that is not general policy.[37] While Hamas' experience in municipal social welfare programs is impressive, many doubt its ability to promote democratic institutions, judicial reform, and bringing the Palestinian constitution to a referendum.

Many recent statements by Hamas are enigmatic and demonstrate both pragmatic and extremist rhetoric. Though Hamas has thus far refused to disarm, there have been statements that some believe express a less maximal position. For example, Khaled Meshaal , leader of Hamas, stated that "resistance can be in a political and diplomatic form."[38] Yet, most assert that as long as Hamas remains militant and its Covenant continues to call for the destruction of Israel, few will take its moderate rhetoric seriously. Unlike the Hamas Covenant, the Hamas election platform did not contain language that calls for the destruction of Israel. However, Hamas spokesman Sami Abu Zuhri stated "the platform refers to details and implementation methods for the next four years, while the Covenant lays out our permanent strategic views."[39] On the other hand, Muaman Bseiso, columnist for the Hamas weekly *Al-Risala*, wrote, "the Covenant is not the Koran, which is unchangeable. I believe that one day it will be changed or replaced according to the views of the Hamas, in order to realize the national interests of the Palestinians."[40]

Hamas' recent statements regarding Israel are also inconsistent. Khaled Meshaal , the leader of Hamas, stated that Hamas does not recognize Israel.[41] Yet, Shaykh Muhammad Abu-Tayr, the second highest ranking member of Hamas, signaled possible shifts within the political circles of Hamas mentioning that "I frankly say Israel does exist. It does exist."[42] Hamas Deputy Ismail Haniyah is widely reported to support dialogue with Israel and the international community. Even though Hamas has made verbal commitments to moderation and dialogue, anti-Israeli language persists. Recently, Mousa Abu Marzouk, Deputy Political Bureau Chief of Hamas, stated, "Israel's are our enemy rather than a partner."[43]

Regional Considerations

In the last few years, the Middle East region has witnessed gains by political Islam. In Egypt, the banned Muslim Brotherhood (running as Independents) ran well in 2005-2006 parliamentary elections. In Iraq, many observers anticipate that politics will likely take on a distinctly religious hue. In southern Lebanon, the militant *Hizballah* (Party of God), plays a visible role in national government. Ultraconservative Wahhabism dominates much of Saudi Arabia's politics, and Iran remains a staunch Shi'a theocracy. Whether a Hamas-led Palestinian government might extend this trend is open to debate. It is clear that Egypt, the largest Arab country and a leader in the region, does not want further instability on its border. On the other hand, there are growing fears that nearby groups like Hizballah and Palestinian refugees in Lebanon may feel more emboldened by the Hamas victory.

It remains unclear whether a Hamas victory will lead to an increase in Iranian influence in the West Bank and Gaza.[44] Although the Hamas victory would appear to bolster the hardline, anti-Israel stand of President Ahmadinejad, many observers believe it is more likely that Hamas and Iran will drift further apart. The State Department report on international terrorism foı 2004 states that Hamas "receives some funding from Iran but primarily relies on donations from Palestinian expatriates around the world and private benefactors in Saudi Arabia, Kuwait, and other Arab states." In many ways, Hamas' alliance with Tehran has always been somewhat unnatural, because Hamas is a Sunni Muslim derivative of the region-wide Muslim Brotherhood organization, while Iran is the center of Shiite Islamic movements. Hamas now has a stake in and interest in Palestinian politics and governance, and is not expected to turn to Iran for instructions or guidance on Palestinian domestic issues.

Issues for Congress

The Future of Palestinian Aid[45]

In fiscal year 2005, the Bush Administration and Congress significantly increased U.S. economic aid to the Palestinians through supplemental appropriations and by reprogramming economic aid which had been appropriated in previous years. President Bush also used his authority to provide $50 million in direct assistance to the Palestinian Authority, marking only the fourth time a U.S. President has used a congressional authorized waiver to channel aid away from USAID programs and directly to the PA.

Following the PLC elections, Administration officials and some Members of Congress have warned the Hamas leadership that the United States will no longer provide assistance to a Hamas-led PA government unless it changes its Covenant to recognize Israel's right to exist and renounces the use of violence. If Hamas should resist such changes, Congress and the Administration could move to alter or halt U.S. assistance altogether to the Palestinians by eliminating the presidential waiver authority to authorize direct aid to the PA or by tightening existing restrictions, including the oversight of Palestinian non governmental organizations working as subcontractors.[46] It is worth noting that the United States currently provides small amounts of ESF aid for projects in Lebanon, despite the participation of Hizballah, a U.S.-designated terrorist group, in parliament and in the current cabinet. However, in Lebanon, Hizballah is part of a larger coalition government, whereas in the West Bank and Gaza, Hamas is poised to be the dominant player in the political arena.

Table 3. U.S. Assistance to the Palestinians, FY2002-FY2006 (Regular and Supplemental Appropriations; Current Year $ in millions)

Account	FY2002 Actual	FY2003 Actual	FY2004 Actual	FY2005 Estimate	FY2006 Estimate
ESF	72.000	124.500	74.558	274.400	150.000
P.L.480 Title II	-	9.984	-	-	-
Total	$72.000	$134.484	$74.558	$274.400	$150.000

Source: U.S. State Department.

Legislation

H.R. 4668 (introduced in the House International Committee on January 31, 2006) would place conditions on assistance to the PA. The President would have to certify, among other things, that the PA is not controlled by an FTO.

H.R. 4681 (Referred to the House Committee on International Relations, and in addition to the Committees on the Judiciary, and Financial Services, for a period to be subsequently determined by the Speaker on February 1, 2006) would require, among other things, that the President certify (every three months after the passage of the bill and every six months thereafter) that no element of the PA is controlled by a foreign terrorist organization (FTO) and no member of an FTO serves in a ministry, agency, or instrumentality of the Palestinian Authority.

S. 2237, the Palestinian Compliance Act of 2006 (introduced in the Senate Foreign Relations Committee on February 1, 2006) would require, among other things, that the President's waiver authority (Section 550 (b) of P.L. 109-102, the FY2006 Foreign Operations Appropriations Act) may only be used if the Palestinian Authority renounces terrorism and recognizes Israel's right to exist and takes appropriate steps to amend the Hamas Covenant to delete statements that are hostile to Israel and that support the use of violence.

S.Con.Res. 79 (passed the Senate on February 1, 2006, and referred to the House International Relations Committee on February 7, 2006) resolves that it is the sense of Congress that no U.S. assistance should be provided directly to the

PA if any representative political party holding a majority of parliamentary seats within the Palestinian Authority maintains a position calling for the destruction of Israel.

Peace Process

Under Abbâs, the PA appeared committed to cooperating with Israel in the peace process. Hamas, for its part, continues to support the killing of Israeli civilians and denies the legitimacy of the state of Israel. On the other hand, standing for elections, toning down its religious rhetoric, and generally holding to a truce might be a harbinger of political and rhetorical moderation on the part of Hamas. Many observers hold that once inside the political sphere Hamas will have little choice but to abandon its violent methods. Hamas leader Isma'il Haniyah stated that Hamas "invites the Quartet Committee to an open an unconditional dialogue."[47] Hamas, however, has a clear and established track record that seems to mitigate any likelihood of political moderation. Additionally, this record suggests that it may perpetrate violence against Israel, which would further complicate matters and marginalize political solutions to the Israel-Palestinian conflict.

Policymakers undoubtedly face a paradigm shift in Arab-Israeli affairs and the peace process. There are those who contend that if a viable solution to the conflict could not be found between Israel and a secular national-liberation movement (Fatah), then an Islamized Palestinian leadership is even less likely to achieve an accord. There are others who claim that Hamas may bring stability, security, and hope to Palestinians and thus create an environment more conducive to peace. Still, nearly all agree that as long as Hamas remains committed to the destruction of Israel and refuses to abandon violence and terror as a political tool, the peace process is likely to remain moribund and Israel may quicken the pace of unilateral withdrawal, emphasizing isolation rather than engagement.

Palestinian Democracy

Some Members of Congress hope that the Palestinian culture of elections may further institutionalize rule of law, and moderate extremist behavior within the West Bank and Gaza. Others fear a democratic process that brings a known terrorist organization into government may legitimize terrorism and not end violence.

Appendix A: Palestinian Elections Timeline

2006

PLC elections.
January 25

Planned municipal re-votes.
February

2005

Second part of the first round of the municipal elections was held.
January 27

Mahmoud Abbas was confirmed as the winner of the Palestinian presidential election.
January 10

Palestinian parliament approved a new line-up of ministers.
February 24

Fourth round of municipal elections.
December 15

Third round of municipal elections.
September 29

Second round of municipal elections.
May 5

Internal Fatah primary elections for the legislature.
November

2004

PA set a January 9 date for presidential elections.
November 14

Arafat died.
November 11

Round one of the municipal elections took place.
December 24

2003

Mahmoud Abbas officially accepted Yasser Arafat's offer of the post of Palestinian prime minister.
March 19

Arafat signed legislation surrendering most of his authority to the prime minister post.
March 18

Arafat nominated PLO Deputy Mahmoud Abbas, as Palestinian prime minister-designate, as part of reforms aimed at reviving peace talks with Israel.
March 7

Yasser Arafat and the Palestinian prime minister-delegate, Mahmoud Abbas, agreed on the composition of the new Palestinian Authority.
April 23

Arafat nominated the speaker of the Palestinian parliament, Ahmed Qureia, to be prime minister.
September 7

Prime Minister Abbas resigned amid a power struggle with Yasser Arafat and an upsurge of violence.
September 6

Palestinian MPs ratified a new cabinet led by the prime minister, Ahmed Qureia.
November 12

2002

In a speech to the Palestinian assembly, Arafat promised reform and elections.
May 15

Yasser Arafat's government was forced to resign to avoid a parliamentary vote of confidence.
September 11

Yasser Arafat appointed a new cabinet.
October 29

Arafat's cabinet called off January's presidential election and legislature because it said that the Israeli military occupation of West Bank cities made a free ballot impossible.
December 22

1996

- In the first Palestinian general elections, Arafat was overwhelmingly elected president of the PA.
- First Palestinian Legislative Council elected.

January 20

1993

Israel and the PLO agreed on an interim peace deal, which established a framework for Palestinian self rule in the West Bank and Gaza.
September 13

APPENDIX B: MUNICIPAL ELECTION RESULTS

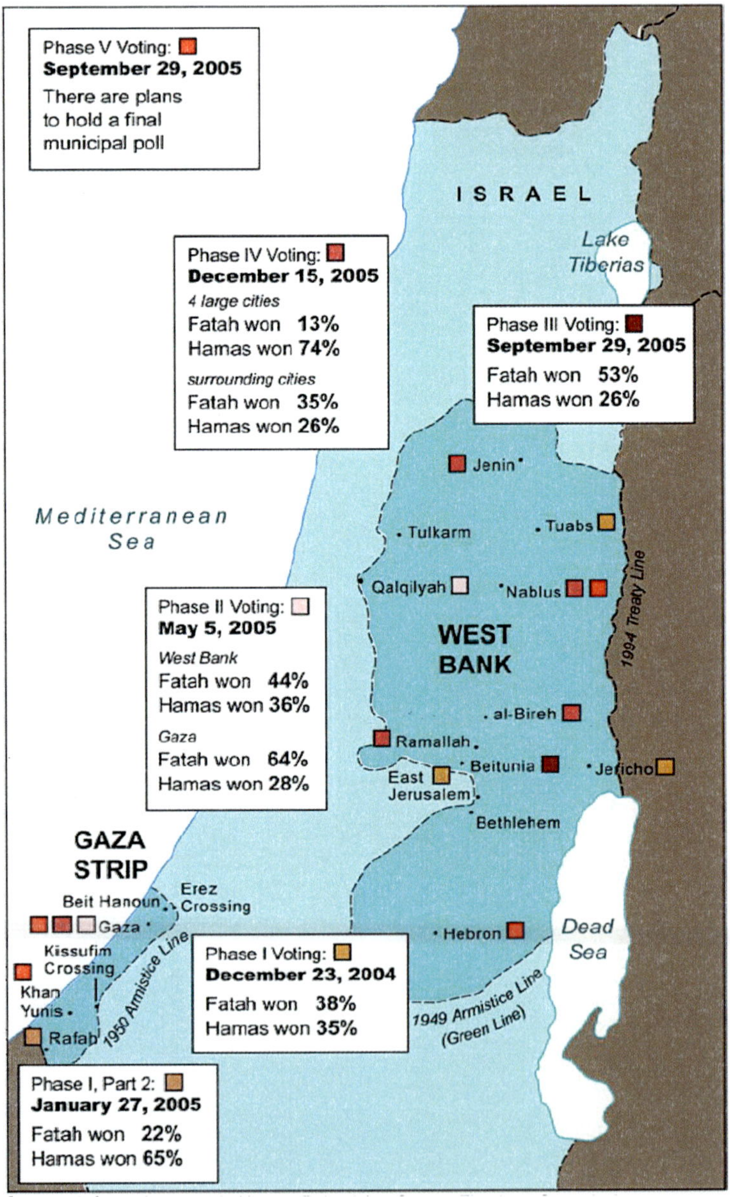

Source: Information provided by the Palestinian Central Elections Commission. Map Resources. Adapted by CRS. (K.Yancey 1/30/06).

References

[1] Hamas Covenant, online at [http://www.yale.edu/lawweb/avalon/mideast/hamas.htm].

[2] Jon O'Neil and Christine Hauser, "Bush Wants Abbas to Remain Palestinian Leader," *CNN Online*, January 26, 2006.

[3] "Abbas Says Armed Intifada Has to Stop," *Al-Sharq al-Awsat* (London), Dec. 14, 2004.

[4] Strategic Assessment Initiative, *Planning Considerations for International Involvement in the Palestinian Security Sector*, the Royal Netherlands Ministry of Foreign Affairs, July, 2005.

[5] "Abbas Might Resign if Policies Opposed," *Associated Press*, January 18, 2006.

[6] Mohammed Daraghmeh, "Palestinian Attorney General Freezes Accounts of Dozens of Corruption Suspects," *Associated Press*, February 6, 2006.

[7] The World Bank, The Palestinian Economy and the Prospects for its Recovery, December 20, 2005.

[8] Ibid.

[9] *Ha'aretz News Service*, "Palestinian official: Saudi Arabia, Qatar promise $33 million in aid to PA," February 1, 2006.

[10] "EU suspends 35 Million Euros in Aid to the Palestinian Authority," *Ha'aretz News Service*, January 17, 2006.

[11] Japan has provided over $800 million to the Palestinians since 1993. Japan Ministry of Foreign Relations, *Japan-Palestinian Authority Relations*, February, 2006.

[12] The PFLP-General Command is currently designated an FTO. Available online at [http://www.state.gov/s/ct/rls/fs/37191.html].

[13] Hamas is the acronym for the Islamic Resistance Movement (or *Harakat al-muqawama al-Islamiya*). Hamas also mean "zeal" in Arabic. For an in-depth analysis of Hamas, See Khaled Hroub's *Hamas: Political Thought and Practic*e, 2002 and Yohan Alexander's *Palestinian Religious Terrorism: Hamas and Islamic Jihad*, 2003.

[14] 1995 Elections Law available online [http://www.elections.ps].

[15] Nathan Brown, "Aftermath of the Hamas Tsunmai," Carnegie Endowment for International Peace, 2006.

[16] Samar Assad, "Palestinian Legislative Elections: The Catalyst for Political Reform," *The Palestine Center*, Number 119, May 17, 2005.

[17] Aluf Benn, "Polls: Fatah Leads Hamas by Up to 11%," *Ha'aretz*, January 25.

[18] "Report on Election Day," Palestinian Initiative for the Promotion of Global Dialogue and Democracy, January 26, 2006.
[19] White House Press Conference, January 26, 2006.
[20] Ibid.
[21] Arnon Regular, "After Landslide, Olmert Says Hamas-led PA Is No Partner," *Ha'aretz News*, January 27, 2006.
[22] *Ha'aretz News Service*, "Likud: Hamas Victory a Direct Result of Disengagement Plan," January 26, 2006.
[23] Laurie Copans, "Netanyahu Stands to Gain in Israeli Election Campaign after Hamas Win," Associated Press, January 30, 2006.
[24] Yoav Stern, "Egypt Demands PA Stop Violence as Condition for Peace Talks," *Ha'aretz Daily*, February 1, 2006.
[25] Statement available online [http://www.ikhwanonline.com].
[26] *Al-Arab al-Yawm* (Jordan), January 27, 2007.
[27] Tehran Voice of the Islamic Republic of Iran Radio, January 27, 2006.
[28] Pakistan Press Release, "Pakistan: Musharraf Urges World To Accept Hamas Victory in Palestinian Election," January 27, 2006.
[29] Sebastian Alison, "European Leaders Tell Hamas: Change or be Shunned," *Reuters*, January 26, 2006.
[30] "Britain's Blair Urges Hamas to Choose Between Democracy, Violence," *Agence Presse*, January 26, 2006.
[31] Ora Koren, "Arab League: Hamas Will Have to Recognize Israel," *Ha'aretz Daily*, January 27, 2006.
[32] The E.U. provided the PA with $605 million in 2005.
[33] Anne Barnard, In Stunning Upset, Hamas Seen as Victor," *Boston Globe*, January 26, 2006.
[34] William Branigin, "Bush: Hamas Must Alter Stance on Israel to Be Partner in Peace," *Washington Post*, January 26, 2006.
[35] Ephraim Lavie, "Hamas' Victory in the Palestinian Elections: What Does it all Mean?" *Tel Aviv Notes Number 159*, Jaffee Center for Strategic Studies, Tel Aviv University, January 29, 2006.
[36] "The Quest for Legitimacy: Electoral Politics In Palestine," *The Palestinian Initiative for the Promotion of Global Dialogue and Democracy*, December, 2005.
[37] Alan Johnston, Hamas Under Pressure Over Vigilantes," *BBC News Service*, April 19, 2005.
[38] International Crisis Group, Enter Hamas: the Challenge of Political Integration, January 18, 2006.
[39] *Al-Hayat Al-Jadida* (Palestinian), January 22, 2006.

[40] The Middle East Media Research Institute, Hamas in Run-up to Elections: Relatively Pragmatic Statements Alongside Extremist Statements, 2006.

[41] Alix Van Buren, "Hamas Leader Khaled Mish'al Refuses To Renounce Resistance to Israeli Occupation," The Republic (Rome), January 27, 2006.

[42] [42] Interview by Ohad Hemo, *Ma'bat Newscast* (Jerusalem), January 13, 2006.

[43] Palestinian Information Center, "Abu-Marzuq: HAMAS To Remain Steadfast on National Constants," January 22, 2006.

[44] For an analysis of Iran, see CRS Report RL32048, *Iran: U.S. Concerns and Policy Responses*, Kenneth Katzman.

[45] For a more detailed analysis of U.S.-Palestinian aid, see CRS Report RS22370, *U.S. Aid to the Palestinians*, by Jeremy M. Sharp.

[46] Section 550 (b) of P.L. 109-102, the FY2006 Foreign Operations Appropriations Act, states that the President may use this waiver if providing direct aid to the PA is important to the national security interests of the United States. By law, the waiver must be accompanied by a report to Congress detailing the steps the Palestinian Authority has taken to arrest terrorists, confiscate weapons and dismantle the terrorist infrastructure. The report also must include a description of how funds will be spent and the accounting procedures in place to ensure that they are properly disbursed.

[47] Al-Jazeera Television Network, January 20, 2006.

In: Politics and Economics of the Middle East ISBN: 978-1-60456-719-9
Editors: W. Evans & D.J. Harris

Chapter 8

QATAR: BACKGROUND AND U.S. RELATIONS*

Jeremy M. Sharp

ABSTRACT

In recent years, the ruler of Qatar, Shaikh Hamad bin Khalifa Al-Thani, has embarked upon a limited course of political liberalization and aligned Qatar firmly with the United States. In 1992, Qatar and the United States concluded a Defense Cooperation Agreement that has been progressively expanded. In April 2003, the Bush Administration announced that the U.S. Combat Air Operations Center for the Middle East will be moved from Prince Sultan Airbase in Saudi Arabia to Qatar's Al-Udeid airbase, which served as a logistics hub for U.S. operations in Afghanistan under Operation Enduring Freedom, as well as a key center for Operation Iraqi Freedom. Camp As-Sayliyah, the largest pre-positioning facility of U.S. equipment in the world, served as the forward command center for CENTCOM personnel during Operation Iraqi Freedom. Qatar also has assisted the United States in the war on terrorism by stepping up its efforts to prevent Al Qaeda from engaging in money laundering. With the third largest proven gas reserves in the world, U.S. companies, such as ExxonMobil, have worked to increase trade and economic ties with Qatar. Qatar has the highest per capita income of any country in the Middle East.

As part of Qatar's experiment with limited political liberalization, the Qatari monarchy started Al Jazeera, the Arab world's first all-news network. In a national referendum in April 2003, Qatari voters approved a new constitution that provides for a partially elected national assembly and grants

---

* Excerpted from CRS Report RL31718, dated March 17, 2004.

women the right to vote and run for office. For further information, see CRS Report RL31889, *The Al-Jazeera News Network: Opportunity or Challenge for U.S. Foreign Policy in the Middle East*, and CRS Report RL31533, *The Persian Gulf: Issues for U.S. Policy, 2003*.

DOMESTIC POLITICAL STRUCTURE

Qatar, a small peninsular state bordering Saudi Arabia in the Persian Gulf, is a constitutional monarchy governed by the Al-Thani family and headed by the Emir, Shaikh Hamad bin Khalifa Al-Thani.[1] The country gained full independence from Britain on September 3, 1971. The Emir is head of the executive branch and appoints members of the Al-Thani family and other notables to a governing Council of Ministers (cabinet), which is headed by the monarch's brother, Prime Minister Abdallah bin Khalifa Al-Thani. The country's newly approved constitution (April 2003) stipulates that the rule of the state is hereditary within the Al-Thani family and that future successors to the throne follow the line of the Emir's male offspring.[2] The constitution also states that legislative authority reside in the hands of a 45-member Advisory Council (*Majlis al-Shura*), two-thirds of which is directly elected and one-third appointed by the Emir from among ministers or others.[3] The Advisory Council has oversight authority over the Council of Ministers and can propose legislation and review budgets. The constitution also empowers the Advisory Council to issue motions of no-confidence against a government minister; the motion must be approved by two-thirds of the Advisory Council. Women have the right to vote in elections and can run for office.

Council members serve four-year terms. National elections for the new Advisory Council will most likely take place in early 2004.

On June 27, 1995, in a bloodless palace coup, Shaikh Hamad replaced his father, Shaikh Khalifa, who had ruled Qatar for 23 years. The former ruler had been living out of the country in Cannes, France most of the time and had turned over many routine affairs of state to his son, Shaikh Hamad, then crown prince and commander of the small armed forces. The ruling Al-Thani family rallied behind the new ruler, who quickly consolidated control. In February 1996, supporters of Shaikh Khalifa unsuccessfully attempted a counter-coup.[4] The coup attempt prompted Shaikh Hamad to initiate civil proceedings against his father to retrieve an alleged \$3-\$12 billion of state assets supposedly in his possession. Saudi Arabian mediation facilitated an out-of-court settlement, and the Emir and his father have reconciled, although the former Emir has not returned to Qatar.

Figure 1. Qatar and Its Neighbors.

Shaikh Hamad, at age 53,[5] has been described as representative of an emerging new generation in Gulf leadership. Like King Abdullah II of Jordan, Shaikh Hamad is British-educated, with degrees from Cambridge University and Sandhurst Military Academy. As part of his modernizing agenda, Shaikh Hamad helped establish the CNN-style satellite news network, Al-Jazeera in 1996. In a major departure from his more conservative-minded father, Shaikh Hamad has borrowed heavily from foreign banks in order to modernize Qatar's energy infrastructure. Shaikh Hamad and his younger generation of advisers have pressed for social, political, and economic liberalization. Qatar also has invested heavily in education reform. In October 2003, Sheikha Mozah, the wife of Sheikh Hamad, helped launch Qatar's new "Education City," a new campus that offers degrees from several U.S. universities including Weill Cornell Medical College, Texas A and M University, Virginia Commonwealth University, and Carnegie Mellon

University. Qatar recently hired the RAND Corporation to evaluate and recommend reform options for Qatar's educational system. RAND also is monitoring the progress of reform in Qatar's schools.

In November 2002, Qatar established diplomatic ties with the Holy See. Qatar plans to grant the Roman Catholic Church and other Christian denominations designated plots of land for the building of churches. Qatar does not ban alcohol, which is available in licensed premises such as the bars of major hotels and clubs. Qatar, like Saudi Arabia, officially adheres to the Wahhabi brand of Sunni Islam; however, in contrast with Saudi Arabia, Wahhabi tenets are not strictly enforced.

ECONOMIC OVERVIEW

Oil and natural gas production is the mainstay of Qatar's robust economy, which has experienced an average annual growth rate of 9% over the last 5 years.[6] Japan, South Korea, and Singapore are the leading importers of oil from Qatar. Qatar Petroleum (QP), the state-owned oil company, has increased its output significantly from 593,000 barrels per day (b/d) in 1999 to over 854,000 b/d in 2002.[7] Qatar is aiming to produce about 1,000,000 b/d by 2004. However, with oil reserves likely to be exhausted by 2020 at current production rates, Qatar is rapidly moving to exploit its natural gas reserves.[8] As part of a long-term development strategy, Qatar has tapped international financial markets and invited foreign investment in recent years in order to finance the expansion of its liquified natural gas (LNG) production.[9] Qatar intends to expand its yearly LNG output, which is not subject to OPEC production quotas, from 4.5 million tons per annum in 2002 to 14 - 18 million tons per annum by 2010. Although Qatar's LNG industry has low capitol costs due to government investment, it has high operational costs, requiring Qatar to develop economies of scale in order to be more competitive with established LNG exporters such as Indonesia and Nigeria.[10]

Qatar has signed several agreements with U.S. energy companies (ConocoPhillips and ExxonMobil) and other international companies to develop facilities to export LNG to the United States, the UK, Spain, Italy, South Korea, Taiwan, and India. Qatar also is in the midst of building the largest gas to liquids (GTL) plant in the world. Under Project Dolphin, Qatar is planning to build underwater pipelines to export natural gas to Kuwait, Oman, and the U.A.E. Qatari government officials estimate that by 2007, gas revenue will outstrip oil income for the first time.[11]

Human Rights and Political Liberalization

The U.S. Department of State Country Report on Human Rights for 2002 states that the government of Qatar "generally respected the human rights of its citizens; however, its record was poor in some areas..."[12] According to the report, the rights of non-citizens are at times abused, particularly among domestic servants from the Phillippines and South East Asia. As in other Gulf countries, expatriate laborers are vulnerable to exploitation by employers who capitalize on their fear of deportation. Citizenship is withheld from foreign workers, who outnumber native Qataris in the labor force by an estimated ratio of more than 5 to 1.[13] In response to Qatar's dependence on foreign labor, the government has embarked on a program of "Qatarization," which is designed to set aside higher-level government and energy jobs for Qataris only.[14] Although the government in 1995 lifted formal censorship of the media, journalists tend to exercise a degree of self-censorship. Al-Jazeera devotes less air time to coverage of Qatari affairs. Al-Jazeera, which does not generate enough advertising revenue to be profitable, is partially dependent on the Qatari government for its financing.[15] Internet service is monitored for pornography and other material considered insulting to Islam. The government maintains strict limits on the freedom of assembly and association. Political parties and demonstrations are not allowed in Qatar, and private professional and cultural associations must register with and are monitored by the state.

Qatar in Brief

Area:	11,437 sq km (slightly smaller than Connecticut)
Population (2002):	793,341
Literacy:	79.4%
Religion:	95% Muslim
Ethnic Groups:	40% Arab, 18% Pakistani, 18% Indian, 10% Iranian, 14% other
GDP (2002):	$28,000 per capita
Inflation (2001):	2.8%
Foreign Debt (2002):	$6 billion

Oil Reserves:	3.7 billion barrels
Gas Reserves:	900 trillion cubic feet
Armed Forces:	11,800 active personnel, 34 tanks, 18 fighter aircraft

Source: The United States Central Intelligence Agency World Factbook 2002.

Since assuming power, Shaikh Hamad has embarked upon a limited course of political liberalization. In April 1998, he permitted about 3,700 business community leaders to elect a Chamber of Commerce, which selected 17 members from a slate of 41 candidates. In November 1998, in a speech before the Advisory Council, Shaikh Hamad signaled his willingness to proceed with political liberalization, declaring that "to meet the requirements of the future...it is necessary to reinforce the role of constitutional institutions, activate meaningful, constructive popular participation in the process of decision-making and supervise proper execution of decisions."[16] In March 1999, the long-anticipated election for a Central Municipal Council occurred. 248 candidates (including 6 women) competed for 29 seats, and all adult Qatari citizens, with the exception of members of the police and armed forces, were allowed to vote and run for office. This was the first time a Gulf country enfranchised all male and female citizens in a nation-wide election.[17] In April 2003, elections for the Municipal Council resulted in the first electoral victory for a Qatari female candidate, Sheikha Yousef Al-Jiffri, an appointed officer at the Education Ministry who ran unopposed.[18] Two other female candidates withdrew from the election for unknown reasons. Although the council functions primarily in an advisory role to the Ministry of Municipal and Agricultural Affairs, some observers view it as a stepping-stone to wider political liberalization. On May 5, 2003, the Emir of Qatar appointed Sheikha bint Ahmed al-Mahmoud, daughter of the Minister of State for Foreign Affairs, as Education Minister. This appointment signified the first appointment ever of a female cabinet minister in any Persian Gulf state.

Some observers and Arab commentators have questioned the timing of Qatar's reforms, calling them symbolic and primarily geared toward satisfying U.S. policy goals of promoting democracy in the region. In response to this criticism, one Qatari politician wrote that "the truth is that this constitution is not a reaction to these events, and as a Qatari politician, I can assert that the democratic trend and the desire to establish a state of institutions and rule of law represents a deep conviction that the Prince of Qatar beholds ... even before he became a Prince."[19]

Foreign Policy

Qatar is a member of the United Nations, the Arab League, the Organization of Islamic Conference, and the Gulf Cooperation Council (GCC), the latter a subregional organization consisting of six states (Saudi Arabia, Kuwait, Bahrain, Qatar, the United Arab Emirates, and Oman) bordering the Persian Gulf and the Gulf of Oman. It is also a member of the Organization of Petroleum Exporting Countries (OPEC).

Gulf States

Qatar's relations with its neighbors have fluctuated over the last decade. Territorial disputes have marred Qatar's relations with Bahrain. In the past, both Qatar and Bahrain have claimed the nearby Hawar island chain, along with the abandoned town of Zubarah on Qatar's northern border. On March 16, 2001, after seven years of deliberations, the International Court of Justice (ICJ) found that Qatar has sovereignty over Zubarah, and that Bahrain has sovereignty over the Hawar islands.[20] Since the resolution of the dispute, Qatar and Bahrain have discussed a plan to construct a 28-mile causeway, aptly named the "Friendship Bridge,"which would connect the two kingdoms.

Relations between the new Emir of Qatar and Saudi rulers were strained in the first few years of his rule. Some Qatari officials accused Saudi Arabia of plotting to restore the former ruler of Qatar in 1996. Since then, Al-Jazeera's treatment of Saudi Arabia in its programming has been the largest point of contention between the two regimes. In protest, Saudi Arabia withdrew its ambassador from Doha in September 2002 in response to an Al-Jazeera program that criticized the kingdom's founder, King Abdul Aziz al-Saud. The following month, Kuwait closed Al-Jazeera's local office in response to an allegedly insulting report on a member of the Kuwait royal family.

Iraq

A combination of factors — strains with Saudi Arabia and Bahrain and aspirations to a more influential role in regional affairs — has contributed to Qatar's increasingly independent foreign policy since 1992. Although it was an active member of the allied coalition formed during the 1990-1991 Gulf crisis and has been a participant in post-war security arrangements, Qatar adopted a conciliatory stance toward both Iraq and Iran before the other members of the GCC did. Qatar restored diplomatic ties with Saddam Hussein's regime shortly after the 1991 Gulf war, hosted visits by the Iraqi Foreign Minister, and called for relaxing economic sanctions against Iraq.

Nevertheless, Qatar played an important logistics role in Operation Iraqi Freedom, providing headquarters for the U.S. Central Command and pre-positioning facilities for U.S. tanks and armored personnel carriers. At the same time, the Al-Jazeera news network, which is privately owned but partially financed and based out of Qatar, was criticized by some U.S. officials for being sensationalistic and slanted in its coverage of the U.S. military operation. Qatar will most likely continue to serve as an important base of operations for U.S. forces in post-war Iraq, particularly after the transfer of the U.S. Combat Air Operations Center from Saudi Arabia to Qatar. On May 8, 2003, President Bush hosted the Emir of Qatar at the White House, thanking him for his steadfast support during Operation Iraqi Freedom and highlighting his role as a reformer.

Arab-Israeli Issues

Although Qatar and Israel do not have formal diplomatic ties, Qatar has been in the forefront of Arab-Israeli talks on expanding economic ties during periods of progress in the peace process. Qatar's position regarding the Arab boycott of Israel is governed by the September 1994 decision by the GCC to terminate enforcement of the indirect boycotts, while maintaining, at least in theory, the primary boycott. Qatar has hosted meetings of multilateral Arab-Israeli working groups and then Israeli Prime Minister Shimon Peres visited in April 1996. In addition, Qatar agreed to the establishment of an Israeli trade mission in Doha, Qatar's capital city, although relations cooled after the peace process slowed down in 1996. Since the beginning of the second Palestinian uprising in 2000, Qatar has claimed to have shut down the office; however, according to Qatari officials, it continued to operate at a very low level.[21] Prior to the start of Operation Iraqi Freedom, the Israeli Foreign Ministry closed the trade mission in Doha and evacuated three Israeli envoys and their families. Israel promised to reopen the office after the war.[22] Despite pressure from some other Arab states, Qatar hosted the fourth annual Middle East/North Africa Economic Conference (MENA) in November 1997. This was a gathering that brought together some Arab and Israeli business and political leaders to discuss regional economic cooperation.

In May 2003, Qatari and Israeli Foreign Ministers met in Paris to discuss ways of reviving the Israeli-Palestinian peace process. The meeting took place only a week after the Emir's visit to Washington DC, prompting speculation that President Bush encouraged Qatari officials to take a more active role in the peace process. Shaikh Hamad has acknowledged that Qatar is keen to play a role in encouraging negotiations between Israelis and Palestinians, but that it is too early to open full diplomatic ties with Israel.

February 2004 Assassination in Doha

According to press accounts, on February 13, 2004, a Chechen guerrilla leader named Zelimkhan Yandarbiyev was allegedly assassinated in a car bombing outside a mosque in Doha.[23] In the past, the Russian government had accused Yandarbiyev of funding Chechen terrorist activity. Qatari authorities reportedly arrested two Russians who may have been involved in the car bombing and have filed criminal charges against them. Russian and Qatari officials have been conducting negotiations over the release of the two Russian detainees.

Defense and Regional Security

With its small territory and narrow population base, Qatar relies to a large degree on external cooperation and support for its security. Qatar, like other Gulf states, contributes military units to a small GCC rapid deployment force of 5,000 - 10,000 known as Peninsula Shield. With a personnel strength of 11,800, Qatar's armed forces are the second smallest in the Middle East. (Bahrain, with an estimated 11,000-member force, has the smallest) France has provided approximately 80% of Qatar's arms inventory. Since the 1991 Gulf war, Qatar has pursued a limited program of force modernization. To date, however, it has not been a purchaser of U.S. weapons.

U.S.-Qatari Relations

A U.S. embassy was established in Doha in 1973, but U.S. relations with Qatar did not blossom until the 1991 Gulf war. During the fighting in January 1991, Qatari armored forces helped coalition troops repel an Iraqi attack on the

Saudi Arabian town of Kafji. The United States promptly recognized the assumption of power by Shaikh Hamad in June 1995. Analysts regard Qatar's exchanges with Israel, though limited, as broadly in accord with U.S. efforts to foster an expanding dialogue between Israel and Arab states.

Trade between the United States and Qatar has increased since the 1990-1991 Gulf war. U.S. exports to Qatar amounted to $320 million in 2001, consisting mainly of machinery and transport equipment. U.S. imports from Qatar, mainly textiles and fertilizers, totaled $501 million in 2001.[24] Although the bulk of Qatar's trade continues to be with a few European countries and Japan, several U.S. firms, including ExxonMobil, Occidental, and Pennzoil are active in the development of Qatar's oil and gas resources. Despite the presence of U.S. firms in the Qatari hydrocarbon industry, the U.S. imports virtually no oil from Qatar. In June 2002, Qatar's Minister of Energy, Abdallah bin Hamad Attiyah, held talks with U.S. Secretary of Energy Spencer Abraham over possible cooperation in the gas sector.

Bilateral defense and security cooperation have expanded since the Gulf war. On June 23, 1992, the United States and Qatar concluded a Defense Cooperation Agreement that provided for U.S. access to Qatari bases, pre-positioning of United States materiel, and combined military exercises.[25] Qatar built Al-Udeid airbase in 1996 at a cost of more than $1 billion. The U.S. government also has invested considerable amounts to upgrade the base in order to handle U.S. aircraft, equipment, and personnel. This investment was rapidly expanded following the terrorist attacks of September 11, 2001. As part of Operation Enduring Freedom, the U.S. Air Force has conducted approximately 14-16 supply flights per day to Afghanistan out of Al-Udeid.

The airbase houses between 5,000-6,500 U.S. troops and civilian contractors. The United States has constructed a 76,000 square foot hangar at Al-Udeid airbase, which can hold a maximum of 40 aircraft. Al-Udeid can accommodate a total of 10,000 troops and 140 aircraft. The base is home to the 379th Air Expeditionary Wing, which includes 17 KC -135 Stratotankers and KC 10-A Extenders for in-flight refueling of attack aircraft and fuel shipments to Afghanistan, which is 2.5 hours away.[26] Most importantly, Al-Udeid now features the region's main combat air-operations center, which had originally been built as a backup to U.S. operations in Saudi Arabia.

Qatar also has allowed the United States to construct the As-Sayliyah Army base, the largest pre-positioning facility of U.S. equipment in the world. The climate-controlled warehouses at As-Sayliyah held hundreds of M1 tanks and Bradley fighting vehicles prior to the recent Iraq war.[27] As-Sayliyah also features a new command center for CENTCOM personnel. Currently, there are approximately 3400 troops and civilian contractors at As-Sayliyah. After the base received warnings of a potential threat in 2000, U.S. personnel were confined to the base for 45 days.

War on Terrorism

In addition to increased military cooperation, Qatar has assisted the United States in the war on terrorism. Qatar has passed a money laundering law, which closed all bank accounts for foreign charities. Also, Qatar National Bank has provided its entire staff with a four-day course on fighting money laundering and terrorist financing.

According to several counterterrorism experts who formerly worked for the U.S. government, Qatar's current Interior Minister and royal family member, Shaikh Abdullah bin Khalid Al-Thani briefly harbored Al Qaeda terrorists in 1996, including the suspected mastermind of the September 11th hijacking plot, Khalid Shaikh Mohammed.[28] The Emir of Qatar appointed Shaikh Abdullah bin Khalid Al-Thani to the post of Interior Minster during an expansion of the cabinet in January 2001. It is unclear what types of discussions the United States has conducted with the government of Qatar regarding the allegations against Qatar's Interior Minister.

CHIEFS OF STATE AND CABINET MEMBERS OF QATAR

Emir	Hamad bin Khalifa Al-Thani
Heir Apparent	Tamim bin Hamad bin Khalifa Al-Thani[29]
Prime Minister	Abdallah bin Khalifa Al-Thani
Deputy Prime Minister	Muhammad bin Khalifa Al-Thani
Foreign Minister	Hamad bin Jassem bin Jabr Al-Thani
Energy Minister	Abdallah bin Hamad Al-Attiyah
Finance Minister	Youssef Hussein Al-Kamal
Ambassador to the United States	Badr Umar Al-Dafa

Source: Shaded Relief Country Map of Qatar, Central Intelligence Agency, 1995.

Figure 2. Country Map of Qatar.

REFERENCES

[1] The term "Shaikh" (or Sheikh or Shaykh) is an honorific title, which can mean a ruler, a tribal leader, or a venerable religious figure. It should be pronounced with a long A (as in "say"), not a long E (as in "see"). The term "Emir" (or Amir), often translated as prince, can also mean a monarch or a ruler in the Gulf region.

[2] The constitution was approved in a nation-wide referendum in which 96.6% of the voters (68,987) approved the constitution and only 3.3.% opposed it (2,145).

[3] Prior to the establishment of a partially elected national assembly, Qatar had a fully-appointed, 35-member advisory council that could only make recommendations to the Council of Ministers. Qatar's old Provisional

Constitution provided for a modified electoral procedure in choosing members of the Council and a three-year term; nevertheless, the Council remained appointive in practice, and terms of the Council members were extended in three or four-year increments since 1975.

[4] Some Qataris believe that Saudi Arabia supported Shaikh Khalifa in his attempt to return to power in Qatar. See, Craig S. Smith, "A Tiny Gulf Kingdom Bets its Stability on Support for U.S.," *The New York Times*, October 24, 2002.

[5] In 1997, the Emir underwent kidney transplant surgery. Since then, there have been no new reports regarding the Emir's health.

[6] Moin A. Siddiqi, "A 21st Century Success Story," *The Middle East*, June 1, 2002.

[7] Qatar is the smallest oil producing member of OPEC. Revenues from petroleum exports account for 60-70% of government revenues.

[8] With proved oil reserves of 3.7 billion barrels, Qatar has far less oil than the major Persian Gulf producers, such as Kuwait (96.5 billion barrels), Iraq (112 billion barrels), and Saudi Arabia (252 billion barrels). However, Qatar has the third largest natural gas reserves behind Russia and Iran. Qatar's supply of natural gas doubled almost overnight in 2002, when surveyors discovered new gas deposits in Qatar's north field.

[9] Qatar's government has a 60-70% stake in two joint partnerships with foreign firms, including ExxonMobil (USA), TotalFinaElf (France), KoGas (South Korea), and Matsui (Japan).

[10] Interview with Qatari executives at Ras Laffan, Qatar's LNG industrial city, January 14, 2003.

[11] "Squaring the Circle," *The Middle East Economic Digest*, October 18, 2002.

[12] Bureau of Democracy, Human Rights, and Labor, Department of State, "Country Report on Human Rights Practices - 2002," March 31, 2003.

[13] The new Qatari constitution does not address the rights of foreign guest workers.

[14] Ibid.

[15] Meeting with Al-Jazeera producer, Mr. Khalid Al Mahmoud, January 11, 2003. Qatar started Al-Jazeera with a $140 million grant. Advertising revenue only covers 35-40% of Al-Jazeera's operating expenses.

[16] "Qatar Plans to Set up First Parliament," *Reuters*, November 16, 1998.

[17] All 6 female candidates were defeated in the elections.

[18] "Qatar Elects First Woman to Council Doha," *Gulf News*, April 8, 2003.

[19] "The Constitution's Referendum: Proof of the Democratic Experience in Qatar," *Dar Al-Hayat*, April 22, 2003.

[20] "The Islands Dispute - Resolved," *The Middle East Economic Digest*, September 28, 2001.

[21] Meeting with the Qatari Minister of State, Ahmed Abdullah al-Mehmood, January 12, 2003.

[22] "Israel Shuts Qatar Mission, To Reduce Staff in Egypt, Jordan, Muaritiania," *Yedi'ot Aharanot*, March 3, 2003, translated by the Foreign Broadcasting Information Service (FBIS), Document ID: GMP20030311000208.

[23] "In Qatar, Standing Up to Putin, *Washington Post*, March 16, 2004.

[24] United States International Trade Commission, "U.S. Trade Balance by Partner Country 2001," online at [http://dataweb.usitc.gov/SCRIPTS/cy_m3_run.asp].

[25] Library of Congress, Federal Research Division (Helen Chapin Metz, ed.) *Persian Gulf States: Country Studies*, Washington, U.S. Government Printing Office, 1994, p. 194. In December 2002, the United States and Qatar signed an agreement to upgrade Qatari military facilities and expand U.S. access to them.

[26] Meeting at Al-Udeid Air Base, January 13, 2003.

[27] Meeting at As-Sayliyah Army Base, January 13, 2003.

[28] "Qatar's Security Chief Suspected of Having Ties to Al Qaeda," *Los Angeles Times*, March 28, 2003.

[29] In August 2003, the Emir named his fourth son as heir apparent, replacing his third oldest son, Jassem bin Hamad Al-Thani, who reportedly was either dissatisfied with his lack of responsibilities, or did not have an interest in continuing to serve as crown prince. The Emir has two other sons, one of whom is a businessman and the other is involved in Islamic charities.

INDEX

9

A

B

C

D

E

F

G

H

J

K

L

M

N

O

P

T

U

Y